The Dynamics of European Integration

The Dynamics of European Integration

Causes and Consequences of Institutional Choices

Thomas König

University of Michigan Press
Ann Arbor

Copyright © 2024 by Thomas König
Some rights reserved

This work is licensed under a Creative Commons Attribution-NonCommercial 4.0 International License. Note to users: A Creative Commons license is only valid when it is applied by the person or entity that holds rights to the licensed work. Works may contain components (e.g., photographs, illustrations, or quotations) to which the rightsholder in the work cannot apply the license. It is ultimately your responsibility to independently evaluate the copyright status of any work or component part of a work you use, in light of your intended use. To view a copy of this license, visit http://creativecommons.org/licenses/by-nc/4.0/

Published in the United States of America by the
University of Michigan Press
Manufactured in the United States of America
Printed on acid-free paper
First published May 2024

A CIP catalog record for this book is available from the British Library.

Library of Congress Cataloging-in-Publication data has been applied for.

ISBN: 978-0-472-13351-2 (hardcover : alk. paper)
ISBN: 978-0-472-03968-5 (paper : alk. paper)
ISBN: 978-0-472-90471-6 (OA ebook)

DOI: https://doi.org/10.3998/mpub.12828486

The University of Michigan Press's open-access publishing program is made possible thanks to additional funding from the University of Michigan Office of the Provost and the generous support of contributing libraries.

CONTENTS

List of Figures	ix
List of Tables	xiii

INTRODUCTION 1

CHAPTER 1
    From Constraining Dissensus to Supranational Consensus? 5
        1.1. Abstract 5
        1.2. Causes and Consequences of Institutional Choices 5
        1.3. (Supra)National Partyism: A Theory of Institutional Choices 9
        1.4. Plan of the Book 14

Part 1

CHAPTER 2
    Causes of Institutional Choices 19
        2.1. Abstract 19
        2.2. Theorizing Causes of European Integration 19
        2.3. Office- and Policy-Seeking Interests 22
        2.4. Power and Capabilities in Interstate Bargains 25
        2.5. Outcomes with(out) Failure and Inefficiency 28

CHAPTER 3
    Design and Competence for European Integration 33
        3.1. Abstract 33
        3.2. Research Design: Issues and Positions 33
        3.3. Amsterdam: Preparing for Enlargement 37
        3.4. Nice: Dealing with Leftovers 42
        3.5. Lisbon: Departure from the Constitution 47

CHAPTER 4
Choices for Europe after Maastricht 53
4.1. Abstract 53
4.2. Examining Hypotheses for a Period of Study 53
4.3. From Amsterdam to Lisbon: A Common Space 55
4.4. Governance Design and Transfer of Competences 59
4.5. Interstate Bargains and Veto Threats 66
4.6. Risk and Efficiency of Outcomes 72

Part 2

CHAPTER 5
Consequences of Choices 83
5.1. Abstract 83
5.2. Theorizing Supranational Governance 83
5.3. Veto Bicameralism and Uncontrolled Delegation 86
5.4. Compliance and Democratic Deficit 91
5.5. Agenda Monopoly and Camp-Building 96
5.6. Affective Polarization and Ideological Alignment 101

CHAPTER 6
Phase I: Technocracism and Compliance 105
6.1. Abstract 105
6.2. Legislative Activities in EU Policy-Making 105
6.3. Uncontrolled Delegation and Threats of Legislative Override 107
6.4. Enforcing Compliance and Informal Policy-Making 116

CHAPTER 7
Phase II: Partisan Conflict and Supranational Camp-Building 122
7.1. Abstract 122
7.2. Party Positions on European Integration 122
7.3. The Critical Juncture of the New Divide 125
7.4. EU Policy-Making and Camp-Building 132
7.5. Portfolios and Polarization 136

CHAPTER 8
Phase III: Polarization and Identity-Formation 148
8.1. Abstract 148
8.2. Public and Partisan Attitudes toward European Integration 148

Contents

    8.3. Governance Design, Policy Competences,
        and Public Support   150
    8.4. Partisan and Public Support of European Integration   161
    8.5. Solidarity and Trust for Co- and Outnationals   169

CHAPTER 9
    Conclusion and Outlook   178

References   185

Index   201

Digital materials related to this title can be found on the Fulcrum platform via the following citable URL: https://doi.org/10.3998/mpub.12828486

FIGURES

Figure 1.1. Causes and Consequences of Institutional Choices — 9
Figure 2.1. The Dual Preference Concept of (Supra)National Partyism — 24
Figure 2.2. Interstate Bargains of Three Member States (Big-3) and Status Quo (SQ) — 26
Figure 2.3. The Summit Game with Knowledge — 28
Figure 2.4. The Summit and Ratification Game with Perceptions — 29
Figure 3.1. The Amsterdam Summit Space — 40
Figure 3.2. The Nice Summit Space — 45
Figure 3.3. The Lisbon Summit Space — 50
Figure 4.1. The Common Space of the Post-Maastricht Period — 57
Figure 4.2. Interaction between Distance to Status Quo and Treaty Outcomes with and without Referendum — 70
Figure 4.3. Preferences of Political Leaders with Referendum Announcement at Amsterdam (green), Nice (red), and Lisbon (blue) — 71
Figure 5.1. Changes of Core Size from Uni- to Bicameralism — 88
Figure 5.2. EU Policy-Making between the European Commission and the (Bicameral) Legislature — 89
Figure 5.3. Compliance and EU Policy-Making of Directives with and without European Parliament (EP) — 92
Figure 5.4. Regular EU Policy-Making and Informal Trilogues for Early Agreement — 94
Figure 5.5. Bicameral Conflict Resolution and Polarization between Pro- and Anti-Integrationists — 98
Figure 5.6. Portfolio Allocation and Agenda-Setting Power of Commissioners — 100
Figure 6.1. Positions of Governmental Representatives and Political Groups of the European Parliament for Competition Policy before and after 2004 European Elections — 109

Figure 6.2. Number of Secondary and Tertiary Legislation in the
  Period 1983 to 2015   111
Figure 6.3. Decisions (black dashed line), Directives (gray dotted line),
  Regulations (gray dashed line), Other Legal Acts (gray solid line) 112
Figure 6.4. Estimation of Executive Activism in the Period 1983 to 2015.
  Dark Shaded = Probability for Secondary Legislation, Gray
  Shaded = Probability of Tertiary Legislation   113
Figure 6.5. Number of Potential Infringements and Infringement Cases 117
Figure 6.6. Share of Directives Approved in First or Second Reading
  Early Agreement or Third Reading Conciliation   118
Figure 6.7. Estimation of Judicial Activism in the Period 1997 to 2008 119
Figure 7.1. Priors for Party Families from the Chapel Hill Expert Survey
  and Contours from Two-Dimensional Kernel Density Estimation
  for Party Families   126
Figure 7.2. Posterior Probability for a One-Dimensional Left/Right
  versus a Two-Dimensional U-shaped Policy Space with Fitted
  Local Polynomial Regression on Each Posterior Draw for the
  Period 1945 to 2017   127
Figure 7.3. Posterior Probability for a One-Dimensional Left/Right
  Policy Space for Each Member State with Fitted Local Polynomial
  Regression on Each Posterior Draw between 1945 and 2017   130
Figure 7.4. Upper Columns on the Right Side = Positional Variation
  of Same Parties, Lower Columns = Positional Variation of All
  Parties for the Period 1999 to 2017   134
Figure 7.5. Density of European Integration Support by Ruling and
  Opposition Parties in the Period 1999 to 2017   137
Figure 7.6. Level of Area-Specific Consensus in the Period from 1979
  to 2019 Measured with Rice's "Index of Voting Likeness"   140
Figure 7.7. Share of Support in Final Votes of Political Groups on
  Legislative Proposals of the European Commission in the Period
  from 1979 to 2019 (EP1 to EP8)   144
Figure 7.8. Share of (Dis)Approval in Votes on Legislative Proposals of the
  European Commission in the Period from 1979 to 2019 of
  Political Groups Weighted by Seat Share in European Parliament   145
Figure 8.1. Turnout at European and General Elections in the Period
  from 1979 to 2019   152
Figure 8.2. Public Support for Governance Design and Transfer of
  Policy Competences   154

Figure 8.3. Group 1: More Satisfaction with Domestic Democracy
   Than with EU Governance in the Period 1999 to 2017   156
Figure 8.4. Group 2: More Satisfaction with EU Governance than with
   Domestic Democracy in the Period 1999 to 2017   157
Figure 8.5. Group 3: Similar Satisfaction with EU Governance and
   Domestic Democracy in the Period 1999 to 2017   158
Figure 8.6. Attitudes toward European Integration: Parties with
   High Governmental Experience (Top 25%-black solid line), Low
   Governmental Experience (Bottom 25%-black dotted line) between
   1979 and 2019, Public Opinion (gray solid line)   162
Figure 8.7. Country-Specific Attitudes toward European Integration:
   Parties with High Governmental Experience (black solid line), Low
   Governmental Experience (black dotted line), Public Opinion
   (gray solid line) between 1979 and 2019   163
Figure 8.8. Country-Specific Attitudes toward European Integration:
   Parties with High Governmental Experience (black solid line), Low
   Governmental Experience (black dotted line), Public Opinion
   (gray solid line) between 1979 and 2019   165
Figure 8.9. Relative Votes of Ruling/Mainstream and Challenger/
   Periphery Parties without Governmental Experience over Past
   Six Elections in the Period 1979 to 2019   168
Figure 8.10. Dictator Game: Solidarity and Ideological Alignment on the
   Left versus Right and the Pro- versus Anti-Integrationist Dimension   172
Figure 8.11. Trust Game: Trust and Ideological Alignment on the Left
   versus Right and the Pro- versus Anti-Integrationist Dimension   172
Figure 8.12. Left versus Right Solidarity and Trust for Co- and
   Outnationals from EU and Non-EU Members of Ruling/Mainstream
   and Challenger/Periphery Parties   174
Figure 8.13. Pro- versus Anti-Integrationist Solidarity and Trust for
   Co- and Outnationals from EU and Non-EU Members of Ruling/
   Mainstream and Challenger/Periphery Parties   175

TABLES

Table 3.1. Factor loadings of the Amsterdam issues   39
Table 3.2. Factor loadings of the Nice summit issues   44
Table 3.3. Factor loadings of the Lisbon summit issues   49
Table 4.1. Descriptive overview   62
Table 4.2. Linear regression of preference foundation   64
Table 4.3. Linear regression of interstate bargains   69
Table 4.4. Preferences, distances, and gains   74
Table 6.1. Secondary and tertiary legislation in areas with exclusive, shared, and coordinated competences   115
Table 7.1. Legislative activities across areas and terms from 1979 to 2019   139

Introduction

Business is about making Money,
Politics about finding Support,
Science about searching for Truth

The classical debates about European integration controversially interpret the foundations of the European Communities and later the European Union (EU). Over several periods of study, the paradigmatic controversies between the schools of (neo-, post)functionalism and (liberal, new) intergovernmentalism center around the question of whether the causes *or* the consequences of the institutional choices for Europe determine European integration. Independent from their theoretical focus, it is impossible to draw inferences on a dynamic period of study from narratives or data alone, nor from the distributions that govern one dataset. Although a growing number of studies infer associations among variables of one dataset for a period of study, this is only possible when the conditions of the data generation process do not change.[1] However, ever since the Maastricht Treaty created the EU in 1993, the conditions of the data generation process change over time because the founding treaties reform the institutional model, membership size varies, and the EU is regularly hit by crises.

The functionalist literature paradigmatically focuses on the consequences of institutional choices for transnational exchange, European lawmaking, and supranational organization in particular by the experts of the European Commission that are considered to promote economic spillover effects for European integration (Stone-Sweet and Sandholtz 1997). In the period after

---

1. The aim of such studies is to assess parameters of a distribution from samples drawn from that distribution. With the help of such parameters, it is possible to infer associations among variables. These tasks are managed well if conditions remain the same. However, these studies cannot make inferences under changing conditions, for example, changes induced by external shocks or crises.

the peak of the Empty Chair crisis in 1965, in which the conflict between the European Commission and France about the common agricultural policy culminated in a blockade of supranational policy-making activities, neofunctionalist scholars stress the role of the experts of the European Court of Justice, which declared the supremacy of European over national law in the mid-1960s (e.g., Burley and Mattli 1993). In contrast to this (neo-) functionalist focus on the consequences, the intergovernmentalist literature paradigmatically emphasizes the role of the heads of state and government, which institutionally design European integration to increase economies of scale and to lower exposure to external shocks in their intergovernmental bargains at summits (Moravcsik 1993, 1998). Similar to this intergovernmentalist focus on the causes of the institutional choices, the more recent literature on differentiated integration posits that exemptions and opt-outs provide alternative designs for European integration (Schimmelfennig and Winzen 2020).

One lesson of the classical debates is that paradigmatic shifts not only change how we analyze European integration but also how we understand the dynamics in a period of study. Compared to the theoretical proclivities of the classical debates, this book aims to provide a unified view of the dynamics of European integration in the period after the Maastricht Treaty created the EU in 1993. It introduces (supra)national partyism as the broadest form of a theory to derive propositions and hypotheses on the causes *and* consequences of the institutional choices for Europe. The empirical implication of this broader theory is that partyism is the most important ideological divide in European integration these days, a dividing -ism following prominent examples such as racism, sexism, classism, and sectarianism that define the classical cleavages of race, gender, class, and religion in Europe (Hahm, Hilpert, and König 2023). However, the dynamic perspective of this book shows that this dividing -ism can also unify Europe when the new cleavage on European integration is fostering the formation of a superordinate supranational identity with solidarity and trust among a majority of Europeans.

Another lesson of the classical debates is that paradigms survive periods of study, which they can hardly explain. According to Max Planck, "a new scientific truth does not triumph by convincing its opponents and making them see the light, but rather because its opponents eventually die, and a new generation grows up that is familiar with it" (Kuhn 1970: 150). This book aims to fascinate a new generation of scholars who are interested in falsifiable predictions of the causes and consequences of the institutional choices for Europe within a dynamic period of study, in which European integration experiences phases of approval and disapproval from political leaders, their

Introduction

parties, and the public. From a dynamic perspective on European integration in the post-Maastricht period, the following analyses examine separately different datasets by using measurement and graphical models, counterfactual analysis, and experimental designs to better understand the causes and consequences of the institutional choices for Europe.

This does not mean that this book ignores the insights and contributions of the classical debates on European integration. In part 1 on the causes, the research design specifies the tripartite framework of liberal intergovernmentalism on the fundamentals of preferences and their changes for governance design and transfer of policy competences, sequential interstate bargains with the implications of additional ratification hurdles, and institutional choices under uncertainty with "differentiating" exemptions and opt-outs in a widening and deepening EU. In part 2 on the consequences, it also reconsiders the three-step approach of postfunctionalism on the institutional mismatch by identifying the critical juncture for the divide between ruling/mainstream versus challenger/periphery parties, the implications of EU policy-making for building of a pro- and an anti-integrationist camp, and how affective polarization in times of supranational problem-solving with mass-mobilizing EU crisis management changes public attitudes and behavior for solidarity and trust among Europeans.

From a methodological point of view, this book aims to set an empirical standard of careful observation, and skepticism about what is significantly observed, given that personal views and omitted variables can distort the interpretation of observation. Examining the dynamics of European integration demands drawing inferences and conclusions from multiple datasets. The data on summit conferences are collectively gathered with Simon Hug on Amsterdam, with Brooke Luetgert on Nice, and with Christine Arnold, Giacomo Benedetto, Ken Benoit, Spyros Balvoukos, Raj Chari, Christophe Crombez, Stephanie Daimer, Han Dorussen, Daniel Finke, Simon Hix, Madeleine Hosli, Simon Hug, Jan Lebbe, Michael Laver, Hartmut Lenz, George Pagoulatos, Paul Pennings, Sven-Oliver Proksch, Tobias Schulz, and George Tsebelis on Lisbon. The data on party manifestos, public opinion, and legislative activities are collected with Hyeonho Hahm, David Hilpert, Dirk Junge, Bernd Luig, Moritz Marbach, and Moritz Osnabrügge. Funding has been provided by the German Research Foundation (DFG) in support of the collaborative research center "The Political Economy of Reforms" (SFB 884).

I also thank Stephanie Daimer, Elena Frech, Paul Heierling, Ursula Horn, Xiao Lu, Guido Ropers, and Alyssa Taylor for their support. I further thank Tanja Börzel, Catherine De Vries, Simon Hix, Verena Kunz, Frank Schimmelfennig, Christina Schneider, Jonathan Slapin, Thomas Winzen, and Nikoleta Yordanova for their helpful comments. The manuscript also profited from several rounds of reviewing—many thanks to the anonymous reviewers for their recommendations and suggestions. All these activities were impossible without the lovely support of my family. Verena and Greta did not complain when I wrote these pages at weekends, evenings, and during our holidays because I had to manage other projects simultaneously. I thank all my colleagues who supported me in these projects and I am particularly grateful for their stimulus to write this book.

CHAPTER 1

From Constraining Dissensus to Supranational Consensus?

1.1. Abstract

This chapter presents the analytical framework of a unified view on the causes and consequences of the institutional choices for Europe. The basic question is whether the institutional reforms of the European Union, which political leaders—as the heads of state and government of the member states—negotiated at three major summits in the post-Maastricht period, divide or unite Europe. Do these political leaders—as the causes—effectively reform a widening and deepening European Union? Do their institutional choices for Europe—as the consequences—foster constraining dissensus or supranational consensus in the post-Maastricht period? It outlines the research design, introduces the broader theory of (supra)national partyism to derive propositions and hypotheses, presents the puzzles addressed and the plan of the book.

1.2. Causes and Consequences of Institutional Choices

Do the institutional reforms of the European Union (EU) divide or unite Europe? Since the creation of the EU by the Maastricht Treaty in 1993, the Amsterdam, Nice, and Lisbon treaties reformed the governance design of the EU and transferred further policy competences to the supranational level of the EU in the post-Maastricht period. Following postfunctionalist scholars, the consequences of these institutional choices for Europe mobilize national identities with a desire for self-rule, which changes supranational governance from permissive consensus to constraining dissensus (Hooghe and Marks 2009, 2019, 2020). Scholars of the growing literature on differentiated integration find multimenu, multispeed, and multitier institutional reforms as the causes, which offer exemptions to overcome constraining dissensus (Kölliker 2001, 2006, Holzinger and Schimmelfennig 2012, Leuffen, Rittberger, and Schimmelfennig 2012, Schimmelfennig and Winzen 2020, Schimmelfennig, Leuffen, and De Vries 2023).

For a long time, the two paradigmatic schools of thought on European integration—functionalism and intergovernmentalism with their derivations—either focus on the consequences, from which postfunctionalism draws inferences on the causes of a "mismatched" institutional model (Hooghe and Marks 2009: 8) or posit the importance of the instiutional choices for the consequences, for which liberal intergovernmentalism infers an institutional equilibrium without democratic deficit (Moravcsik 2002: 603). To better understand the dynamics of European integration in the post-Maastricht period, this book studies the causes *and* consequences of the institutional choices for Europe, which reform the EU after 1993. In this period, European integration experiences phases of approval and disapproval from political leaders, their parties, and the public, which cannot be inferred from narratives or data alone, nor from the distributions that govern one dataset.

Since the Maastricht Treaty in 1993, the Amsterdam (1999), Nice (2003), and Lisbon (2009) treaties reform the EU, while several crises—the Constitutional crisis (2005), the Great Recession with the following European debt crisis (2009/2010), and the Migrant crisis (2015)—reveal the shortcomings of supranational problem-solving with mass-mobilizing EU crisis management. Ever since, public support for European integration declines, popularly coined Euroscepticism (Taggart 1998, Hobolt and De Vries 2016). However, despite their success in general elections in the aftermath of the Great Recession and the Migrant crisis, Eurosceptic parties surprisingly fail to achieve an electoral breakthrough in the 2019 European election. Furthermore, the EU is able to establish the Next Generation Fund in the aftermath of Covid-19 and demonstrates supranational consensus that is necessary for approving sanctions against the Russian invasion into Ukraine. To examine these dynamics, this book distinguishes between the pre- and the post-Maastricht period for two reasons:

- Corresponding to the founding of the EU, the Maastricht Treaty transfers policy competences for sensitive areas and changes governance design by introducing the codecision procedure (Steunenberg 1994,

Crombez 1996, 1997, Garrett and Tsebelis 1996), which establishes veto bicameralism with regulated supranational competences. In veto bicameralism, the two chambers, the Council and the European Parliament must approve legislative proposals of the European Commission. Despite widening and deepening, the reform of the role and composition of the European Commission fails, which has a supranational agenda monopoly to draft legislative proposals. This changes EU policy-making toward technocracism and camp-building.

- The permissive consensus without differences between partisan and public attitudes toward European integration ends, first at referendums on the Maastricht, Nice, and Lisbon treaties, which reveal sporadically "punctuated politicization" (Grande and Kriesi 2016), second at times of supranational problem-solving with mass-mobilizing EU crisis management. Ever since, growing Euroscepticism with the rise of anti-integrationist challenger parties from the left and right periphery of the party spectrum changes party competition and government formation in several member states (Hobolt and De Vries 2016, De Vries and Hobolt 2020).

In this post-Maastricht period, widening by the accession of Austria, Finland, and Sweden in 1995, and especially by accessions from Central and Eastern Europe in 2004 and 2007 increases the heterogeneity of interests, which reduces the potential of choices for Europe (König and Bräuninger 2004), while deepening by further transfers of policy competences for sensitive areas—such as monetary and fiscal, migration and asylum, economic and environmental, and foreign and defense—raises the salience of interests, which politicizes the choices for Europe (De Wilde 2011). For postfunctionalism, this politicization is constraining supranational governance (Hooghe and Marks 2009), while others conceive it either as a temporary phenomenon (Rauh, Bes, and Schoonvelde 2020) or a necessary condition for democratic responsiveness (Schneider 2018).

From a static perspective on European integration, in which the conditions for data generation would not change, the analysis of widening and deepening predicts a dividing rather than uniting of Europe when the potential of choices does not allow changing of the status quo in the EU, which faces fundamental crises and challenges. When the heterogeneity and salience of interests increases among a growing number of (institutional and partisan) veto players (Tsebelis 2002), a lower potential of choices is associated with reduced EU legislative activity (Crombez and Hix 2015) and lower EU policy-making efficiency (Schulz and König 2000), more bureaucratic politics (Junge, König, and Luig 2015) and noncompliance (König and Mäder 2014), and higher polarization of partisan (Hix 2008) and public opinion (Hobolt and De Vries 2015).

From a dynamic perspective on European integration, the conditions for data generation change in the period of study. Compared to the Amsterdam and Nice treaties, the number of the heads of state and government almost doubles at interstate bargains of the Lisbon Treaty (Finke et al. 2012). Furthermore, these treaties change the institutional and material foundations of supranational governance. Another change concerns external shocks by crises, which regularly hit the EU and demand supranational problem-solving with mass-mobilizing EU crisis management. All of this implies that inferences on the dynamics of European integration cannot be drawn from the distributions that govern one dataset, nor from narratives or data alone. Jones, Kelemen, and Meunier (2021: 1519) describe these dynamics as a pattern of failing forward: "in an initial phase, lowest common denominator intergovernmental bargains led to the creation of incomplete institutions, which in turn sowed the seeds of future crises."

To better understand the creation of incomplete institutions, this book argues that two games are played when the heads of state and government make institutional choices for Europe in interstate bargains, the interstate summit game and the national game of party competition. In the interstate summit game, policy- and office-seeking political leaders pursue country-specific interests in supranational governance design and party-specific interests in transfers of policy competences (König 2018). For example, political leaders from larger countries prefer a more proportional allocation of supranational offices that reflects population size, while political leaders of ruling/mainstream parties with governmental experience support the further transfer of policy competences. According to Figure 1.1, their institutional choices for Europe establish veto bicameralism with regulated supranational competences in the post-Maastricht period.

In addition to the causes of the institutional choices for Europe, Figure 1.1 also illustrates their consequences for supranational governance, which according to Jones, Kelemen, and Meunier (2021: 1519) "sowed the seeds of future crises, which then propelled deeper integration through reformed but still incomplete institutions—thus setting the stage for the process to move integration forward." To identify the empirical implications of incomplete

From Constraining Dissensus to Supranational Consensus?

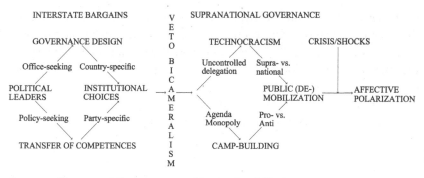

Figure 1.1. Causes and Consequences of Institutional Choices

institutions for supranational governance, this book distinguishes between the EU policy-making game and the supranational game of party competition with affective polarization of issues on European integration through exogenous shocks and crises.

In the first phase of deepening, uncontrolled delegation through a lower threat of legislative override fosters supranational technocracism, in which supranational experts prioritize supranational over national norms. In the second phase of widening, the failure to reform the composition and role of the European Commission promotes supranational camp-building in EU policy-making between pro-integrationist ruling/mainstream and anti-integrationist challenger/periphery parties with few moderates in between (Proksch and Lo 2012). While these changes only sporadically mobilize the public when a referendum is required for treaty ratification in the initial phases of the post-Maastricht period, supranational problem-solving with mass-mobilizing EU crisis management leads to affective polarization with emotional mobilization and ideological alignment along the divide between the existing two camps in the third phase. Similar to the analysis of the causes of the institutional choices for Europe, inferences on their consequences cannot be drawn from the distributions that govern one dataset, nor from narratives or data alone.

1.3. (Supra)National Partyism: A Theory of Institutional Choices

From a dynamic perspective on European integration in the post-Maastricht period, this book introduces (supra)national partyism (SNP) as a broader theory to derive propositions and hypotheses on the causes and consequences of the institutional choices for Europe. Compared to the paradigmatic schools of the classical debates, SNP offers falsifiable predictions about changes of the causes with the making of Amsterdam, Nice, and Lisbon treaties, and changes of the consequences for supranational governance with decreasing support of European integration in the beginning and increasing support in the most recent post-Maastricht period. There are two reasons to call this broader theory SNP:

- First, like other -isms, such as racism, sexism, classism, and sectarianism that define the classical social cleavages of race, gender, class, and religion in Europe, partyism contends that partisan identification is the major cleavage in European integration, which fosters in- and outgroup-building along party lines (e.g., Sunstein 2015, Iyengar, Sood, and Lelkes 2012, Iyengar and Westwood 2015, Westwood et al. 2018). Although partisan in- and outgroup-building are responsible for affective polarization in Europe (Hahm, Hilpert, and König 2023), it is also a precondition for ideological alignment along the pro- versus anti-integrationist camps with the formation of a superordinate supranational identity of solidarity and trust among Europeans.
- Second, two of the four games that this book introduces to better understand the dynamics of European integration, explicitly address their partisan foundation, the first in party competition at the national and the second at the supranational level. Thereby, the parentheses underscore that the supranational party system still consists of multiple national party systems, in which electoral competition is organized. They also underline the dynamic perspective of SNP, which perceives affective polarization as a means to an end, not an end in itself.[1]

Compared to the paradigmatic schools of the classical debates, which emphasize the role of either governments at major summits or supranational institutions in EU policy-making for European integration, SNP identifies the key actors, who seek offices and policies for their countries and parties as their delegated agents at summits and in EU policy-making (see also Hix and Lord 1997, Hix 2008, Hix and Hagemann 2009). This dual conception of their pref-

---

1. In my analysis of the causes, I originally called this theory national partyism because it combines the interstate summit with the national party game (König 2018).

erence fundamentals differs from the country-specific conception of liberal intergovernmentalism and the party-specific approach of postfunctionalism. SNP also shows under which conditions vote-seeking strategies are pursued to receive concessions at the bargaining table, and under which conditions these strategies may increase the risk of failure and inefficiency of the outcomes of their institutional choices.

Concerning the propositions and hypotheses on changes of the consequences of the institutional choices for Europe, SNP investigates the interactions between the supranational executive, judiciary, and legislature in the EU policy-making game. At the first step, SNP identifies the critical juncture for the divide between ruling/mainstream and challenger/periphery parties on European integration, which secondly consolidates by supranational camp-building in EU policy-making. While these implications are of little relevance for the public in the initial phases of deepening and widening, the public ideologically aligns with the pro- and anti-integrationist camps at times of supranational problem-solving with mass-mobilizing EU crisis management at the third step. Distinguishing between these three steps or phases, this book aims to provide a more dynamic understanding of the consequences for European integration in the post-Maastricht period.

In the first part of the book, the propositions and hypotheses of SNP on the causes of the country- and party-specific fundamentals of preferences, vote-seeking strategies in interstate bargains, and outcomes of their institutional choices are empirically examined with data of the Amsterdam, Nice, and Lisbon summits. The analyses explore changes of choices on the two important dimensions of interstate bargains, supranational governance design and transfer of policy competences to the level of the EU. They show that political leaders trade off office- and policy-seeking interests on supranational form and function, use referendums to receive concessions at the bargaining table, and finally agree on veto bicameralism with regulated supranational competences for EU policy-making.

In the second part of the book, the propositions and hypotheses of SNP on the consequences of supranational technocracism, camp-building, and affective polarization with the formation of a superordinate supranational identity are presented and examined with data on EU policy-making, partisan and public attitudes toward European integration. The analyses reveal systematic trends toward supranational technocracism and building of a pro- and an anti-integrationist camp in the EU policy-making game. They also identify affective polarization in the supranational game of party competition with ideological alignment at times of supranational problem-solving with mass-mobilizing EU crisis management. Finally, they show that similar levels of solidarity and trust exist among co- and EU outnationals but discrimination of Non-EU outnationals, which suggests the formation of a superordinate supranational identity.

In addition to the empirical examination of the causes and consequences of the institutional choices for Europe, this book aims to answer important puzzles in the post-Maastricht history of European integration, such as the integration paradox of new intergovernmentalism regarding the further transfers of functions without reforming the EU (Bickerton, Hodson, and Puetter 2015), the democratic deficit paradox of announcing more referendums in order to enhance democracy though they were ultimately ignored when political leaders agreed to continue with European integration (Finke et al. 2012), the parliamentarization paradox of strengthening the role of the European Parliament though legislative proposals are negotiated in informal trilogues (Reh, Héritier, Bressanelli, and Koop 2011), and the challenger paradox of ruling/mainstream parties, which commonly support the overemphasis of the goal of European integration, which promotes the rise of anti-integrationist challenger/periphery parties (De Vries and Hobolt 2020).

For scholars of politicization (e.g., De Wilde 2011, De Wilde and Zürn 2012, Rauh 2016), it introduces theories of delegation and party competition into the study of the global interactions that is still dominated by theories of trade and economic transactions on goods and services. Accordingly, vote-seeking political leaders pursue the office-seeking interests of their countries and the policy-seeking interests of their parties. Concerning the informational theory of legislative organization (e.g., Gilligan and Krehbiel 1987), representatives are interested in acquiring special expertise and power in supranational offices, while they experience policy-seeking benefits from further integration following the distributive theory of legislative organization (e.g., Weingast and Marshall 1988). Accordingly, representatives of ruling/mainstream parties are more likely to support European integration, while those of challenger/periphery parties reject it. These incentives may establish a new cleavage when the voters align along this divide in times of crises and their management.

Compared to bargaining theories of international relations, which predominantly focus on variation of country-specific interests that are negotiated in an environment of low cost complete and perfect information (Moravcsik and Schimmelfennig 2019), SNP identifies a two-dimensional bargaining space for a period of study and considers the implications of an environment of incomplete and imperfect information for the power distribution and outcomes at interstate bargains. While two- or multidimensional bargaining spaces offer trading-off utilities for compromise, considering the incompleteness and imperfectness of the environment can explain why some "weaker" vote-seeking political leaders, who signal high domestic ratification hurdles, are able to dominate interstate bargains by their domestic veto threats (Hug and König 2002, Slapin 2008). However, when more political leaders pursue this vote-seeking strategy, the increase of uncertainty may explain incomplete contracting with unintended consequences, such as the failure of summits and involuntary defection by referendums.

To scholars interested in the empirical implications of theoretical models, the analyses will present rich data and methods for examining the causes and consequences of the institutional choices for Europe in the post-Maastricht period. Analyzing the dynamics of European integration demands drawing conclusions for a period of study, which cannot be inferred from narratives or the data alone, nor from the distributions that govern one dataset. Remarkably, although a growing number of empirical studies on European integration attempt to answer these questions by inferring associations among variables of one dataset, this is only possible when the conditions of the data generation process remain the same. To outline associations among variables under changing conditions in the post-Maastricht period, the following analyses use measurement models to combine datasets and examine separately different datasets by graphical models, counterfactional analysis, and experimental designs.

For those interested in the future of European integration, the findings describe lessons about the institutional reforms of the EU and their dynamics. Scholars of liberal intergovernmentalism continue to defend the benefits of further integration due to economies of scale, lower exposure to external shocks, and more power in the international system without considering the possibility of an institutional mismatch, which is the starting point of post-functionalism. Taking into account the causes and consequences of the institutional choices for Europe, SNP can explain why political leaders agree on incomplete and imperfect institutions, and which implications these have for EU policy-making in the first place. However, these imperfect institutional choices may be a necessary condition for affective polarization in supranational party competition in the second place, which can finally promote the formation of a superordinate supranational identity with solidarity and trust among a majority of Europeans.

1.4. Plan of the Book

In Part 1 on the causes of the institutional choices, chapter 2 sets up propositions and hypotheses on the making of treaties and treaty amendments, providing explanations for the fundamentals of preferences, interstate bargains, and institutional choices of political leaders and their changes in the period of study. The central argument is that the choices on the reforms of the EU in the post-Maastricht period can be understood as a change of three factors: a change of relative importance toward country- and party-specific preferences; a change of interstate bargains toward sequential choices under incomplete and imperfect information; and a change toward outcomes with unintended consequences that foster supranational technocracism and camp-building. The general goal of the chapter is to outline simple, parsimonious explanations for the causes of the institutional choices for Europe.

Chapter 3 introduces data and a measurement model for the study of three summits as the major turning points in the post-Maastricht history of European integration. Although the observable issues and the positions of the political leaders vary across summits, the exploration of their latent preferences reveals an inherent structural conflict on supranational governance design and the transfer of policy competences. Due to the deepening and widening of the EU, the conflict on governance design unsurprisingly increases during the ratification process of the Constitutional Treaty, in particular by the accession of a high number of new members from Eastern and Central Europe. For some (sensitive) areas, such as defense, foreign policy, taxation, and asylum, introducing veto bicameralism with regulated supranational competences also matters for the transfer of policy competences.

For the empirical examination of the propositions and hypotheses of SNP on the causes of the institutional choices, chapter 4 integrates the summit-specific preferences into a common space for the period of study. This integration is a necessary condition for examining the propositions and hypotheses on the fundamentals of preferences and interstate bargains in the post-Maastricht period. Confirming the propositions on office- and policy-seeking, the findings suggest that political leaders perform a dual role as delegated agents of their countries on governance design and of their parties on the transfer of policy competences. Over time, the environment of their interstate bargains changes toward more uncertainty, in which vote-seeking political leaders use domestic veto threats to receive concessions. With higher uncertainty, the increasing popularity of this strategy not only provokes summit and referendum failure, but it also sporadically mobilizes the masses, and survival of the ratification process becomes the dominant goal at the end of this reform process.

In Part 2, chapter 5 begins with the study of the consequences of the institutional choices for Europe. It sets up propositions and hypotheses on EU policy-making, and partisan and public attitudes toward European integration. The central argument is that veto bicameralism with regulated supranational competences reduces the threat of legislative override for activism of supranational executive and judicial experts, which establishes supranational technocracism. Furthermore, the failure to reform the role and composition of the European Commission promotes supranational camp-building of pro-integrationist ruling/mainstream parties and anti-integrationist challenger/periphery parties, which have different office- and policy-seeking benefits from European integration. Finally, it predicts affective polarization when partisans ideologically align along the existing pro- and anti-integrationist divide in times of mass-mobilizing supranational problem-solving with EU crisis management.

Chapter 6 investigates the propositions and hypotheses of SNP on supranational technocracism. The analysis of about 120,000 legal acts shows that centralizing delegated regulations and decisions dominate EU policy-making. The trend toward uncontrolled supranational delegation is also visible for shared areas, which the subsidiarity principle aims to protect against supranational activism. Compared to supranational activism of executive experts, which increases with a lower threat of legislative override by a larger size of the legislative core, the member states can conditionally constrain judicial activism by sending uncontested signals to the European Court of Justice. In addition to reducing the threat of legislative override, the larger size of the legislative core also increases the risk of enforcement conflicts about compliance, which the European Commission attempts to reduce by involving the European Parliament in the making of directives. Another strategy to avoid enforcement conflicts about compliance is to approve early agreements in informal trilogues with the Council presidency and a delegation of the European Parliament at the expense of transparency and accountability.

Chapter 7 examines the implications of the institutional choices for supranational camp-building in EU policy-making. According to SNP, ruling/mainstream parties support European integration for office- and policy-seeking benefits, which stands in opposition to challenger parties from the periphery of the party spectrum. The analysis of their configuration in the national game of party competition reveals that the critical juncture for the divide between ruling/mainstream and challenger/periphery parties on European integration is the time of accession. The analysis of the supranational voting patterns confirms the proposition that this divide consolidates in the supranational game of party competition in EU policy-making of the post-Maastricht period. Following SNP, this is of little public relevance in the initial phases of the post-Maastricht period, in which the public is only sporadically mobilized on issues of European integration when a referendum is required for ratification.

Chapter 8 explores changes in public support of European integration. Confirming the proposition of SNP, the public disapproves the agenda monopoly of the European Commission and uncontrolled supranational delegation in EU policy-making. While the public interest in European integration declines during the initial phases of deepening and widening, this changes in times of supranational problem-solving with mass-mobilizing EU crisis management. The experimental analyses reveal a similar level of affective polarization among partisans on the left versus right and the pro- versus anti-integrationist dimension at the end of the period of study. Furthermore, except for right-leaning supporters of challenger/periphery parties, both camps show similar levels of solidarity and trust for co- and EU outnationals, while only left-leaning supporters of ruling/mainstream and challenger/periphery parties do not discriminate against non-EU outnationals.

Chapter 9 concludes by distinguishing two perspectives on European integration: one "differentiating" possibility would be to renationalize policy competences for sensitive areas. For such differentiated integration, it is important to distinguish between EU migration and immigration, which, according to postfunctionalism, mobilizes national identities and a desire for self-rule. If this desire evolves against non-EU outnationals from immigration, the recommendation would be to secure external borders, while a desire for self-rule against EU outnationals from EU migration would need to constrain free movement in the common market. Another possibility would be to reform the institutional model toward a supranational party democracy, which can overcome supranational cooperation and coordination deficits. Compared to current descriptive representation by country-specific population size, a more active representation principle in supranational party competition can reduce "My Population First" nativism by internalizing the costs of electoral nationalism, which is likely to rise in times of supranational problem-solving with mass-mobilizing EU crisis management.

Part 1

CHAPTER 2

Causes of Institutional Choices

2.1. Abstract

This chapter presents the theoretical framework for studying the causes of the institutional choices for Europe. After a short introduction into the fundamental reform questions in the period of study, propositions and hypotheses on the fundamentals of preferences of political leaders, their strategies at sequential interstate bargains, and outcomes of the institutional choices are introduced from a game-theoretical perspective. According to SNP, political leaders pursue country-specific office-seeking and party-specific policy-seeking interests. Over time, the vote-seeking strategy to announce referendums for ratification changes the power distribution at interstate bargains and the outcomes toward the lowest common denominator with risk of failure and inefficiency in a widening and deepening EU.

2.2. Theorizing Causes of European Integration

Compared to the classical debates between the schools of (neo-, post)functionalism and (liberal, new) intergovernmentalism, which focus either on the causes *or* the consequences,[1] SNP theorizes the causes *and* consequences of the institutional choices for Europe. Since the Maastricht Treaty, these choices aim to reform the EU by answering four fundamental questions:

---

1. While (liberal, new) intergovernmentalism concentrates on the part of governments and national economic interests at major summits as the causes, (neo-, post) functionalism focuses on the role of supranational institutions and global economic interests in EU policy-making as the consequences (e.g., Haas 1958, Hoffmann 1966, Lindberg and Scheingold 1970, Moravcsik 1998, 2018, Sandholtz and Stone Sweet 1998, Bickerton, Hodson, and Puetter 2015, Hooghe and Marks 2009, 2019).

- How can the institutional choices for Europe prepare for widening from 12 to 25 and more member states, which differ in their economic, cultural, and political backgrounds, but need to approve and comply with EU policies commonly?
- How can the institutional choices for Europe provide efficiency for deepening within a common market without borders, in which policy competences for sensitive areas such as monetary and fiscal, migration and asylum, economic and environmental, and foreign and defense politicize EU policy-making?
- How can the institutional choices for Europe settle disputes about the priority of supranational over national norms, which raise partisan and public conflicts between pro- and anti-integrationists in the national and supranational games of party competition?
- How can the institutional choices for Europe balance the relationship between long-term responsibility for the goal of European integration and short-term responsiveness to the distinct public demands in times of supranational problem-solving and EU crisis management?

For many scholars, the postwar period of permissive consensus ends at the beginning of the 1990s with the events around the Maastricht Treaty. While the French voters approved the founding treaty of the EU by only 51 percent, known as the "petit oui," the Danish voters surprisingly rejected it in June 1992. However, this could not stop ratification, and the Danish voters, after Denmark received one-sided concessions, approved the Maastricht Treaty in a second referendum in 1993.

Only a few years before, the Single European Act (1987) set the ambitious objective of establishing a common market that increases competition, specialization, and economies of scale, and the finally ratified Maastricht Treaty creates the EU with the premise of "further steps to be taken to advance European integration" (TEU: 3–5). Accordingly, further policy competences in more sensitive areas such as common security and defense, justice and home affairs, and a common asylum system are transferred, including the introduction of EU citizenship and the Eurozone of a monetary union under the so-called Maastricht criteria.

In the post-Maastricht period, the institutional choices for Europe establish the subsidiarity principle for areas of shared competences between the domestic and the EU level, and veto bicameralism, in which the bicameral chambers—the Council and the European Parliament—need to approve legislative proposals of the European Commission to take supranational action that can be better achieved at the EU level. This introduces veto bicameralism with agenda-setting monopoly of the European Commission under regulated supranational competences for the post-Maastricht period, in which the EU "shall take action, in accordance with the principle of subsidiarity, only if and in so far as the objectives of the proposed action cannot be sufficiently achieved by the member states" (Article 5 TEU).[2]

Although political leaders reach agreement on the reform of the EU and ratify the Amsterdam, Nice, and Lisbon treaties, König (2018) argues that it is unlikely that they intentionally make institutional choices, which ultimately reduce their power as

- their representatives can hardly control supranational delegation in EU policy-making, and
- their ruling/mainstream parties are challenged by the rise of populist movements and Eurosceptic parties.

This puzzling outcome rather suggests that the treaties are imperfect and establish incomplete institutions (Jones, Kelemen, and Meunier 2021) with so-called leftovers and unintended consequences.[3] For example, in addition to their inability to reform the role and composition of the European Commission, the treaties do not introduce a right of initiative for the (bicameral) legislature, clarify the horizontal and vertical division of policy competences, simplify the EU's legislative instruments, and achieve that "decisions are taken as closely as possible to the people," as declared in Article 1 TEU and reiterated by the Laeken declaration.

Instead of advocating one answer to the four fundamental questions on the institutional choices for Europe—the preparation for enlargement, the provision of efficiency for deepening, the balance between supranational and national norms, as well as between responsibility and responsiveness, this book introduces a set of propositions and hypotheses to better understand their

---

2. Only the European Commission can propose legislative proposals, while it can (but does not have to) respond to invitations to do so from the European Council, the Council of the EU, the European Parliament, and a successful European Citizens' initiative.

3. The limited reforms of the Amsterdam Treaty became known as the infamous "Amsterdam leftovers" (Yataganas 2001: 243, Laursen 2002: 5), which became the "Nice hangovers" that hardly prepared the EU for enlargement by the countries from Central and Eastern Europe (König and Bräuninger 2004).

causes. In doing so, it follows a methodological standard that derives propositions and hypotheses from general theories, such as on preference fundamentals from office- and policy-seeking theories, strategies at interstate bargains from games of sequential choices, and outcomes from theories of collective decision-making under uncertainty. These propositions and hypotheses are embedded into the broader theory of SNP, which emphasizes partyism as a crucial element in the post-Maastricht history of European integration.

2.3. Office- and Policy-Seeking Interests

To describe the motivation of the heads of state and government as delegated agents of their countries and parties, SNP assumes that they pursue coherent rational strategies to implement their underlying latent preferences. Underlying latent means that the fundamentals of these preferences cannot be directly observed but only inferred from functional positions, which political leaders articulate for each issue at the bargaining table. Political leaders articulate these positions "as if" they are rational, which stipulates that they advocate actions and outcomes they prefer. This assumption is weakly defined, which proposes that they strictly prefer one position to another or are indifferent between them.[4]

According to liberal intergovernmentalism, political leaders pursue national economic (commercial) interests, which vary by issues and countries concurrent with foreign economic policy (Moravcsik and Schimmelfennig 2019: 66). This proposition on the fundamental goals of political leaders is derived from endogenous political economy theories of trade and transactions. SNP posits that political leaders pursue the office-seeking interests of their countries on governance design and the policy-seeking interests of their parties on transfers of policy competences in the interstate summit game. Following the office-seeking theory of Riker (1962), political leaders maximize their country-specific benefits by controlling supranational offices within the governance design of the EU. These offices provide access to acquiring special expertise and power in EU policy-making. Typical examples concern the country-specific number of European Commissioners and the descriptive allocation of seats in the European Parliament and of voting

---

4. Formally, their ordering can be presented by the utility function $U(x)$: $x_1 > x_2$ if and only if $U(x_1) > U(x_2)$.

Causes of Institutional Choices

weights in the Council to population size, which are highly contested in the post-Maastricht period. From this office-seeking proposition follows the first hypothesis on the fundamentals of political leaders' preferences on supranational governance design:

- $H_{cau}1$. Political leaders pursue country-specific interests in the governance design of the EU.

In addition to country-specific office-seeking, political leaders also represent their parties in the national game of party competition. In the EU, most political leaders have the status of prime minister or chancellor, who are accountable to their partisan majority in parliament. Although some political leaders are directly elected, they need their parties for organizing electoral campaigns and support for policy-making. According to De Swaan (1973), political leaders maximize their partisan benefits from policy outcomes. Following the distributive theory of legislative organization of Weingast and Marshall (1988), parties respond positively to European integration when they have experienced partisan-ideological benefits from EU policy-making (König and Luig 2017). From this policy-seeking proposition follows the second hypothesis on the fundamentals of political leaders' preferences on transfers of policy competences:

- $H_{cau}2$. Political leaders pursue party-specific interests in the transfer of policy competences to the level of the EU.

SNP proposes with office- and policy-seeking a dual conception of preference fundamentals, which means that political leaders have country- and party-specific utilities. As shown in Figure 2.1, the indifference curves between the country- and party-specific fundamentals of their preferences trade off utility on one for utility on the other. If political leaders treat both sources of utility equally, their indifference curves will be straight lines (U1 to U5). However, if they are more concerned about one than the other, then the indifference curves will go up- or downward, depending on their relative office- and policy-seeking importance for each political leader.

When political leaders perform a dual role as the delegated agents of their countries in seeking benefits from offices and of their parties in seeking benefits from policies, their indifference curves can change over time reflecting the relative weight of individual office- and policy-seeking. Compared

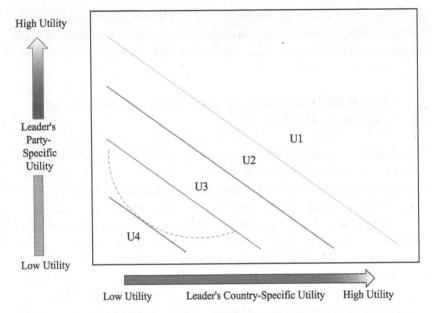

Figure 2.1. The Dual Preference Concept of (Supra)National Partyism

to country-specific office-seeking interests, the party composition of government can periodically change in the representative democracies of the member states. This suggests more variation in shifts of party-specific policy-seeking interests in the transfer of policy competences. For example, while most German parties prefer an allocation of power and offices according to population size, a governmental change can shift the German focus from transfers of market-oriented competences preferred by a government consisting of Liberal-conservative parties to equality and sustainability, which are preferred by a government of Left-green parties. According to this proposition, the third hypothesis is about the timing of a shift in political leaders' preferences:

- $H_{cau}3$. The preferences of political leaders are more likely to shift when the partisan composition of the government changes.

Unlike trends in economic circumstances and pressures from globalization, SNP expects that shifts in preferences resemble a dynamic electoral process with governmental changes, which are also affected by the electoral support of challenger/periphery parties (De Vries and Hobolt 2020). When issues of European integration become more salient due to their redistributive and emotional nature for the electorate, that is, during the migrant and Covid-19 crises, major concessions can also be economic, such as the EU-Turkey refugee pact and the Next Generation fund. Accordingly, preferences describe motivations and conditions, under which political leaders are assumed to behave in interstate bargains. Given preferences, bargaining theories use different assumptions on the informational environment and the strategies, which ultimately determine the power and capabilities in those bargains.

2.4. Power and Capabilities in Interstate Bargains

In addition to preferences for different procedures that assign power and capabilities for EU policy-making (e.g., Crombez 1996, 2000, Tsebelis and Garrett 2001), SNP also considers the preferences for the transfer of policy competences as an important component of interstate bargains, which can explain "why the signatories of a treaty selected one set of institutional arrangements over another" (Garrett and Tsebelis 1996: 270). From a game-theoretic perspective, SNP conceptualizes the interstate bargaining space as multidimensional and distinguishes between games of one- and two-stage sequential choices, in which the Council presidency can propose compromise for treaty approval. The first describes a game without (one stage) and the second with domestic ratification (two stages).

Another important distinction concerns the conception of the informational environment, in which these interstate bargains take place. When it is assumed that the Council presidency, which is responsible for the preparation of summits, makes proposals in an environment of complete and perfect information, a differentiation between political leaders and other actors of their domestic arena in a game with two stages is obsolete. In such an environment, which Moravcsik and Schimmelfennig (2019: 68) describe as a situation in which information and ideas are low-cost and widely evenly distributed among governments and domestic actors, the Council presidency can act as an effective entrepreneur in a one-stage game by initiating, mediating, and mobilizing coalitions among the political leaders of the member states (Tallberg 2004, 2006, Thomson 2008).

According to liberal intergovernmentalism, the willingness to compromise is itself primarily a function of preferences, not capabilities or power

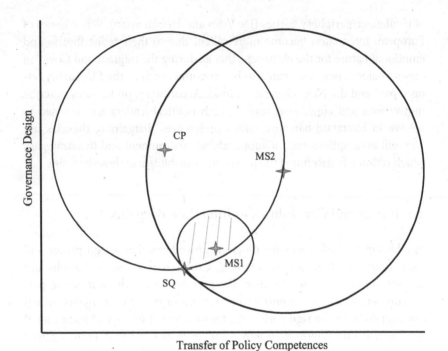

Figure 2.2. Interstate Bargains of Three Member States (Big-3) and Status Quo (SQ)

(Moravcsik 1992: 523). In the pre-Maastricht period, the preferences of the Big-3 of France, Germany, and the United Kingdom with their relative gains from institutional choices are accordingly decisive for treaty approval (Moravcsik 1998). For SNP, the Council presidency performs an important role in interstate bargains of sequential choices when the member states are willing to change the status quo. Figure 2.2 shows the Big-3 in a two-dimensional space of interstate bargains, one as the Council presidency (CP), and two member states MS1 and MS2, which need to approve a treaty in a two-dimensional bargaining space. The dimensions concern governance design and transfer of policy competences.

The shaded winset limits the space for approval of a treaty to the points from the intersection of the indifference curves of all three actors to the status quo (SQ). The larger the winset, the larger the potential of choices for Europe. For example, if MS1 would share the preference of MS2, the winset will enormously expand to the intersection of their similar indifference curves with that of CP. Similarly, if a member state would prefer the maintenance of the status quo, the winset will be empty and no point for treaty approval will exist. From this proposition on the size of the winset follows the fourth hypothesis on interstate bargains:

- $H_{cau}4$. Member states are more likely to approve a treaty in interstate bargains, the more distant they are from the status quo.

In interstate bargains of sequential choices, the Council presidency can successfully propose compromise to a member state that prefers to maintain the status quo. Compared to the 15 member states that negotiated the Amsterdam and Nice treaties, the Lisbon Treaty required the approval of 25 member states. Accordingly, widening may already explain why the conditions of interstate bargains change in the post-Maastricht period. Apart from widening, the conditions may also change when a noncooperative member state prefers summit failure over treaty approval and announces a referendum for ratification as a veto threat. To find approval for a treaty in this situation, the Council presidency needs to offer further concessions, which please the (voters of the) noncooperative member state. Figure 2.3 shows two scenarios with a cooperative and a noncooperative member state, in which they prefer to maintain the status quo (first preference).

In the first scenario, the cooperative member state prefers treaty approval (second preference) over summit failure (third preference) to save, for example, reputation and audience costs, while a member state favors summit failure (second preference) over treaty approval (third preference) in the noncooperative second scenario. When the Council presidency prefers a change of the status quo, it can only achieve approval for a treaty if the noncooperative member state becomes more cooperative. Vice versa, a noncooperative member state can demand further concessions, the more it is in favor of failure. From this proposition on the (non)cooperative type of member state follows the fifth hypothesis on power distribution in interstate bargains:

- $H_{cau}5$: A noncooperative member state is more powerful in interstate bargains, the more it favors failure over approval.

In an environment of incomplete and imperfect knowledge, the Council presidency needs to form a belief about the (non)cooperative type of member state by the probability p that it is likely to prefer treaty approval over summit failure, such that $1>p>0$. One way to infer this (non)cooperative type is pub-

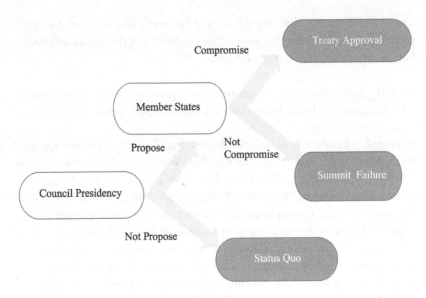

Figure 2.3. The Summit Game with Knowledge: Scenario (1): Preference equals Status Quo > Treaty Approval > Summit Failure. Scenario (2): Preference equals Status Quo > Summit Failure > Treaty Approval

lic support of European integration, which is decisive when a referendum is announced for ratification or when the voters already rejected the ratification of a treaty. However, for 25 or more member states, it becomes difficult, if not impossible, to correctly infer this (non)cooperative type. According to SNP, this change of the environment is responsible for scholarly debates about the patterns of European integration in the post-Maastricht period.

2.5. Outcomes with(out) Failure and Inefficiency

For liberal intergovernmentalism, the distribution of gains and efficiency determines the outcomes of interstate bargains in an environment of low costs and complete information (Moravcsik 1998: 51). Efficiency means that political leaders can achieve an optimal outcome, which does not leave potential gains at the bargaining table. In sequential interstate bargains, the Council presidency can behave as an effective entrepreneur and secure efficiency in an environment of complete and perfect information (Tallberg 2004, 2006).

Causes of Institutional Choices

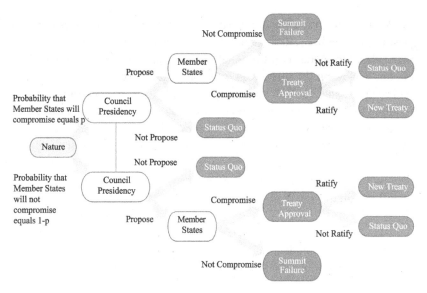

Figure 2.4. The Summit and Ratification Game with Perceptions: Scenario (1): Probability that Preference equals Status Quo > Treaty Approval > Summit Failure. Scenario (2): Probability that Preference equals Status Quo > Summit Failure > Treaty Approval

The simple reason is that the possibility of failure and inefficiency is excluded as the Council presidency would not make a proposal when it knows that a member state prefers failure over treaty approval.

Treaty approval depends on the outcome of the institutional choices. In the game-theoretical literature, two types of outcomes are distinguished, the first is a "weighted" compromise without consideration of the status quo, which may correspond to a Nash solution (Achen 2006), the second is the lowest common denominator, which emphasizes the veto power of status quo–prone (Slapin 2011) and eventually non-cooperative political leaders with credible veto threat (König 2018). According to interstate bargains of sequential choices in Figure 2.4, a new treaty not only requires approval by political leaders in the interstate summit game, but it also needs to be ratified in the national game of party competition. This additional requirement may reduce the size of the winset when the national game of party competition sets higher hurdles for treaty ratification than for government formation itself (König and Hug 2000).

At this ratification stage, a variety of domestic ratification procedures exist in the member states, ranging from simple to five-sixths parliamentary majorities, bicameral (constitutional) majorities, and ratification via referendum. Following the literature on two-level games, this establishes a second stage in sequential interstate bargains, in which successful ratification is required for treaty approval (Putnam 1988, Iida 1993, Pahre 1997). According to Hug and König (2002), this can be achieved by dropping contested issues from the bargaining table at the interstate summit game, which reduces the outcome of the institutional choices for Europe to the lowest common denominator. From this proposition on treaty ratification follows the sixth hypothesis on the outcome of institutional choices:

- $H_{cau}6$. In an environment of complete and perfect information, the lowest common denominator is the outcome of two-stage sequential choices without risk of failure and inefficiency.

Unlike the 15 member states at Amsterdam and Nice, the Lisbon Treaty required that 25 member states with diverse economic, cultural, and political backgrounds approve and ratify the institutional choices for Europe (Finke et al. 2012). According to SNP, widening increases not only the heterogeneity and salience of national interests but also the informational demand of the Council presidency about the national game of party competition. In this environment, the Council presidency needs to form a belief about the preference ordering of each type of member state and its domestic ratification type. For example, even if one only distinguishes between a domestic type that is likely to ratify or not in the national game of party competition, two potential types need to be considered for each member state, a cooperative and a noncooperative domestic type.[5]

When the Council presidency needs to form a belief about the preference ordering of 25 or more member states for treaty approval over summit and ratification failure, this is likely to raise the error term for the misperception of the Council presidency. This error term further increases when higher uncertainty exists about the outcome of a referendum. According to Finke and König (2009), treaty-friendly political leaders call for a referendum when

---

5. Hug and Tsebelis (2002) further distinguish between different types of referendums for ratification.

the risk of parliamentary ratification failure is higher, such as in Denmark. However, the authors also find that political leaders become more noncooperative and announce a referendum with a risk of failure when they expect little gains from treaty approval. Compared to parliamentary ratification in the national game of party competition, referendums not only increase the risk of ratification failure but also of inefficiency when additional one-sided concessions and opt-outs are necessary for final ratification. Compared to differentiated integration with concessions at interstate bargains, repeating negative referendums requires to make further one-sided concessions and opt-outs. From this proposition on referendum announcement follows the seventh hypothesis on the risk of failure and inefficiency of institutional choices:

- $H_{cau}7$. In an uncertain environment, the announcement of referendums increases the risk of failure and inefficiency of institutional choices for Europe.

For SNP, the informational environment changes over time. In particular, deepening and widening make it more difficult to approve and ratify treaties in the post-Maastricht period. This change has implications not only for preferences and power at interstate bargains but also the risk of failure and inefficiency of the institutional choices for Europe. Under these conditions, not only a noncooperative member state can dominate interstate bargains but the risk of failure and inefficiency also increases with higher popularity of this strategy. Briefly summarized, SNP posits that

- political leaders are office- and policy-seeking, which predicts that they pursue the interests of their countries and parties, which are more likely to shift by government change in the post-Maastricht period;
- the distance to the status quo determines power and outcomes, which predicts that outcomes reflect the lowest common denominator, which is likely in an environment of complete and perfect information;
- higher uncertainty by a widening and deepening EU but also due to the announcement of more referendums raises the risk of failure and inefficiency.

But why should one believe in the propositions and hypotheses of a new theory about the causes of the institutional choices more than in existing insights from prominent schools of thought, such as (liberal, new) intergovernmentalism? SNP offers to examine the explanatory power of the propositions and hypotheses, for which the next chapter presents the research design and data on political leaders' preferences, their interstate bargains, and outcomes of the institutional choices at summit conferences in the post-Maastricht period.

CHAPTER 3

Design and Competence for European Integration

3.1. Abstract

This chapter presents the research design for examining the propositions and hypotheses on the causes of the institutional choice for Europe in the post-Maastricht period. In addition to introducing the methodological standards, the issues and positions of the political leaders of the member states are presented as the input variables for the empirical estimation of summit spaces with latent dimensions and preferences. These spaces are explored for the Amsterdam, Nice, and Lisbon summits, which are the major turning points in the history of the post-Maastricht period. They reveal a structure that is characterized by two dimensions, governance design and transfer of policy competences, in which the preferences of political leaders and the outcomes of their interstate bargains are located in the period of study.

3.2. Research Design: Issues and Positions

For examining the propositions and hypotheses on the causes of the institutional choices for Europe in the post-Maastricht period, a research design is required that allows us to validate the empirical findings for a series of summits. In the pre-Maastricht period, for example, the number of political leaders changed from 6 to 12 until 1992, while the three major summit conferences during the post-Maastricht period experience an influx from 12 to 25 member states (excluding Bulgaria and Romania, which joined the EU in 2007) until the signing of the Lisbon Treaty in 2007. Empirically, this variation includes not only the number of political leaders but also the issues that are discussed and approved at each summit, and the context of their institutional choices, which also varies over time.

The research design of this book adheres to three methodological standards for the evaluation of the propositions and hypotheses on the causes of the institutional choices for Europe in the period of study: the first is disaggregation by data collection of all observable issue-positions pursued by political leaders at each summit. These data need to generate sufficient observations to identify the latent dimensions with preferences of political leaders and outcomes of their interstate bargains at each summit in a second step. Third, when these latent dimensions and preferences of political leaders can be aggregated into a common post-Maastricht space, this will allow the empirical examination of the propositions and hypotheses on the causes of the institutional choices for Europe regarding the fundamentals of preferences, strategies at interstate bargains, and the type of outcomes of institutional choices for the whole period of study.

More specifically, the data collection comprises three major turning points in the post-Maastricht history: the Amsterdam, Nice, and Lisbon summits with treaties and treaty amendments. While each summit is a unique event in the sense that different sets of issues are discussed, and while a different number of political leaders participate in those interstate bargains, most of the existing literature focuses on individual summits to draw inferences on their preferences and institutional choices (e.g., Moravcsik and Nicolaidis 1999, Yataganas 2001, Laursen 2002, 2005, 2008). For each summit, a specific set of observable issue-positions can be used to examine their bargains for the making of a treaty (e.g., Hug and König 2002, Tallberg 2002, König 2005, Thurner and Pappi 2009, Slapin 2008, 2011). When the issue-specific positions of the political leaders have a similar pattern, they can be reduced to latent dimensions, on which political leaders pursue more general (latent) preferences, which are not directly observable.

To identify the fundamentals of the preferences of political leaders on latent dimensions, which reflect the structure of the observable issue-positions, a measurement model is required that can also secure the comparability of the data across summits for a period of study: if similar latent dimensions can be identified for Amsterdam, Nice, and Lisbon, the follow-up question is whether a common space exists, which allows the examination of the propositions and hypotheses on the causes of the institutional choices for Europe in the post-Maastricht period. Methodologically, the estimation requires bridging the different sets of issues, respectively the latent dimensions of each summit into a common post-Maastricht space. This common space renders it possible to answer three main questions:

- First, what is the source of the preference fundamentals of political leaders who negotiate the form of governance design and function of supranational policy competences? Do these leaders pursue country-specific office-seeking and party-specific policy-seeking interests, which shift by governmental changes, as SNP posits?
- Second, how does an increasing number of political leaders negotiate governance design and transfer of policy competences? Do vote-seeking leaders dominate interstate bargains, in particular, if they have high domestic ratification constraints, as SNP contends?
- Finally, how about their institutional choices? Do the outcomes reflect the lowest common denominator with risk of failure and inefficiency, such that survival of ratification becomes the dominant goal, as SNP predicts?

For the study of the post-Maastricht period, the issue-specific positions of all political leaders across all major summits are gathered by Thurner, Pappi, and Stoiber (2002) for Amsterdam, König and Luetgert (2003) for Nice, and König, Daimer, and Finke (2008) for Lisbon. These positions are collected through expert interviews of the delegated participants. Before the summits concluded, most of the interviews were conducted with the responsible delegation of political leaders. The three datasets contain between 32 and 61 issues with responses from between 15 (Amsterdam and Nice) and 25 (Lisbon) political leaders on their issue-specific positions. All datasets are generated by researchers who did not intend to examine the explanatory power of propositions and hypotheses for a period of study.[1]

Theoretically, it is possible that the political leaders' positions, outcomes, and status quo—respectively their ordering on the scales—are identical across all issues. In this unlikely case, the set of issues can be reduced to a single dimension without loss of information on the data structure. This one-

---

1. The dataset of Thurner, Pappi, and Stoiber (2002), for example, is collected to study the multilevel negotiations with the coordination of informal administrative networks and the empowerment of administrative leadership, which are expected to shape the dynamics and outcomes of the Amsterdam Treaty. The data on the Nice Treaty are collected for the study of the positional changes of the political leaders through public (dis)approval during the summit conference (König and Luetgert 2003). Finally, the data collection for the Lisbon Treaty begins with an analysis of the delegates of the Laeken Convention, which set the agenda for the following summit conference on the Constitutional Treaty, which ultimately became the Lisbon Treaty (Finke et al. 2012).

dimensionality, which is often used for simplification of theoretical solutions, would facilitate drawing statistical inferences on the latent preferences of political leaders as their ordering is always the same.[2] However, if this ordering is empirically different across issues, the question arises about the number of dimensions to which a space can be reduced without (significant) loss of information on the data structure.

When the observable positions of the political leaders, as well as the locations of the status quo and the outcomes, vary across issues, and when the set of issues with the positions of political leaders, as well as the locations of the status quo and the outcomes, change over time, the methodological challenge is to estimate a space with latent dimensions, on which political leaders pursue more general latent preferences. One disadvantage of this estimation is that it reduces variation among observable issues to a fewer number of latent dimensions. However, measuring political leaders' issue-specific positions faces several potential sources of error. First, the issues and their alternatives must be identified. Second, if more than two positions on one issue exist, they must be ordered. And finally, the data concerning which positions political leaders support must be generated. All of these steps are potential sources of measurement error, which need to be related to the loss of information on the data structure, as the orderings of political leaders may not perfectly fit into a lower dimensional estimation of a space.

Estimating spaces substantively means that both the dimensions and preferences are latent, that is, one cannot directly observe the nature of the dimensions and the location of these preferences on them. With the knowledge about the location of the status quo at hand, it is possible to pre-order the alternatives of the issues along their pro- and anti-integrationist ordering, which is an important step to avoid an arbitrary aggregation of the issue-specific positions. Because the scales of the observable issues may differ by the number of positions, that is, dichotomous scales with two positions and scales with three or more positions, and so forth, their estimation requires a statistical measurement model (Jackman 2008, Benoit and Laver 2012). Following item response theory this measurement model reduces the orderings of the issues by employing

---

2. Oftentimes, one-dimensional simplifications are used for illustrations, such as to show the implication of a median voter for agenda setting, the location of a (weighted) bargaining solution, etc.

- latent variables to model the presence of measurement error. Like factor analysis, item response theory conceives latent variables to be continuous but assumes that observables are discrete, or, ordered, and
- probabilistic reasoning to facilitate inference from observational data to more broadly conceived preferences.[3]

3.3. Amsterdam: Preparing for Enlargement

One of the major challenges in the post-Maastricht period are the accessions from Eastern and Central European countries, which end the post-war division of Europe. In view of the approaching Eastern enlargement, the political leaders decide to form a group of representatives from the European Commission, the European Parliament, and the member states in March 1994 to prepare a new intergovernmental conference that lasted from June 1995 to April 1997. The European Council already decided in June 1993 in Copenhagen to offer membership to the applicant countries from Eastern and Central Europe. Following the formal signing of this treaty in Amsterdam by the 15 political leaders in October 1997, the European Parliament endorses the Amsterdam Treaty, and after two referendums and 13 decisions by national parliaments, the 15 member states finally conclude the ratification procedure and the treaty enters into force in May 1999.

After Maastricht, the number of political leaders not only changes over time but also the sets of issues, which are discussed at each summit afterward. A revision clause of the Maastricht Treaty already prescribes that any amendments have to be made in accordance with the objectives for the creation of an ever closer union among the peoples of Europe, the promotion of economic and social progress which is balanced and sustainable, an assertion of the identity of the EU on the international scene, protection of the rights and interests of nationals in the member states, development of closer cooperation in the fields of Justice and Home Affairs, and respect for the principle

---

3. Observations are y_{ij}, which are represented by the political leaders i ($i = 1, \ldots, n$) and issues j ($j = 1, \ldots, m$) with k ($k = 1, \ldots, K_j$) positional alternatives as $p(y_{ij} = K_j) = 1 - F\,(\gamma j, K_{j-1} - \Phi_i \lambda_j)$, where $F\,(\cdot)$ is the C.D.F. of a multivariate normal distribution. The parameter of interest is Φ_i, a vector that describes the latent preferences of political leaders i, while the vector λ_j indicates the loading of issues j on each dimension. γ_{jk} is a cut point parameter relating the latent "utility" (the product $\Phi_i \lambda_j$) to the probability corresponding to a response for each kth alternative.

of subsidiarity. Table 3.1 lists the Amsterdam issues and their loadings on the two dimensions, which are statistically identified.

The Amsterdam set of issues, which a preparation group elaborates, comprises two dimensions regarding governance design and the transfer of policy competences to promote the functioning of the common market. During the summit, the issues of qualified majority voting (QMV), flexibility, and strengthening parliamentary powers play a similarly important role as the further transfer of policy competences, including those for employment, the Common Foreign and Security Policies (CFSP), and Justice and Home Affairs (JHA) (Moravcsik and Nicolaidis 1999: 66). In addition to revising and expanding the application of the bicameral codecision procedure to sensitive areas such as internal market, employment, environment, and foreign affairs, in which the European Parliament (EP) becomes a colegislator with veto power, the Amsterdam Treaty introduces flexibility by "enhanced cooperation," a restrictive procedure that enables a smaller set of member states to take action where it was formerly not commonly possible (Thurner and Pappi 2009: 11).

Furthermore, in addition to JHA and CFSP, which also establish the position of a high representative of the EU in foreign affairs, the Schengen Agreement, which abolishes internal border checks, becomes part of the treaty. Except for Ireland and the United Kingdom, the EU sets out the conditions for entry into the Schengen area with legal acts, though it requires approval by the bicameral legislature of the Council and the European Parliament. The new areas of Freedom, Security, and Justice assure the free movement of persons in conjunction with appropriate measures "with respect to external border controls, immigration, asylum and the prevention and combating of crime" (CONF/4001/97: 11).

Like the decision on the introduction of a common currency at Maastricht, the transfer of these policy competences is accompanied by fundamental conflicts about governance design in Amsterdam. Although political leaders commonly agree on the need to reform EU governance design in preparation for an enlarged EU, the Amsterdam Treaty cannot resolve conflicts on the limitation of the number of Commissioners and the rebalance of the voting weights for qualified majority voting (QMV) in the Council, while the application of the bicameral codecision is expanded in further policy areas. Overall, the limited reforms of the governance design become known as the infamous "Amsterdam leftovers" (Yataganas 2001: 243, Laursen 2002: 5). Even though political leaders praise the Amsterdam Treaty as a necessary

Table 3.1. Factor loadings of the Amsterdam issues

Issue	Dimension 1	Dimension 2
Commission (number)	1	0
Commission (composition)	0.74	0.5
Commission (legislative powers)	−0.98	0.74
Subsidiarity (introduction)	0.48	−0.35
Scope of Codecision	−0.77	0.5
JHA (competences)	−0.56	0.28
JHA (application of QMV)	−0.61	0.45
JHA (democratic control)	−0.87	0.63
JHA (judicial control)	−0.53	0.29
National Parliaments (powers)	0.23	0.1
Employment (objective)	−0.67	0.38
Employment (chapter)	−0.47	−0.12
Fundamental Rights (introduction)	−0.62	0.3
Defense	0	1
Fundamental Rights (monitoring)	−0.32	0.78
Transparency of Council Meetings	−0.13	0.26
Citizenship of the Union	−0.11	0.87
CFSP (planning and preparation)	−0.33	0.98
CFSP (application of QMV)	−0.59	0.91
CFSP (implementation and representation)	−0.42	1.12
CFSP (WEU)	−0.17	0.9
QMV (extension of application)	−0.29	0.62
QMV (principle or case-wise)	−0.03	0.63
QMV (voting threshold)	−0.16	−0.27
QMV (voting weights)	0.89	1
QMV (dual majority)	0.35	0.87
Codecision (environment)	0.21	−0.03
Codecision (internal market)	−0.51	0.32
Codecision (employment)	0.24	0.29
Codecision (foreign)	0.49	1.09
Enhanced Cooperation (flexibility)	0.63	1.07
Enhanced Cooperation (conditions)	0.24	0.69
EP (electoral rules)	0.08	0.34
EP (budgetary powers)	−0.15	0.88
New Policy Competences	−0.37	0.31
Employment (monitoring)	−0.34	−0.3
Environment (exceptions)	0.01	−0.56
Taxation	0.43	0.08
Tourism	0.21	0.75

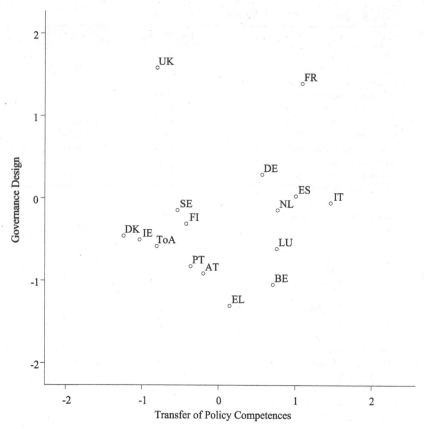

Figure 3.1. The Amsterdam Summit Space with AT: Austria, BE: Belgium, DE: Germany, DK: Denmark, EL: Greece, ES: Spain, FI: Finland, FR: France, IE: Ireland, IT: Italy, LU: Luxembourg, NL: Netherlands, PT: Portugal, SE: Sweden, UK: United Kingdom, ToA: Treaty outcome Amsterdam

step toward European integration after overcoming the ratification hurdles of two referendums in Denmark and Ireland and a constitutional amendment in France, the leftovers exemplify the need for further reform.

Figure 3.1 shows the estimation of two dimensions—a vertical on governance design and a horizontal axis on the transfer of policy competences—with the configuration of political leaders' preferences.[4] The preferences

---

4. The two-dimensional model is identified via exclusions by $y_{ji} = g(\lambda_{j,1} \Phi_{i,1} + \lambda_{j,2} \Phi_{i,2} - \gamma_j)$, where $g(\cdot)$ is a general function that relates the parameters to the observed responses y_{ji}.

Design and Competence for European Integration   41

indicated by the more extreme political leaders are used to interpret their direction, that is, on the y-axis more (proportional) asymmetry on top versus more (equal) symmetry of power and offices in governance design on the bottom, and on the x-axis less on the left versus more transfer of policy competences on the right side of Figure 3.1. The outcome of the Amsterdam Treaty (ToA) is surrounded by a group of countries, which are considered to have bargained surprisingly well (Moravcsik and Nicolaidis 1999: 75). Tallberg (2006: 123) describes this group as a Northern alliance between the political leaders from Sweden (SE), Finland (FI), and Denmark (DK), while the estimation suggests the additional inclusion of Ireland (IE) in this group as one of the two countries that ratifies via referendum. Similar to Denmark and Ireland, the United Kingdom (UK) is located slightly to the left side of the outcome on the x-axis, which means that the British prime minister does not support a further transfer of policy competences. In contrast to the preference of political leaders from these three countries, all others are in favor of transferring more policy competences from the national level to the EU, in particular from the founding members Italy (IT), France (FR), Belgium (BE), Luxembourg (LU), the Netherlands (NL), Germany (DE) along with Spain (ES).

Compared to the ordering on the x-axis on the transfer of policy competences, the configuration on the y-axis indicates a higher level of conflict in governance design. On the one side, the political leaders of the United Kingdom (UK) and France (FR), and only to some extent of Germany (DE), are in favor of a more proportional allocation of power and offices in relation to population size. This "proportionalist" group stands in contrast to the preferences of political leaders from smaller countries such as Greece (EL), Belgium (BE), Austria (AT), and Portugal (PT), which prefer to apply a "one state one vote" principle for the allocation of offices and power. This group is especially opposed to giving up leadership posts, even though this risks doubling the number of supranational executive and judicial offices in the event of the upcoming Eastern enlargement.

At the summit, most of the discussions relate to this conflict on governance design (Laursen 2002: 575). On the three main issues regarding the size

---

When a leader's $\Phi_{i,1} = \Phi_{i,2} = 0$, $y_{ji} = g(\gamma_j)$ for all j's, the γ parameters are identified by setting one point in both dimensions to the origin. Markov-Chain-Monte-Carlo simulations fit with the Bayesian approach to statistical analysis in which unknown parameters are treated as random and represented with probability distributions.

of the European Commission, changes in the Council voting weights, and the expansion of qualified majority voting in the first pillar, only an agreement on the latter is reached in Amsterdam. According to Laursen (2002: 586), the "question of weighting of votes turned out to be a real battle between the small and big member states ... a zero-sum game, which made it impossible to find a solution in Amsterdam in June 1997." However, the political leaders agree to introduce the possibility of early agreements, which offer the Council presidency and a delegation of the European Parliament a simplification of the bicameral procedure through informal trilogue meetings with the European Commission—an agreement with fundamental implications for the accountability and transparency of EU policy-making in the post-Maastricht period (Reh et al. 2011).

3.4. Nice: Dealing with Leftovers

Only a few months after the Amsterdam Treaty comes into force, the Treaty of Nice is already negotiated at a summit conference in December 2000 dealing mainly with the leftovers from the Amsterdam Treaty, in particular with the three institutional issues on governance design of weighting votes in the Council, increased use of qualified majority voting, and the size and composition of the European Commission. The Nice summit explicitly starts with the aim to reform the EU's governance design before Eastern enlargement, which is becoming not only a matter of credible commitment but also a question of balancing EU policy-making efficiency and democratic legitimacy.

Policy-making efficiency mainly concerns the increased use of qualified majority voting in the Council to reduce the higher gridlock risk in the event of enlargement, where the results lead to its expanded application in 31 policy areas (Maurer 2005: 175). Furthermore, the issue of easier enhanced cooperation relates to efficiency, while the size of the European Commission and the hotly debated reweighting of Council votes raises more conflict about democratic legitimacy. The political leaders from the smaller countries do not accept the perspective of a supranational executive and judiciary in which their country would not be represented, while the reweighting of Council votes is seen as "politically and symbolically important" (Laursen 2006: 410). Under the new chancellor Gerhard Schröder, unified Germany demands a representation principle that reflects population size, which stands in contrast not only to the preferences of political leaders from smaller countries

Design and Competence for European Integration 43

but also to the French postwar prerogative to tame (unified) Germany (Katzenstein 1997). In preparation for the Nice summit, a high number of reweighting proposals for qualified majority voting (QMV) are circulated, which ultimately leads to the application of a triple majority criterion that decreases instead of increases policy-making efficiency by a higher gridlock risk in the legislature. Blocking minorities can be established through either the number of countries, a threshold of their weighted votes, or population size. In particular, the application of the bicameral codecision procedure is extended for a high number of policy areas and subareas, including fundamental rights, and asylum and immigration. Compared to previous summits, less attention is paid to the transfer of policy competences from the national to the EU level (Laursen 2006: 2). However, the European Council in Helsinki (1999) decides to develop the EU's defense policy and to draft a Charter of Fundamental Rights, which are dealt with in a parallel process of the Nice summit. In some countries, such as the UK and DK, this charter raises concerns about democratic legitimacy in case of judicial activism of the European Court of Justice. Table 3.2 lists the Nice issues and their loadings on the two dimensions.

The high number of institutional and organizational issues and the dominance of QMV issues underline the focus on governance design at Nice. While the extension of QMV reveals specific concerns about taxation and social security, shipping, and the film industry (Laursen 2006: 10), the estimation suggests that the transfer of further policy competences also plays an important role at the Nice summit. On closer inspection, the loading patterns reveal that several QMV and composition issues are also loading on the policy transfer dimension, which may indicate the nonseparability of those preferences (Finke 2010a). Figure 3.2 illustrates the configuration at Nice, which shows—except for Denmark (DK)—the most variation on the vertical axis of governance design.

Interestingly, the political leaders from Italy (IT) and the United Kingdom (UK), represented for the first time by Tony Blair from the Labour Party, are more closely related on matters of governance design to the German preference represented by the Social Democrat Gerhard Schröder than the French preference represented by the Republican Jacques Chirac. Like Amsterdam, the "proportionalist" group of Italian (IT), German (DE), and British (UK) political leaders stands in opposition to the group of those from smaller countries such as the Netherlands (NL), Luxembourg (LU), Greece (EL), Sweden (SE), and Portugal (PT), which continue to favor "the one state one vote"

Table 3.2. Factor loadings of the Nice summit issues

Issue	Dimension 1	Dimension 2
Commission (number)	1	0
Commission (internal organization)	0.73	0.25
Commission (organization)	−0.2	0.14
ECJ (composition)	−0.17	−0.07
ECA (composition)	0.09	0.01
EP (allocation of seats)	−0.14	−0.26
Closer Cooperation	−0.09	0
Codecision (education)	−1.14	0.2
Codecison (fundamental rights)	−1.05	0.45
Codecision (employment)	−1.05	0.24
Codecision (culture)	−0.87	0.19
Codecision (health and social)	−0.84	0.43
Codecision (monetary)	−0.66	0.15
Codecision (drugs)	−0.63	0.17
Codecision (development)	−0.58	−0.23
Codecision (research)	−0.57	−0.2
Codecision (environment)	−0.48	−0.04
Codecision (working rights)	−0.46	0.46
Codecision (media)	−0.41	0.18
Codecision (economic)	−0.36	−0.37
Codecision (foreign)	−0.33	0.24
Codecision (defence)	−0.24	0.54
Codecision (VAT)	−0.23	−0.32
Codecision (social)	−0.14	0.09
Codecision (immigration)	−0.13	0.56
Codecision (agriculture)	−0.13	−0.44
Codecision (asylum)	0.02	0.49
Codecision (general rule)	0.54	0.54
Public Prosecutor	0	1
Committee of Regions (composition)	−0.34	−0.73
ECOSOC (composition)	−0.34	−0.73
Commission (accountability)	0.08	0.24
QMV (voting weights)	0.19	0.28
QMV (principle or case-wise extension)	0.24	0.49
QMV (foreign non-EU countries)	0.38	−0.15

solution for the allocation of offices and power. The group in-between consists of political leaders from Spain (ES), Finland (FI), Ireland (IE), Belgium (BE), France (FR), and Austria (AT), who find their preference for governance design closely reflected in the Nice Treaty. Concerning the size and composition of the European Commission, a decision is postponed to the time after Eastern enlargement, and the triple majority in Council voting reflects the status quo of the voting threshold. Compared to these hotly debated institu-

Design and Competence for European Integration

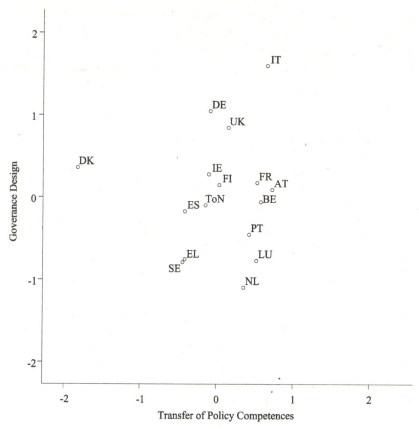

Figure 3.2. The Nice Summit Space with AT: Austria, BE: Belgium, DE: Germany, DK: Denmark, EL: Greece, ES: Spain, FI: Finland, FR: France, IE: Ireland, IT: Italy, LU: Luxembourg, NL: Netherlands, PT: Portugal, SE: Sweden, UK: United Kingdom, ToN: Treaty outcome Nice

tional issues for preparing enlargement, the expansion of veto bicameralism remains uncontested.

The horizontal axis refers to the further transfer of policy competences, where the major issues concern easier enhanced cooperation and the extension of qualified majority voting in the Council with the expansion of veto bicameralism to sensitive policy areas. Most obviously, the preference of the Danish (DK) political leader diverges from those of other leaders at Nice. After the negative Danish referendum on participation in the Euro in September 2000, which took place during the Nice summit, the Danish Social Democratic prime minister Poul Nyrup Rasmussen makes efforts to avoid another referendum. As the transfer of policy competences from the national to the EU requires a five-sixths majority in the Danish parliament, ratification by an ordinary parliamentary majority followed by a referendum has formerly been an easier solution for ratification in Denmark (König and Hug 2000).

To ratify Maastricht after the No-vote of the Danish voters, Denmark already negotiated three exemptions regarding the transfer of policy competences on citizenship, justice and home affairs, and defense policy—issues that were negotiated in parallel to the reform of governance design at Nice. Furthermore, the Danish preference is opposed to the extension of a Council qualified majority voting in sensitive policy areas, such as social policy, easier use of enhanced cooperation due to the fear of marginalization, and the introduction of a surveillance mechanism by the Charter on Fundamental Rights.

Although the Nice Treaty does not solve the institutional issues for preparing Eastern enlargement and the final agreement closely reflects the Irish status quo–prone preference, the Irish voters surprisingly reject it in a first referendum in June 2001, and a second referendum is needed. In Ireland, the transfer of the defense policy raises public concerns about Irish neutrality, which lead to the rejection of the first Irish referendum. On closer inspection of the referendum process, the noncooperative Irish government shows modest enthusiasm in campaigning for support of the first agreement, which the majority of the Irish rejects with a low turnout of only 34 percent. Only after receiving an opt-out from defense, the more cooperative Irish ruling parties massively campaign for support of the modified agreement in the second referendum.

Compared to Amsterdam, the Nice Treaty expands the application of Council qualified majority voting and strengthens the role of national parliaments to increase democratic legitimacy for EU policy-making in sensitive policy areas. In addition to facilitating enhanced cooperation, the Nice Treaty further integrates the area of Common Foreign and Security, the area of Freedom, Security and Justice, and expands veto bicameralism in several policy areas, such as consumer protection, tourism, commercial policy, education, and research. In particular, the disunity between political leaders from France and unified Germany concerning the allocation of power and offices prohibits a more effective institutional reform of the EU.

Accordingly, the Nice Treaty cannot resolve the leftovers of the Amsterdam Treaty, which become so-called hangovers when preparing for the enlargement of the countries from Central and Eastern Europe. The partly chaotic discussions about the reweighting of the Council voting weights shows that another method is required to prepare the next summit. Already in parallel to the interstate bargains at Nice, the political leaders establish the convention method used for the drafting of the Charter of Fundamental Rights that has been chaired by former German president Roman Herzog. The convention—which is composed of governmental representatives, representatives from the European Commission, European Parliament, and national parliaments—drafts the Charter after 30 meetings in nine months. In the end, no votes are taken and the charter's draft is sent to the political leaders for approval.

3.5. Lisbon: Departure from the Constitution

The negotiations of the Lisbon Treaty start with the impression that the two former treaties, the Amsterdam and the Nice treaties, failed to prepare the EU for the accession of the 10 to 12 countries from Eastern and Central Europe. At Laeken (2001), the 15 political leaders set the key issues to be discussed at a convention on the future of Europe, whose inaugural session already takes place in 2002 before the Nice Treaty comes into force. These issues include the division of policy competences between the EU and the member states, the simplification of the EU's legislative instruments, the maintenance of the interinstitutional balance, the improvement of EU policy-making, and the constitutionalizing of the treaties.

Following the experience with the Charter on Fundamental Rights, the political leaders decide to convene a convention and appoint the former French president Giscard d'Estaing as the convention's president. The convention is composed of governmental representatives, representatives from the European Commission, European Parliament, and national parliaments, including delegates from 13 accession and candidate countries. The purpose of this inclusive composition with 207 members and 13 observers, of which only 66 have the right to vote (each country has one governmental and two parliamentary representatives) is twofold: first, it shall provide the legitimacy for constitution-building; second, it shall avoid ratification failure (König 2005: 259).

The convention establishes eleven thematic working groups and goes through three phases: (1) a listening phase during the first six months, (2) an analysis phase through early 2003, and (3) a drafting phase during the remaining months in 2003 (Laursen 2008: 5). Without taking a vote, the convention presents a draft for a constitution in June 2003. However, even though governmental delegates were participating in the convention, several political leaders immediately call the finality of the constitutional text into question. Instead of presenting a wish list, Valérie Giscard d'Estaing governed the process toward a coherent constitutional proposal by establishing a committee system (Proksch 2007), steering the agenda (Tsebelis 2006), and making decisions by consensus (König and Slapin 2006). Under the Italian presidency, the summit starts in 2003 with fundamental reservations against the constitutional text, in particular for a change of the Council's voting threshold, the Common Foreign and Security Policy, and the Charter of Fundamental Rights. Furthermore, the issue of the size and composition of the European Commission is left unsolved. However, the trend of the two previous summits to expand the codecision procedure is completed by establishing veto bicameralism as the standard procedure for EU policy-making. Table 3.3 lists the Nice issues and their loadings on the two dimensions.

Because political leaders cannot find an agreement under the Italian presidency led by Silvio Berlusconi, the Rome summit concludes without finding an agreement until a compromise is presented by the Irish presidency at a new summit in 2004. The political leaders accept the compromise, but an unprecedented number of eleven leaders announces ratification by referendum. Among those are countries with and without referendum tradition, parties with more pro- and anti-integrationist attitudes, and popular and unpopular political leaders (König and Finke 2009: 350). After the political leaders from Spain, Luxembourg, Denmark, the Netherlands, Portugal, and the Czech Republic, British prime minister Tony Blair announces a referendum, followed by French president Jacques Chirac. Figure 3.3 shows the preference distribution of political leaders on governance design and transfer of policy competences in Lisbon.

Like previous configurations, the political leaders from larger countries, such as Italy (IT), Germany (DE), and France (FR) prefer a more proportional distribution of offices and power, which stands in contrast to the preferences of political leaders from smaller countries, such as Slovakia (SK) and Cyprus (CY). Most of the political leaders from the accession countries are located on the bottom half of the governance design dimension, which suggests a preference for an equal distribution of power and offices. Compared to Amsterdam and Nice, the British preference (UK) moves to the center of the con-

Table 3.3. Factor loadings of the Lisbon summit issues

Issue	Dimension 1	Dimension 2	Issue	Dimension 1	Dimension 2
Commission (number)	1	0	Codecision (social security)	−0.15	0.46
Council Presidency (nomination)	−0.35	−0.05	Codecision (fundamental rights)	−0.14	0.36
ECJ (scope)	−0.3	0.08	Codecision (ASFJ)	−0.08	0.4
Subsidiarity	0.22	−0.2	Codecision (taxation)	−0.07	0.9
EP (right of initiative)	−0.4	−0.07	Codecision (social)	0.1	0.37
Right of Initiative (Council)	0.18	−0.11	QMV (voting threshold)	0.12	0.52
SGP (flexibility)	−0.28	−0.12	QMV (regional)	−0.06	0.06
SGP (debt criterion)	−0.11	0.12	QMV (economic)	−0.05	0.48
Commission (appointment president)	0.04	−0.14	QMV (social security)	0.01	0.57
Common Security and Defence	0	1	QMV (monetary)	0.02	0.5
Enhanced Cooperation	0.48	0.79	QMV (internal market)	0.23	0.26
Competence (AFSJ)	0.13	0.6	QMV (defence)	0.26	0.8
Competence (economic)	−0.26	0.67	QMV (taxation)	0.42	0.75
Competence (foreign)	0.12	0.77	QMV (foreign)	0.44	0.62
Competence (health)	−0.22	0.45	QMV (social)	0.53	0.46
Competence (social)	−0.21	0.82	QMV (employment)	0.17	0.57
Competence (taxation)	−0.2	0.8	MFA (appointment role of EP)	−0.13	−0.54
Competence (tourism)	−0.13	0	MFA (appointment role of Commission)	0.05	0.36
Competence (research)	−0.09	0.79	MFA (external representation)	0	0.44
Competence (environment)	−0.6	0.39	External Borders (management)	0.03	0.34
Competence (regional)	−0.57	0.43	Council Presidency (organization)	0.12	0.48
Competence (employment)	−0.56	0.54	EP (budgetary powers)	−0.01	0.07
Competence (education)	−0.44	0.48	Right of Initiative (Citizens)	0.18	0.41
Competence (agriculture)	−0.43	0.19	Right of Withdrawal	−0.06	−0.47
Codecision (economic)	−0.48	0.04	Commission (appointment)	0	0.7
Codecision (monetary)	−0.43	0.11	Religious Reference	0.13	−0.44
Codecision (employment)	−0.3	0.43	Full employment (objective)	−0.22	0.61
Codecision (internal market)	−0.3	0.21	Competitiveness (objective)	0.1	0.3
Codecision (defence)	−0.29	0.49	Social Market Economy (objective)	0.41	0.3
Codecision (foreign)	−0.29	0.49	Employment (chapter)	−0.26	0.6
Codecision (agriculture)	−0.23	0.03	Migration and Asylum (chapter)	0.47	0.61
Codecision (region)	−0.21	0.22			

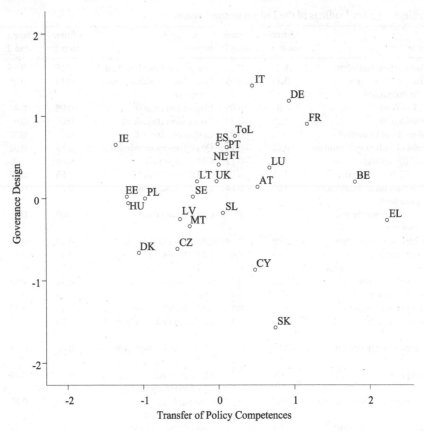

Figure 3.3. The Lisbon Summit Space with AT: Austria, BE: Belgium, CY: Cyprus, CZ: Czech Republic, DE: Germany, DK: Denmark, EE: Estonia, EL: Greece, ES: Spain, FI: Finland, FR: France, HU: Hungary, IE: Ireland, IT: Italy, LU: Luxembourg, LT: Lithuania, LV: Latvia, MT: Malta, NL: Netherlands, PL: Poland, PT: Portugal, SE: Sweden, SK: Slovakia, SL: Slovenia, UK: United Kingdom, ToL: Treaty outcome Lisbon

figuration, in which the final outcome—the Lisbon Treaty—is located. The formerly successful couple, Denmark (DK) and Ireland (IE), which resisted a further transfer of policy competences from the national to the EU level in previous rounds of treaty revisions in the post-Maastricht period, are now joined by leaders from Poland (PL), Hungary (HU), and Estonia (EE).

The ratification process starts with parliamentary approval in Lithuania, Hungary, Slovenia, Slovakia, Italy, and Germany followed by a consultative referendum in Spain, and parliamentary approval in Austria. Most surprisingly, the French voters reject the Constitutional treaty in a referendum, followed by a No-vote of the voters in the Netherlands. Although Greece, Malta, Cyprus, Finland, Latvia, Belgium, and Estonia continue with parliamentary ratification, the political leaders from the Czech Republic, Denmark, Ireland, Poland, Portugal, Sweden, and the United Kingdom postpone their ratification processes after the negative French and Dutch referendums. This leads to a so-called reflection period, which lasts until the French presidential election in the spring of 2007.

Under the German presidency, a compromise is reached, which removes the more symbolic constitutional elements from the text, while the political leaders agree to continue with parliamentary ratification, where possible. At the Lisbon summit, the political leaders sign the treaty, but the Irish voters reject it in a mandatory referendum in 2008. The analysis of Finke and König (2009) suggests that the German presidency pursues a risky strategy, and the noncooperative Irish ruling parties have little incentive to campaign for ratification, which led to a turnout of only 53.1 percent by a margin of 53.4 to 46.6 percent against the treaty. Consequently, Ireland receives additional concessions, and the treaty is approved in a second Irish referendum in 2009 by a margin of 67.1 to 32.9 percent with a turnout of 59 percent.

Briefly summarized, the exploration of the three major summits in the post-Maastricht period shows that the political leaders cannot achieve their original reform goals:

- First and foremost, they promise to improve the efficiency of EU policy-making. They lower the voting threshold in the Council, which however more than doubles membership size. Furthermore, they add with the European Parliament an institutional veto player that is likely to increase the size of the legislative core.
- Second, they fail to reform the composition of the European Commission. Only a protocol laid down the provision that "the Commission shall comprise one national of each of the Member States, provided that, by that date, the weighting of the votes in the Council has been modified (. . .) in a manner acceptable to all Member States." A more extensive reform would have to be implemented at a later date, "at least one year before the membership of the European Union exceeds twenty," but the exact terms are not specified.
- Third, they do not establish the right to initiate legislative proposals

for the European Parliament or the Council to constrain the agenda monopoly of the European Commission. As a result, the European Commission continues to prioritize supranational over national norms, which fosters the building of two camps with few moderates in between.

To examine the propositions and hypotheses on these institutional choices for Europe in the period of study, the identification of a common space for a series of summits is a necessary condition. However, scaling differences are likely to exist not only for the issues of each summit but also across these summits. Put differently, if no common space can be identified, each summit would be "sui generis" and exclude any periodic generalization of the findings. If, however latent dimensions and preferences structure the institutional choices for Europe in the period of study, an examination of the propositions and hypotheses on preference fundamentals, strategies at interstate bargains, and outcomes of their institutional choices is possible. This examination should be statistically rigorous in the sense that the propositions and hypotheses are falsifiable.

CHAPTER 4

Choices for Europe after Maastricht

4.1. Abstract

This chapter identifies the structure of the space in which the institutional choices for Europe are made in the post-Maastricht period. This common space allows us to examine propositions and hypotheses on the fundamentals of political leaders' preferences, their strategies at interstate bargains, and the outcomes of their institutional choices in the post-Maastricht period. The findings show that political leaders pursue country-specific office-seeking and party-specific policy-seeking interests, which shift at times of government changes. Vote-seeking political leaders with referendum threat are particularly powerful at Amsterdam and Nice, where outcomes reflect the lowest common denominator. However, the higher uncertainty by more referendum announcements in Lisbon leads to institutional choices for Europe with the risk of failure and inefficiency.

4.2. Examining Hypotheses for a Period of Study

One central argument of SNP is that the history of the post-Maastricht period can be understood by a change in the relative importance of country- and party-specific preferences. Another example for this change concerns the announcement of British prime minister David Cameron before the general election to hold a referendum about EU membership (König 2018). The British prime minister proposed to renegotiate the country-specific terms of British EU membership, on which the public can decide.[1] Although the Brit-

---

1. These terms concern an emergency brake mechanism, which would allow member countries to limit access to in-work benefits for new EU immigrants, a red card mechanism, which would allow a member state of the Council with the support of other members

ish voters appreciated the announcement and the prime minister's Conservative party surprisingly won the general election, the party could not settle its ideological dispute on EU membership in the referendum campaign, which signaled that the prime minister ineffectively renegotiated the British membership terms (König and Lu 2020).[2]

A second central argument of SNP posits that interstate bargains change from one-stage toward two-stage sequential choices under uncertainty. This change has crucial implications for the power distribution and the risk of failure and inefficiency of outcomes. This is also exemplified by the interstate bargains between the British prime minister and the political leaders of the other member states on the British terms of EU membership, which the British voters finally rejected. The political leaders of the other member states did or could not offer sufficient compromise to settle the ideological dispute within the Conservative party, from which the British voters could finally infer ineffective renegotiations of British membership terms. Historically, it was possible to settle a similar dispute in the Labour party of prime minister Harold Wilson to avoid the risk of referendum failure in the beginning of the 1970s (König and Lu 2020).[3]

Of course, the British example is only a special case that exemplifies the change of the relative importance of country- and party-specific preferences, an environment of incomplete and imperfect information, and an outcome with risk of failure and inefficiency. For a more general evaluation of the prop-

---

to return a recommendation to the European Parliament for further changes, a mechanism on the free movement rules to make it easier for countries to deport the EU immigrants and on their child care benefits that would reflect the standard of living in the country where the child lives and the amount of child benefits that would normally be paid in that country, to limit the ability of a non-EU national to gain the right to live and work anywhere in the EU, a system for non-Eurozone members to object to rules being passed that might harm them but it will not give them a legal opt-out.

2. Similar to David Cameron, Prime Minister Harold Wilson from the Labour party announced holding a referendum at the beginning of the 1970s. Both prime ministers surprisingly won the general election, renegotiated the terms, suspended the constitutional convention of cabinet collective responsibility, and recommended to remain. While the voters supported Harold Wilson's membership proposal with a high turnout of 64 percent and 67 percent in favor, 52 percent of the voters with a turnout of 72.2 percent rejected the remaining proposal of David Cameron.

3. Whether the credibility of the British partnership or the heterogeneity of the other member states' preferences reduced the number of concessions that would have been necessary to convince the Conservative party and the British voters of British EU membership, remains an open question.

ositions and hypotheses on the fundamentals of political leaders' preferences, their strategies at interstate bargains, and the outcomes of their institutional choices, the data on the three summits of Amsterdam, Nice, and Lisbon are used to estimate a common space, which allows examining their explanatory power for the period of study.

The exploration of the three summits already shows that typical issues on governance design are the allocation of offices in the European Commission, the design of voting rules and policy-making procedures, the rules for enhanced cooperation, the duration, rotation and composition of the Council presidency, the allocation of seats in the European Parliament, the Committee of Regions, and the Economic and Social Committee. Regarding the transfers of policy competences, the issues include (sensitive) policy areas, enhanced cooperation, fundamental and human rights, and the financial endowment of supranational institutions and their political accountability (Finke 2010b: 84).

4.3. From Amsterdam to Lisbon: A Common Space

Until now, the spaces of each summit conference at Amsterdam, Nice, and Lisbon are explored individually. They show the configuration of the political leaders' preferences at each summit, which suggests variation across issues, countries, and changes over time. However, these explorations cannot reveal the fundamentals of preference changes, the timing of shifts in preferences, and the different speed of integration within a period under study nor clarify policy consistency and demands, which can be economic or partisan. Furthermore, the exploratory analyses of the individual summits cannot identify the changes in the bargaining strategies and outcomes in the post-Maastricht period, which result from the power distribution and the context with the underlying distribution of information. This refers to the different sets of propositions and hypotheses that SNP proposes for the study of the causes of the institutional choice for Europe in the post-Maastricht period.

Although these summits differ not only in the substance of the negotiated issues but also in the number of participating political leaders, the exploratory analyses already reveal that their latent preferences can be reduced to two dimensions, namely governance design and the transfer of policy competences. On governance design, the configuration of the preferences indicates a conflict pattern between political leaders from large and smaller countries, while Denmark and Ireland—two countries profiting from economic integration—oppose the further transfer of policy competences. A typical and often discussed governance design issue concerns the reduction of the number of European Commissioners and the distribution of the voting weights in the Council, the latter however sometimes loading on both dimensions. Similarly, defense is discussed at all three summits, which belongs to the dimension of the transfer of policy competences.

In addition to the exploration of these individual spaces, the evaluation of the explanatory power of the factors for the period under study requires estimating a common space. Considering all dependencies among variables and sources of uncertainty, this estimation requires mapping the positions of the 15 political leaders on the 44 Amsterdam issues and 32 Nice issues as well as those of the 25 political leaders on the 62 Lisbon issues into a common space (see also Hug and Schulz 2005, Finke 2009). For this purpose, the Lisbon outcome is used as the point of origin, for which no uncertainty measures are assumed to exist (note that this has no substantive implication but determines the relative location of the coordinate system). Two bridge issues, the number of European Commissioners and the policy competence for defense, are further used for identification, which are a priori known to load only on one dimension across the summits. Together with the Lisbon outcome, these two issues jointly identify the model.[4]

To trace shifts of preferences in the period of study, triangles mark the political leaders' latent preferences on the two dimensions for the Amsterdam Treaty, dots for the Nice Treaty, and diamonds for the Lisbon Treaty in Figure 4.1.[5] Across the three summits, most issues loading on the first dimension concerning the governance design of the EU, such as the composition of the European Commission, the application of veto bicameralism, and so on, while the loading pattern of the second dimension indicates the transfer of policy competences from the national to the EU level, such as for regional, educational and research policies. The estimation also locates the outcomes of the treaties, with the Lisbon outcome (ToL) fixed in the middle,

---

4. When an issue j^* does not load on the first dimension ($\lambda_{j^*,1} = 0$), the lambda parameter can be set for this issue on the second dimension to 1 ($\lambda_{j^*,2} = 1$). When another issue j^* does not load on the second dimension ($\lambda_{j^*,2} = 0$), the lambda parameter for this issue can be set to ($\lambda_{j^*,1} = 1$) to impose the scale of the first dimension.

5. The estimation of the common space is relatively robust (for governance design, the correlation without Amsterdam is 0.97, without Nice 0.98, and for transfer of policy competences 0.96 without Amsterdam and 0.97 without Nice); furthermore, preferences of leaders are reestimated for robustness check without Amsterdam and Nice outcomes.

Choices for Europe after Maastricht

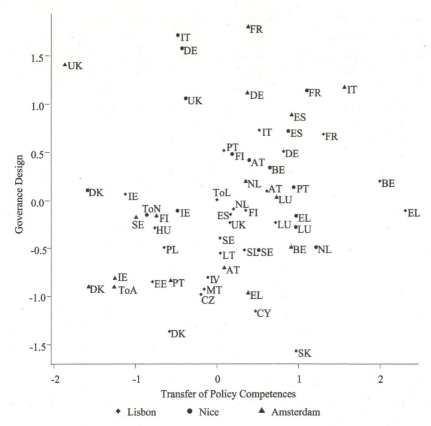

Figure 4.1. The Common Space of the Post-Maastricht Period with AT: Austria, BE: Belgium, CY: Cyprus, CZ: Czech Republic, DE: Germany, DK: Denmark, EE: Estonia, EL: Greece, ES: Spain, FI: Finland, FR: France, HU: Hungary, IE: Ireland, IT: Italy, LU: Luxembourg, LT: Lithuania, LV: Latvia, MT: Malta, NL: Netherlands, PL: Poland, PT: Portugal, SE: Sweden, SK: Slovakia, SL: Slovenia, UK: United Kingdom, ToA: Treaty outcome Amsterdam, ToN: Treaty outcome Nice, ToL: Treaty outcome Lisbon

the Amsterdam outcome (ToA) on the lower left side, and the Nice outcome (ToN) almost in between.

The latent preferences of the Big-3 from France (FR), Germany (DE), and the United Kingdom (UK) are—except for the British preference for the Lisbon Treaty—located in the upper part of the space, which indicates their favor for a more proportional allocation of offices and power according to population size. Compared to this conflict about the number of Commissioners and the allocation of voting weights in the Council, the issues concerning the application and expansion of the codecision procedure load on both dimensions.[6] Similar to this group are the preferences of the political leaders from Italy (IT) and Spain (ES), which illustrates the similarity between political leaders from large countries. It is noteworthy that the political leaders from these countries pursue more moderate preferences on governance design in Lisbon as compared to Amsterdam and Nice. Almost in opposition to this group, we find the Danish (DK) and Irish (IE) preferences, which correspond to those of several Eastern European countries in Lisbon. This suggests the level of conflict does not decrease in governance design over time because a larger number of political leaders from smaller countries favor the "one state one post" allocation rule. This is a result of enlargement by Eastern and Central European countries, which prefer a more equal distribution of power and offices.

Regarding the transfer of policy competences, the British preference shifts from less at Amsterdam to more transfers at Nice and Lisbon. On closer inspection, more variation exists among political leaders regarding the transfers of competences, which is particularly supported by political leaders from Greece (EL) and Belgium (BE) at Lisbon. Compared to the permissive consensus on European integration in the pre-Maastricht period, which resulted from the fact that the transfer of national sovereignty was of little relevance for party competition in the member states (Bardi, Bartolini, and Trechsel 2014), the ideological interests of political parties and their (national) concerns become more important in the post-Maastricht period. With the transfer of more salient redistributive policy competences, such as competition, and monetary and fiscal policies, European affairs become more prominent in party competition of the member states. On governance design, the conflict between political leaders from large and smaller member states remains more persistent. Compared to the outcomes of Amsterdam and Nice, which are located close to the status quo–prone leaders from Denmark and Ireland, the outcome of the Lisbon Treaty is more centrally located. The common space nicely illustrates the variation and the timing of shifts in preferences of each political leader in the post-Maastricht period.

---

6. The estimation reveals that about one-fourth of the 138 issues only load on governance design, more than one-third only on transfer of policy competences, and more than one-third on both dimensions, see also Finke (2010b: 86).

For the evaluation of the hypotheses on preference fundamentals, interstate bargains, and outcomes, the estimation of a common post-Maastricht space across the Amsterdam, Nice, and Lisbon summits is a necessary condition that reveals the (latent) preference changes and distances to the outcome for the period of study. Because most of the issues vary across summits, it would be difficult to directly compare the issue-specific distances between the respective alternatives, and impossible to inspect the changes in their preferences otherwise. Interestingly, the issues on the codecision procedure load on both dimensions, which suggests that the expansion of veto bicameralism remains relatively uncontested. Which factors determine the changes in preferences, and whether their distances are explained by one- or two-stage sequential choices is an empirical question, which can be answered with the estimators of the common post-Maastricht space.

4.4. Governance Design and Transfer of Competences

The data on the Amsterdam, Nice, and Lisbon summits cover 2,690 issue-specific positions with 15 to 25 political leaders, which can be reduced to 55 cases (2x15 plus 1x25) for each dimension by their mapping into a common policy space. In the post-Maastricht period, only the political leaders from Ireland, Prime Minister Patrick Ahern, joins the three summits. Despite this personnel continuity, the Irish preference shifts over time, in particular on the governance design dimension. Similar variation exists for political leaders who join two of the three summits, such as the Belgian prime minister Guy Verhofstadt, the Danish prime minister Poul Nyrup Rasmussen, the Finish prime minister Paavo Lipponen, the French president Jacques Chirac, and the British prime minister Tony Blair.

Compared to the preference shifts of these political leaders, the Conservative Spanish prime minister Jose Maria Aznar pursues a relatively similar preference at Amsterdam and Nice, which changes when Social Democratic prime minister Rose Louis Zapatero represents Spain in Lisbon. The most proportionalist preference on governance design comes from the French president Jacques Chirac, the Italian prime minister Giuliano Amato, and the German chancellor Gerhard Schröder, which stand in contrast to the preferences of the Slovakian prime minister Robert Fico and the Cypriot prime minister Tassos Papadopolous. British prime minister Tony Blair is against a further transfer of policy competences at the Amsterdam summit, followed by Danish prime minister Poul Nyrup Rasmussen at Amsterdam and Nice. The Belgian prime minister Guy Verhofstadt and the Greek prime minister Kostas Karamanlis are mostly in favor of a further transfer of policy competences from the national to the level of the EU at Lisbon. Overall, political leaders often shift preferences in the post-Maastricht period.

On closer inspection of the common post-Maastricht space, the third hypothesis on the variation and timing of preference shifts can already be answered. According to Table 4.1, the preferences of political leaders vary not only by country and issues but also by party affiliation over time. Furthermore, the shifts in their preferences often reflect government change. Because the preference changes of political leaders vary by dimension, as the second and third columns of Table 4.1 show, the hypotheses on their fundamentals are examined separately. The table also describes indicators, for instance, GDP per capita, GDP percent of export, and partisan characteristics such as governmental experience and the party's support for European integration, which operationalize the propositions on their country- and party-specific preference fundamentals.[7] GDP per capita, which distinguishes between rich existing and poorer new member states, is highest in Luxembourg, followed by Ireland and Sweden. Unsurprisingly, the lowest GDP per capita is found in the poorer and smaller accession countries from Central and Eastern Europe, such as Poland and Lithuania. Exports as a share of GDP are highest in Ireland, followed by Hungary and Belgium. Except for the United Kingdom, this share is rising in all other member states over time.

Partisan support for European integration varies within and across countries. To account for this factor the support of a political leader's party for European integration and the days of governmental experience of this party are used. Days in governmental experience reflect the status as ruling/mainstream parties, while a party's support is measured by the party's programmatic positive and negative manifesto statements on European integration (König and Luig 2017: 368). The highest partisan support comes from Spain, Germany, Italy, France, and Austria in the post-Maastricht period. However, these values differ by party affiliation, for example, the Conservative parties of Jose Maria Aznar, Helmut Kohl, Romano Prodi, Jacques Chirac,

---

7. To avoid autocorrelation between GDP and GDP percent of export, GDP per capita is used, while further analysis is run with GDP only to approximate member state size. However, as the accession countries from Eastern and Central Europe are smaller and poorer, GDP per capita reflects Eastern enlargement respectively the divide between existing and new member states.

Choices for Europe after Maastricht 61

and Wolfgang Schüssel provide the highest support, which seems to reflect their ideological experiences with outcomes and the view of their supporters. Once these political leaders are replaced, most of them by Social Democratic competitors, the partisan support for further transfers of policy competences drastically declines. High variation within and across countries also exists for governmental experience with the Polish Donald Tusk as a newcomer and the Luxembourg Jean-Claude Juncker, who is by far the most experienced political leader in the post-Maastricht period.

To compare the explanatory power of these estimators for the fundamentals of political leaders' preferences, the Bayes factors quantify their effect.[8] The methodological advantage of the use of Bayes factors is that it automatically, and quite naturally, includes a penalty for overfitting by including too many variables (Stegmueller 2013). The first three columns of Table 4.2 list the results of governance design, which indicate that only GDP per capita and export ratio to GDP matter for political leaders' preferences on this dimension.[9]

Confirming $H_{cau}1$, a higher GDP per capita correlates with a preference for more proportionality, while a higher share of exports is negatively associated with this preference. Accordingly, the country-specific conflict pattern on this dimension distinguishes political leaders from importing and exporting countries rather than periphery and core countries, as suggested by liberal intergovernmentalism. Countries with a higher share of exports, such as Luxembourg, Belgium, Ireland, and the Netherlands, but also the new periphery countries from Eastern and Central Europe, such as Hungary, Slovakia, Lithuania, Latvia, Estonia, Slovenia, Czech Republic, and Cyprus belong to this group, while GDP per capita mainly distinguishes the groups of existing richer and larger from new poorer and smaller member states. The Bayes factor results show that including other measures reduces the explanatory power of the country-specific factors, which underscores their relevance for this dimension. Note that the conflict on this dimension is increasingly polarized with the entrance of Eastern and Central European countries in the post-Maastricht period.

The last three columns of Table 4.2 show that the picture changes for

8. Unlike a likelihood-ratio test, a Bayesian model comparison does not depend on any single set of parameters, as it integrates all parameters in each model (concerning the respective priors).
9. Running the analysis with GDP shows that the difference between large and small is decisive.

Table 4.1. Descriptive overview

	Country	IGC	Gov Design	Trans Comp	Cabinet	Cabinet party	GDP p.c.	Exports (% of GDP)	Experience (in days)	EUSupp
1	AT	A	-0.70	0.09	Klima I	SPÖ	23500.00	37.11	1038	2.25
2	AT	N	0.41	0.40	Schuessel I	ÖVP	27400.00	44.69	357	2.35
3	AT	R	0.09	0.61	Gusenbauer	SPÖ	34000.00	52.49	336	1.96
4	BE	A	-0.49	0.91	Dehaene II	CVP	22100.00	63.90	6757	1.96
5	BE	N	0.33	0.65	Verhofstadt I	VLD	25900.00	71.02	563	0.98
6	BE	R	0.19	2.00	Verhofstadt III	VLD	32500.00	77.49	3075	1.83
7	CY	R	-1.15	0.47	Papadopoulos II	DIKO	22900.00	53.82	1749	1.18
8	CZ	R	-0.98	-0.19	Topolanek II	ODS	13400.00	66.55	465	0.52
9	DE	A	1.10	0.37	Kohl V	CDU	24000.00	25.39	5477	2.41
10	DE	N	1.57	-0.43	Schroeder I	SPD	26700.00	31.87	822	0.00
11	DE	R	0.50	0.81	Merkel I	CDU	31000.00	43.01	751	0.09
12	DK	A	-0.90	-1.58	Rasmussen N III	Sd	29000.00	37.81	1711	0.00
13	DK	N	0.10	-1.59	Rasmussen N IV	Sd	34400.00	45.60	2923	-0.44
14	DK	R	-1.36	-0.58	Rasmussen F III	V	42800.00	51.34	2207	0.00
15	EE	R	-0.85	-0.79	Ansip II	ERe	12100.00	63.20	974	1.71
16	ES	A	0.88	0.91	Aznar I	PP	13000.00	25.75	516	2.71
17	ES	N	0.71	0.87	Aznar II	PP	17200.00	27.86	1728	1.91
18	ES	R	-0.15	0.17	Zapatero I	PSOE	23900.00	25.71	1335	1.78
19	FI	A	-0.17	-0.74	Lipponen I	SSDP	21800.00	37.80	903	1.59
20	FI	N	0.47	0.19	Lipponen II	SSDP	27800.00	39.71	2115	0.00
21	FI	R	-0.11	0.35	Vanhanen II	KESK	35300.00	44.00	1701	1.55
22	FR	A	1.79	0.38	Chirac	RPR/UMP	21500.00	25.24	869	2.38
23	FR	N	1.13	1.10	Chirac	RPR/UMP	25200.00	27.79	2081	2.38
24	FR	R	0.68	1.30	Sarkozy	UMP	30400.00	27.13	4593	2.16
25	GB	A	1.39	-1.87	Blair I	Labour	23300.00	27.10	153	1.50
26	GB	N	1.05	-0.38	Blair I	Labour	30500.00	26.06	1365	1.50
27	GB	R	-0.24	0.16	Brown	Labour	36500.00	25.64	3877	1.42
28	GR	A	-0.97	0.38	Simitis II	PASOK	11900.00	16.22	1438	2.24
29	GR	N	-0.17	0.97	Simitis II	PASOK	14000.00	22.79	2650	2.32
30	GR	R	-0.11	2.31	Karamanlis Kos II	ND	21100.00	22.52	1360	0.00

31	HU	R	−0.29	−0.76	Gyurcsany II	MSZP	10100.00	78.33	2026	1.84
32	IE	A	−0.82	−1.26	Ahern I	FF	21700.00	77.16	98	0.60
33	IE	N	−0.11	−0.48	Ahern I	FF	31600.00	95.37	1310	0.60
34	IE	R	0.06	−1.13	Ahern III	FF	44800.00	80.84	3822	1.18
35	IT	A	1.16	1.56	Prodi I	PpP	19200	24.19	503	2.38
36	IT	N	1.7	−0.48	Amato II	DSa	22800	25.72	821	1.56
37	IT	R	0.72	0.52	Prodi II	Unione	27400	27.41	575	2.41
38	LT	R	−0.55	0.04	Kirkilas	LSDP	9000	50.42	2352	1.29
39	LU	A	0.02	0.73	Juncker I	CSV	41400	118.87	6654	0.78
40	LU	N	−0.28	0.96	Juncker II	CSV	53200	148.69	7866	1.08
41	LU	R	−0.24	0.72	Juncker III	CSV	76500	184.18	10378	1.29
42	LV	R	−0.8	−0.11	Kalvitis III	TP	10300	38.52	1106	0
43	MT	R	−0.93	−0.15	Gonzi I	PN	14200	89.22	1359	1.91
44	NL	A	0.19	0.35	Kok I	PvdA	23300	60.68	1137	0.69
45	NL	N	−0.49	1.21	Kok II	PvdA	29700	63.82	2349	1.84
46	NL	R	−0.1	0.2	Balkenende V	CDA	37400	70.27	1970	0.98
47	PL	R	−0.49	−0.65	Tusk I	PO	8200	38.82	19	2.26
48	PT	A	−0.84	−0.56	Guterres I	PS	10200	27.15	705	1.55
49	PT	N	0.13	0.94	Guterres II	PS	13100	27.42	1917	1.37
50	PT	R	0.51	0.09	Socrates I	PS	16600	31.01	1006	1.42
51	SE	A	−0.18	−0.99	Persson I	SAP	26400	40.05	1092	2.05
52	SE	N	−0.52	0.51	Persson II	SAP	30100	43.75	2304	2.34
53	SE	R	−0.4	0.04	Reinfeldt I	MSP	39000	48.26	434	2.14
54	SK	R	−1.57	0.97	Fico I	Smer	10400	83.5	527	1.76
55	SL	R	−0.52	0.34	Jansa I	SDS	17400	67.6	1105	1.51

Table 4.2. Linear regression of preference foundation

	Dependent variable:					
	Design dimension			Transfer dimension		
	(1)	(2)	(3)	(4)	(5)	(6)
GDP p.c.	0.00003***		0.00003**	0.00000		−0.00001
	(0.00001)		(0.00001)	(0.00001)		(0.00001)
Ratio (Export/ GDP)	−0.014***		−0.014***	0.001		−0.002
	(0.004)		(0.004)	(0.005)		(0.005)
Cabinet experience (days)		−0.00001	0.00002		0.0001**	0.0001*
		(0.0001)	(0.0001)		(0.0001)	(0.0001)
EU position		0.189	0.162		0.314**	0.287*
		(0.135)	(0.127)		(0.138)	(0.147)
Constant	0.042	−0.274	−0.235	0.066	−0.501*	−0.310
	(0.231)	(0.250)	(0.345)	(0.284)	(0.255)	(0.399)
Observations	55	55	55	55	55	55
Adjusted R^2	0.197	0.001	0.196	−0.035	0.114	0.086
Bayes Factor±	27.939	0.238	8.001	0.114	3.130	0.607
	+/−0%	+/−0.01%	+/−0%	+/−0.01%	+/−0%	+/−0%

Note: The unit of GDP p.c. is Euro per capita. Thus, the values of this coefficient are relatively small. For example, 0.00003 means an increase of ten thousand Euros per capita contributes to 0.3 change in the dependent variable.
The same is true for the cabinet experience which was measured by days.
*p < 0.1; **p < 0.05; ***p < 0.01
±Reference (denominator): Intercept only.

the transfer of further policy competences dimension where only partisan-ideological factors matter. This confirms the second hypothesis ($H_{cau}2$) on the party-specific interest in the transfer of policy competences: both governmental experience and the support of the leader's party for European integration promote the further transfer of policy competences. The first is particularly driven by the experience of the Conservative leaders Jean-Claude Juncker (Luxembourg), Jean-Luc Dehaene (Belgium), and Helmut Kohl (Germany). Again, the other country-specific measures reduce the explanatory power of the partisan-ideological factors on this dimension.

The results lend support for the first and second office-seeking and policy-seeking propositions of SNP regarding the predicted fundamentals of country-specific preferences on governance design ($H_{cau}1$) and party-specific preferences on the further transfer of policy competences ($H_{cau}2$). The country- and party-specific interests of political leaders offer a distinction between the further transfer of policy competences and governance design, which are identified as the latent dimensions of the post-Maastricht period. On the first dimension of governance design, political leaders are office-seeking by either favoring a proportional or equal allocation rule for power and offices, while their policy-seeking interests are decisive for the second dimension on the transfer of policy competences from the national to the level of the EU.

The change toward country- and party-specific fundamentals of preferences is associated with political leaders' backgrounds. Notably, political leaders of Conservative parties from new member states—economically disadvantaged competitively within the common market—favor the further transfer of competences, supported by political leaders from Belgium, France, Greece, and Italy. Over time, their preferences change with the change of the party affiliation of the leaders of those member states. Regarding governance design, the country-specific component determines the conflict measured by GDP per capita and the export ratio to GDP. In particular, new members, who set high importance on trade in the economy, form a group that prefers to continue with the "one state one vote" allocation rule for power and offices, which assures each member state access to the supranational executive and judiciary at the expense of more than doubling their size through enlargements in the post-Maastricht period.

This group stands in opposition to the group of larger and richer countries, which favors more proportionality in the allocation of power and offices according to population size. Both groups, however, support the expansion of the codecision procedure of veto bicameralism. The post-Maastricht estimators also show that preferences vary not only by country and issue, but also change over time to changes in government, which confirms the third hypothesis of SNP about the timing of preference shifts ($H_{cau}3$). The party-oriented preference shifts of political leaders suggest that demands are concurrent with partisan ideology in the national game of party competition rather than foreign economic policy. In contrast to the original idea of Jean Monnet, who was skeptical of, if not against European integration as an issue of electoral competition due to the volatility of voters' interests, the "uploading" of policy competences for sensitive policy areas is a precondition for the politicization of European integration (Börzel and Panke 2013).

In addition to variation and timing in shifts of preferences, the findings suggest that the bargaining demands are mainly political. On governance design, the country-specific factors indicate a conflict between political leaders from large/rich importing and smaller/poorer exporting countries rather than between core and periphery countries. Their concerns relate to the country-specific distribution of power and offices, which define the office-seeking advantages of the ruling/mainstream parties. The more important dimension of the further transfer of policy competences is however explained by partisan-ideological factors, such as the political leader's party support of European integration and governmental experience. This relates the summit game of interstate bargains to the national game of party competition, in which vote-seeking political leaders may attempt to maximize support from their voters by demanding more concessions.

This does not mean that macroeconomic interests do not play a role in the post-Maastricht period. In particular, the accessions of countries from Central and Eastern Europe sharpen the cleavage between new/poorer and older/richer member states, culminating in a country-specific conflict about governance design. In this conflict, one group prefers a more proportional allocation of power and offices that reflect population size. The group of political leaders from smaller and poorer member states, by contrast, favors the "one state one office" allocation rule with more equal distribution, including voting weights and seats in the EU's bodies. This inherent conflict intensifies with the accessions of new member states in the post-Maastricht period, which may also change the environment in which political leaders make institutional choices at interstate bargains. How this change in the environment changes the strategies of political leaders at interstate bargains, and how this change of strategies impacts the outcomes of their institutional choices is part of the following analyses.

4.5. Interstate Bargains and Veto Threats

Following SNP, the change toward country-specific office-seeking and party-specific policy-seeking interests with accessions from 12 to 25 is predicted to change the environment in which the interstate bargains take place in the post-Maastricht period. The Danish rejection of the Maastricht Treaty in 1992, along with the "petit oui" of the French voters, already signals the end of the permissive consensus on European integration that existed among European elites in the pre-Maastricht period (Hooghe and Marks 2019). As treaties can only come into force once every member state concludes ratification, the Edinburgh Agreement, negotiated in the months following the negative Danish referendum, provides Denmark with four one-sided exceptions. These opt-outs concern the European Monetary Union, the Common Security and Defence Policy, Justice and Home Affairs, and the citizenship of the EU. With these opt-outs, the Danish voters accept the Maastricht Treaty in a second referendum held in 1993.

The events around the Constitutional Treaty indicate that interstate bargains change from an environment of complete and perfect information toward an environment in which the Council presidency needs to form a belief about the (non)cooperative type of a growing number of member states in the post-Maastricht period. This change is already indicated by the first important treaty in the post-Maastricht period, the Amsterdam Treaty (1999), which is composed of 13 Protocols, 51 Declarations adopted at the Amsterdam summit, eight Declarations by the member states plus amendments set out in 15 Articles of the final treaty. Despite some reservations, the European Parliament endorses the treaty, and after two referendums and 13 parliamentary approvals, the member states finally conclude the ratification procedure of a treaty, which becomes famous for the many leftovers—in particular for governance design issues that could not be solved in preparation of enlargement by Central and Eastern European countries.

During the negotiations of the Nice Treaty, dissent among political leaders becomes apparent as the German chancellor Gerhard Schröder demands a higher (voting) weight for unified Germany. This demand provokes resistance from French president Jacques Chirac, who insists that the symbolic parity between France and Germany be maintained. Instead of increasing EU policy-making efficiency in preparation for enlargement by Central and Eastern European countries, the treaty increases the voting threshold in the Council by introducing a triple majority criterion, the number of seats in the European Parliament, and delays the reduction of the number of Commissioners. Before the summit, the entering of the Eurosceptic Freedom Party (FPÖ) into the Austrian government already raises ideological concerns about the rise of Euroscepticism. For the first time, the other 14 political leaders approve boycotting Austria because "the admission of the Austrian Free Democrats (FPÖ) into a coalition government legitimizes the extreme right in Europe" (Meret 2010). And finally, the Irish voters reject the Nice Treaty in the initial referendum, which requires further concessions with opt-outs presented in the Seville Declaration of

2002 that provides the necessary support for the Irish voters in a second referendum.

Both treaties, the Amsterdam and the Nice treaties conclude at the lowest common denominator despite approaching enlargement ($H_{cau}6$). Denmark and Ireland are the two most powerful countries because they receive one-sided concessions to change their noncooperative attitude ($H_{cau}5$). In turn, the Laeken declaration (2001) adopts committing the EU to greater democracy, transparency, and efficiency, and sets out a process by which a treaty should be created for the people of Europe. This process establishes with the European Convention a new instrument that, under the chairmanship of the former French president Valéry Giscard d'Estaing, drafts a document for a constitution (König, Luetgert, and Dannwolf 2006). Under the Italian presidency, the signing of the document fails in 2003, and a compromise on the Constitutional Treaty can only be reached in 2004.

However, despite the ratification experiences with previous referendums, an unprecedented number of eleven political leaders announces referendums for the ratification of the Constitutional Treaty. In May and June 2004, the negative referendums in France and the Netherlands stop the ratification process, and a reflection period begins until a compromise is reached in 2007. It removes the constitutional elements from the document which ultimately becomes the Lisbon Treaty. Instead of ratification by referendums, the political leaders finally agree to ratify the Lisbon Treaty in their parliaments, which is possible except for the mandatory Irish referendum. In 2008, the Irish voters however reject the treaty, and further one-sided concessions with opt-outs for Ireland are required until the Irish voters approve it in a second referendum (Finke et al. 2012).

All of this suggests that the environment changes in the post-Maastricht period, in which the Constitutional Treaty does not survive ratification. According to SNP, the risk of failure and inefficiency increases in an uncertain environment ($H_{cau}7$). The more political leaders pursue a vote-seeking strategy to receive concessions by announcing referendums with a veto threat, the higher the risk of failure and inefficiency. Against this, liberal intergovernmentalism predicts that the threat to reject and to move on without a particular member state is used to counterbalance the power of status quo–prone leaders and to reestablish the distribution of power and gains (Moravcsik 1991: 26), which do not affect the ratification process (Moravcsik 1993: 515). Table 4.3 lists the findings on interstate bargains in the two-dimensional post-Maastricht space.

Table 4.3. Linear regression of interstate bargains

	Dependent variable: Euclidean distance to outcomes	
	(1)	(2)
Distance Centroid (Big 3)	0.158	0.228*
	(0.106)	(0.116)
Big 3		0.651
		(0.459)
Distance SQ	0.781***	0.774***
	(0.089)	(0.086)
Referendum		0.307
		(0.283)
Nice	1.203***	1.117***
	(0.249)	(0.247)
Lisbon	1.020***	0.963***
	(0.249)	(0.231)
Distance Centroid (Big 3) X Big 3		−0.244
		(0.374)
Distance SQ X Referendum		−0.307**
		(0.140)
Constant	−1.528***	−1.606***
	(0.482)	(0.496)
Observations	55	55
Adjusted R²	0.680	0.734
F Statistic	29.750***	19.602***
	(df = 4; 50)	(df = 8; 46)

Note: *p < 0.1; **p < 0.05; ***p < 0.01

For the pre-Maastricht period, it has been argued that the relative distance of the Big-3 of France, Germany, and the United Kingdom to the outcome is decisive without risk of failure and inefficiency in an environment of low cost complete and perfect information (Moravcsik 1998, Moravcsik and Schimmelfennig 2019). In such an environment, the Council presidency only needs to know that the member states prefer treaty approval over failure. In the post-Maastricht period, the distance to the centroid of the Big-3, which locates the outcome in the middle of their preferences, can hardly account for the outcomes. While it is only significant at the 10 percent level of model 2, the nonsignificant interaction effect shows that the centroid does not matter. Confirming $H_{cau}4$, the distance of the member states to the status quo provides a highly significant finding on their approval of treaties in the period of study. For substantive interpretation of the interaction effect

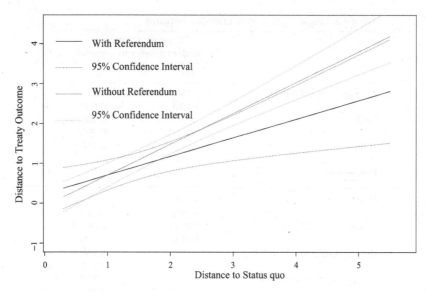

Figure 4.2. Interaction between Distance to Status Quo and Treaty Outcomes with and without Referendum

with referendum announcement, Figure 4.2 provides additional insight into this mechanism. The figure shows that the announcement of referendums, indicated by the solid line, is particularly important for the final distance to the outcome. When the distance to the status quo increases, the distance to the outcome is getting larger without announcing a referendum. This suggests that a member state has more power to shorten the distance to the outcome when the announcement of a referendum increases the perception of being a noncooperative type ($H_{cau}5$). Figure 4.3 shows the outcomes of the Amsterdam, Nice, and Lisbon treaties as well as the member states announcing referendums.

Using the Maastricht Treaty as a reference, the connecting line to the Amsterdam Treaty illustrates that the treaty expands policy competences on the horizontal axis and moves the design along the vertical axis by expanding the application of the codecision procedure. Denmark (DK), Ireland (IE), and partly Portugal (PT), which originally announced referendums, are very closely located to the status quo and the Amsterdam outcome. The Nice Treaty is more ambitious in changing governance design—as the long line on the vertical axis indicates—even though it introduces a triple majority voting rule for the Council. However, as the previous chapters showed, the applica-

Choices for Europe after Maastricht

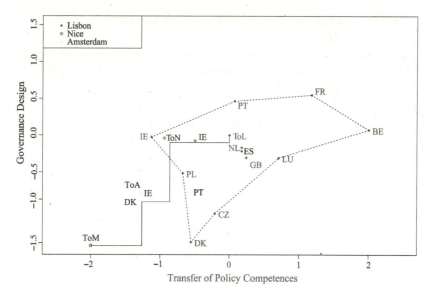

Figure 4.3. Preferences of Political Leaders with Referendum Announcement at Amsterdam (green), Nice (red), and Lisbon (blue) with ToM: Treaty outcome Maastricht, ToA: Treaty outcome Amsterdam, ToN: Treaty outcome Nice, ToL: Treaty outcome Lisbon, BE: Belgium, CZ: Czech Republic, DK: Denmark, ES: Spain, FR: France, IE: Ireland, LU: Luxembourg, NL: Netherlands, PL: Poland, PT: Portugal

tion of the codecision procedure is expanded to further policy areas, including sensitive areas. Ireland, which requires two referendums to approve the Nice Treaty, is the actor closest to the status quo and the outcome (followed by Denmark). Confirming $H_{cau}6$, the political leaders of these two member states have a credible veto threat that enables them to postpone institutional reforms that most political leaders want to implement before the enlargement by Central and Eastern European countries. Despite an overwhelming majority of political leaders preferring further transfers of policy competences, they can block further changes at these summits. This also shows that those who profit economically from European integration do not necessarily support a reform of the EU.

Although the Lisbon Treaty is negotiated by 25 political leaders, the outcome—after summit and referendum failures—goes one step further regarding the further transfer of policy competences on the horizontal axis. One reason for the modest change of governance design is that the expansion of the codecision procedure, which is becoming the standard procedure for EU policy-making across almost all areas, is also loading on the policy competence transfer dimension. Instead of first transferring competences of (sensitive) policy areas under unanimity, which are secondly transferred to qualified majority voting in the Council—a stepwise deepening process that governed the pre-Maastricht period—the policy competences for these areas are directly transferred into qualified majority voting in the (standard) codecision procedure of veto bicameralism.

As the dotted line connecting referendum announcements shows, the outcome of the Lisbon Treaty is surrounded by those announcing a referendum as a veto threat, which makes it difficult to make concessions in one or another direction. This time, the counterinitiation of referendum announcements by member states of higher distance to the status quo reduces the power of the status quo–prone noncooperative member states. Consequently, the outcome is located in the middle of the referendum announcing member states in the two-stage sequential choice game under uncertainty. Except for the mandatory referendum in Ireland, these announcements are annulled after a reflection period, which paves the way for final parliamentary ratification in the national game of party competition. However, this strategy initially fails due to the Irish voters' rejection in 2008. This allows the new Irish prime minister Brian Cowen to renegotiate the terms and receive one-sided opt-outs, ultimately leading to the Lisbon Treaty's approval in a second Irish referendum in 2009.

4.6. Risk and Efficiency of Outcomes

One of the major discussions in the post-Maastricht period center around risk and efficiency of outcomes of the institutional choices for Europe. Following Moravcsik (1998), efficiency means optimal outcomes, which do not leave potential gains at the bargaining table, while their distribution determines who is winning and losing in interstate bargains. For postfunctionalism, inefficiency by an institutional mismatch is the starting point for the argument on the rise of populism and Euroscepticism in the post-Maastricht period (Hooghe and Marks 2009, 2018). SNP specifies the conditions under which the outcomes of interstate bargains bear the risk of failure and inefficiency. Even if the member states prefer the status quo, the Council presidency can act as an effective entrepreneur and present a proposal that member states prefer against failure. In an environment of complete and perfect information, Hug and König (2002) show that approval can be reached by dropping contested issues from the bargaining table, which reduces the outcome to the lowest common denominator ($H_{cau}6$).

Failure and inefficiency are more likely when the Council presidency operates under uncertainty. In the post-Maastricht period, the accession from 12 to 15 and from 15 to 25 member states and the announcement of an increasing number of referendums makes it more difficult for the Council presidency to infer the (non)cooperative type of each member state. Compared to the interstate bargains of the Maastricht Treaty, in which 12 member states were involved, the Council presidency needs to form a belief about the (non)cooperative type of 25 or more member states, which increases the error term of the Council presidency. This suggests that the informational environment changes over time in the post-Maastricht period. Therefore, failure becomes more likely, that is, summit and ratification failure, which require further one-sided concessions or opt-outs. In addition to summit failure at Rome (2003) under the Italian Council presidency, the Constitutional Treaty is not ratified after negative referendums in France and the Netherlands, and the Nice and Lisbon treaties require a repetition of the first negative referendums in Ireland.

According to SNP, these failures support the view of a change in the informational environment toward higher uncertainty about the member states' (non)cooperative type, which announces an unprecedented number of referendums for the ratification of the Constitutional Treaty (Finke and König 2009). Instead of imposing costs on unorganized or unrepresented groups, as articulated by liberal intergovernmentalism, the vote-seeking strategy of announcing referendums also allows populist movements to mobilize masses against further integration by a new treaty. When the mainstream/ruling parties of political leaders, who usually support European integration for office- and policy-seeking interests, remain silent to receive one-sided concessions at the bargaining table, these movements are able to dominate ratification campaigns, and further concessions are needed to overcome public concerns.

Under these dynamic conditions, SNP predicts a change in the goal toward the survival of ratification, which political leaders can finally achieve by not only committing to ratify the Lisbon Treaty—except for the mandatory Irish referendum—in the national game of party competition, but also offering one-sided concessions to noncooperative Irish ruling parties, which did not campaign for ratification of the first version of the Lisbon Treaty.

Compared to ratification by referendum, the dual role of political leaders as delegated agents of their countries and their parties provides more control over parliamentary ratification. However, because the Irish voters reject the Lisbon Treaty in the first mandatory referendum, additional one-sided concessions are necessary for Ireland to overcome public concerns. To survive ratification, efficiency comes at a risk, which means that some member states bear losses from the second version of the Lisbon Treaty.

Admittedly, it is difficult to evaluate gains and losses from interstate bargains as well as to estimate the efficiency of outcomes. If efficiency means the ratio of useful output to total input, then the existence of leftovers at Amsterdam and Nice which should be resolved by the Constitutional Treaty, already indicates a modest efficiency, which is further reduced by dropping issues from the Constitutional Treaty to find agreement on the Lisbon Treaty. Another possibility to evaluate efficiency is to compare the distances of political leaders' preferences on governance design and transfers of competences to the status quo and the outcome. If their distance to the status quo is higher than to the outcome, they are likely to profit from a new treaty, while a higher distance to the outcome than to the status quo would indicate inefficiency. In Table 4.4, the columns on governance design and transfer of competences list the location of the treaties and political leaders' preferences, the following columns their distance to the outcomes and the status quo in the common space, and the final column the distribution of gains (and losses).

Table 4.4. Preferences, distances, and gains

Name	IGC	Governance Design	Transfer Competences	Distance to Outcome	Distance to Status quo	Distribution of Gains
Maastricht		−2	−1.5			
Amsterdam		−0.85	−1.27			
Nice		−0.04	−0.94			
Lisbon		0	0			
Austria	Amsterdam	−0.64	0.07	1.36	2.08	0.72
Belgium	Amsterdam	−0.41	0.9	2.22	2.88	0.66
Denmark	Amsterdam	−0.9	−1.57	0.3	1.11	0.81
Finland	Amsterdam	−0.14	−0.76	0.88	2	1.12
France	Amsterdam	1.84	0.33	3.14	4.26	1.12
Germany	Amsterdam	1.18	0.32	2.59	3.67	1.08
Greece	Amsterdam	−0.87	0.39	1.66	2.2	0.54
Ireland	Amsterdam	−0.79	−1.27	0.07	1.23	1.17
Italy	Amsterdam	1.27	1.52	3.51	4.45	0.94
Luxembourg	Amsterdam	0.11	0.7	2.2	3.05	0.85
Netherlands	Amsterdam	0.25	0.33	1.95	2.9	0.95
Portugal	Amsterdam	−0.76	−0.57	0.71	1.55	0.84

Table 4.4—Continued

Name	IGC	Governance Design	Transfer Competences	Distance to Outcome	Distance to Status quo	Distribution of Gains
Spain	Amsterdam	0.96	0.88	2.82	3.8	0.98
Sweden	Amsterdam	−0.15	−1	0.75	1.92	1.16
UKingdom	Amsterdam	1.41	−1.95	2.37	3.44	1.08
Austria	Nice	0.42	0.4	1.42	2.11	0.69
Belgium	Nice	0.32	0.66	1.63	2.26	0.62
Germany	Nice	1.56	−0.43	1.68	2.56	0.88
Denmark	Nice	0.11	−1.62	0.7	1.03	0.33
Spain	Nice	0.69	0.86	1.94	2.63	0.69
France	Nice	1.12	1.11	2.35	3.09	0.74
Finland	Nice	0.49	0.18	1.24	1.98	0.74
Greece	Nice	−0.19	0.97	1.91	2.34	0.42
Italy	Nice	1.73	−0.47	1.83	2.71	0.88
Ireland	Nice	−0.08	−0.5	0.45	1.1	0.65
Luxembourg	Nice	−0.28	0.96	1.92	2.31	0.39
Netherlands	Nice	−0.5	1.2	2.19	2.5	0.31
Portugal	Nice	0.12	0.94	1.89	2.42	0.53
Sweden	Nice	−0.5	0.49	1.5	1.8	0.3
UKingdom	Nice	1.02	−0.37	1.2	2.08	0.88
Austria	Lisbon	0	0.64	0.64	1.58	0.94
Belgium	Lisbon	0.07	2	2	2.95	0.94
Cyprus	Lisbon	−1.21	0.56	1.33	1.9	0.57
CzechRep.	Lisbon	−1.06	−0.21	1.08	1.26	0.18
Denmark	Lisbon	−1.45	−0.55	1.55	1.46	−0.09
Estonia	Lisbon	−0.93	−0.76	1.2	0.91	−0.3
Finland	Lisbon	−0.24	0.3	0.38	1.26	0.87
France	Lisbon	0.55	1.18	1.3	2.2	0.9
Germany	Lisbon	0.43	0.82	0.93	1.82	0.9
Greece	Lisbon	−0.15	2.33	2.33	3.27	0.94
Hungary	Lisbon	−0.38	−0.75	0.84	0.39	−0.45
Ireland	Lisbon	−0.03	−1.13	1.13	0.19	−0.94
Italy	Lisbon	0.64	0.49	0.81	1.58	0.78
Latvia	Lisbon	−0.88	−0.14	0.9	1.17	0.27
Lithuania	Lisbon	−0.62	0.01	0.62	1.12	0.49
Luxembourg	Lisbon	−0.31	0.71	0.77	1.67	0.9
Malta	Lisbon	−0.98	−0.12	0.99	1.25	0.26
Netherlands	Lisbon	−0.17	0.18	0.24	1.12	0.88
Poland	Lisbon	−0.52	−0.67	0.85	0.55	−0.3
Portugal	Lisbon	0.46	0.08	0.47	1.13	0.66
Slovakia	Lisbon	−1.64	1.03	1.94	2.54	0.6
Slovenia	Lisbon	−0.63	0.39	0.74	1.46	0.72
Spain	Lisbon	−0.21	0.18	0.28	1.13	0.85
Sweden	Lisbon	−0.48	−0.08	0.49	0.97	0.48
UKingdom	Lisbon	−0.3	0.24	0.39	1.21	0.82

Except for the United Kingdom at Lisbon, the political leaders from large countries such as France, Germany, Italy, and Spain pursue similar preferences on governance design across all summit conferences in the post-Maastricht period, which political leaders from smaller member states are opposed to. This picture changes for the transfer of further policy competences, where Denmark, Ireland, and the United Kingdom are mostly in opposition, while Belgium, Greece, Portugal, and Spain are mainly in favor of a further transfer of competences to the EU level. Some countries, such as France, Italy, Germany, and Spain have almost always high distances to both the outcome and the status quo, while countries like Denmark and Ireland have short distances to both. This explains why both groups have sometimes very similar benefits.

Although the Amsterdam and Nice treaties conclude on the lowest common denominator ($H_{cau}6$), they are efficient because they improve all political leaders compared to the status quo with a relatively similar distribution of gains (with Sweden and the Netherlands with the lowest benefits from Nice, while Sweden and Ireland profit the most from Amsterdam). This changes with the Lisbon Treaty, leaving political leaders with benefits and losses. The political leaders from Denmark, Estonia, Hungary, Ireland, and Poland could not stop the treaty despite their closer distance to the status quo, which confirms $H_{cau}7$ on the risk of inefficiency under higher uncertainty. Austria, Belgium, Finland, France, Germany, Greece, Luxembourg, Netherlands, and Spain all come out winners, albeit for different reasons. For example, the political leaders from Belgium and Greece are able to maximize their gains from large distances to both the outcome and the status quo, while smaller distances to both provide Germany and the Netherlands with a similar record.

These country-specific results underline how the environment changes over time. For example, Ireland belongs to the group of winners at Amsterdam and Nice but has good reason to reject the Lisbon Treaty. The political leaders from Poland, Hungary, and Estonia are skeptical about the Constitutional Treaty and lose to the outcome of the Lisbon Treaty. Compared to Amsterdam and Nice, this finding supports the claim of SNP that survival of the ratification process becomes the dominant goal for the Lisbon Treaty. In addition to the interstate summit game, the second stage of ratification becomes more important for the outcome. In some countries, a qualified majority is necessary for ratification in parliament, which can set higher ratification hurdles than a referendum (Hug and Tsebelis 2002). While the analysis shows that announcing a referendum serves as a vote-seeking strategy to achieve a bargaining advantage at the Amsterdam and Nice summits, the announcement of multiple referendums by political leaders with diverse preferences for the ratification of the Constitutional Treaty increases uncertainty to a degree which promotes the risk of failure and inefficiency.

In sum, the findings confirm the hypotheses of SNP on the causes of the institutional choices for Europe and answer important puzzles, such as the integration paradox of new intergovernmentalism and the democratic deficit paradox of the proximity principle, according to which decisions should be taken as close as possible to the preferences of the citizens. Accordingly, political leaders trade off preferences on governance design and transfer of policy competences, which can explain why further transfers are approved without effectively reforming the institutional model of the EU. Furthermore, the announcement of referendums is a successful vote-seeking strategy to receive concessions at the bargaining table, which however increases the risk of failure and inefficiency when this strategy is applied from a higher number of political leaders with diverse preferences.

The analyses of the common space confirm the hypotheses on the country-specific office-seeking and the party-specific policy-seeking interests of political leaders on governance design ($H_{cau}1$) and transfers of policy competences ($H_{cau}2$). The political leaders need to consider two games when they decide about governance design and transfer of policy competences, the interstate summit and the national game of party competition. The analyses also support the third hypothesis ($H_{cau}3$) on the shifts of political leaders' preferences resulting from government changes in the national game of party competition, which change the political leaders' configuration in the interstate summit game.

For making institutional choices at interstate bargains in the post-Maastricht period, a larger distance from the status quo makes approval more likely ($H_{cau}4$). Furthermore, because treaties need to be ratified in the national game of party competition, in particular a few noncooperative member states with a close preference to the status quo are powerful in the interstate bargains of the Amsterdam and Nice treaties ($H_{cau}5$). Their credible veto threat produces outcomes at the lowest common denominator ($H_{cau}6$). The analysis also confirms the hypothesis on the interaction between the distance to the status quo with the announcement of a referendum. This vote-seeking strategy is very successful at the Amsterdam and Nice interstate bargains, but it increases the risk of failure and inefficiency at the interstate bargains of the Constitutional Treaty, which finally becomes the Lisbon Treaty ($H_{cau}7$).

Survival of ratification—after the rejection of the Constitutional Treaty, a reflection period, and another negative referendum on the first version—becomes the primary goal of the Lisbon Treaty. Ireland rejects the proposal of the German presidency, which—according to the findings—is unlikely to profit from the new treaty. Similarly, the skeptical political leaders from the new member states of Estonia, Hungary, and Poland are unlikely to win from the new treaty accordingly. Although these empirical findings warrant a cautious interpretation, the events around the Lisbon Treaty indicate incomplete contracting among the 25 member states. This incompleteness does neither mean that the Lisbon Treaty is invalid nor unenforceable. It only means that the institutional choices may have ineffectively reformed the EU with a high likelihood of unintended consequences.

Briefly summarized, the empirical examination of the propositions and hypotheses of SNP on the causes of the institutional choices for Europe shows that

- office- and policy-seeking political leaders pursue the interests of their countries and parties on governance design and transfer of policy competences in a widening and deepening EU;
- the distance to the status quo determines the power of political leaders with credible domestic veto threats and outcomes at the lowest common denominator at Amsterdam and Nice in the beginning of the post-Maastricht period;
- this changes to higher uncertainty with the failure of the Constitutional Treaty and the inefficiency of institutional choices for Europe as the survival of ratification becomes the dominant goal for the Lisbon Treaty in the post-Maastricht period.

For SNP, failure and inefficiency of institutional choices for Europe have important implications for EU policy-making, and partisan and public attitudes toward European integration in the post-Maastricht period. Failure like the rejection of the Constitutional Treaty postpones the reforming of the institutional model of the EU despite Eastern enlargement. It shows that only a very few vote-seeking political leaders can break down institutional reform processes by announcing referendums, even if their ratification procedures allow for ratification in the national game of party competition. This also increases the likelihood of incomplete contracting, which only partially prepares for Eastern enlargement, and fails to provide policy-making efficiency, a balance between supranational and national norms in EU policy-making as well as between responsibility and responsiveness to the distinct public demands.

Part 2

CHAPTER 5

Consequences of Choices

5.1. Abstract

This chapter presents the theoretical framework for studying the consequences of the institutional choices for Europe, which establish veto bicameralism with regulated supranational competences. Despite widening and deepening, these choices fail to reform the composition and role of the European Commission, which has agenda monopoly in EU policy-making. After a short discussion of the existing literature on the consequences of the institutional choices for Europe, propositions and hypotheses on supranational technocracism and camp-building with affective polarization are presented. These consequences change the game in EU policy-making, the supranational game of party competition, and public support for European integration in the post-Maastricht period.

5.2. Theorizing Supranational Governance

Following the functionalist approach of Jean Monnet, integration cannot be achieved by party competition because the voters have neither the necessary expertise nor the time to make informed decisions. Following this argument, the European Coal and Steel Community—as the precursor of the European Communities and the EU—was established as a technocratic trustee model to integrate the coal and steel industries of the six founding members Belgium, France, Germany, Italy, Luxembourg, and the Netherlands by the supranational experts of the high authority—today's European Commission. In this trustee model, the supranational experts autonomously regulate policy-making (Majone 1996). They are committed to their responsibility for achieving the goal of European integration (the key word here being "responsible"), while electoral party competition fosters that their representatives are responsive to the distinct public demands (emphasis on being "responsive").

For a long time, the technocratic trustee model of functional integration has stimulated the scholarly debate about the predominant role of supranational institutions in EU policy-making, such as the European Commission and the European Court of Justice (e.g., Haas 1958, Burley and Mattli 1993, Sandholtz and Stone Sweet 2012). According to Haas (1958: 18) "as impracticable as it is unnecessary to have recourse to general public opinion surveys, or even to surveys of specifically interested groups. . . . It suffices to single out and define the political elites in the participating countries, to study their reactions to integration, and to assess changes in attitude on their part." For Lindberg and Scheingold (1970) a permissive consensus about functional integration existed because the political elites did not oppose this technocratic type of European integration.

Compared to Majone's (1996) regulatory state, one implication of this technocratic trustee model of functional integration is that it does not mobilize the masses, which consequently reduces political participation when ruling/mainstream parties show little responsiveness to distinct public demands (Stimson, Mackuen, and Erikson 1995, König 2018). Without political controversies in the chief national arenas, the public does not call into question the existing elite consensus about European integration (Reif and Schmitt 1980). However, Lindberg and Scheingold (1970: 277) already indicate that this consensus might not last forever: "if the Community were to broaden its scope or increase its institutional capacities markedly, . . . there [would] be reason to suspect that the level of support or its relationship to the political process would be significantly altered."

For scholars of postfunctionalism (Hooghe and Marks 2009, 2018), politicization (de Wilde and Zürn 2012, Hutter, Grande, and Kriesi 2016, Rauh 2016), and globalization (Kriesi et al. 2006, Kriesi et al. 2012, Grande and Kriesi 2016), this happens with the further transfer of policy competences of sensitive areas to the supranational level of the EU. Compared to the optimistic view of functionalist integration, which emphasizes positive spillovers from the transfer of policy competences for European integration (Rosamond 2000), postfunctionalism points to the negative consequences of this transfer into an institutionally mismatched EU. It considers that mass politics in elections, referendums, and party primaries open the door to the mobilization of national identities, which generates a new transnational cleavage with increasing Euroscepticism (Hooghe and Marks 2019).

Specifying the politicization thesis of European integration as "an increase in polarization of opinions, interests or values and the extent to which they are publicly advanced towards policy formulation within the EU" (de Wilde 2011: 566–67), De Vries (2018) explains the rise of Euroscepticism as political differentials between the public's support of a policy and a regime as well as between the national and EU level (see also Sánchez-Cuenca 2000). Schneider (2018) shows that European affairs become more important in national (electoral) politics, in which responsive governments need to defend their positions on European issues at least around election time (see also Wratil 2019). While the public did not pay much attention to European issues in the pre-Maastricht period of permissive consensus (Mair 2000), "the elite has had to make room for a more Eurosceptical public" (Hooghe and Marks 2009: 9). Evidence for this change provides the emergence of a new transnational cleavage that—according to postfunctionalism—emerges from the mobilization of national identities and the demand for self-rule among dealigned voters (Marks et al. 2017, Hooghe and Marks 2018).

In the post-Maastricht period, four fundamental questions concerned the consequences of the institutional choices for EU policy-making:

- How does the institutional choice to empower the European Parliament, which becomes a co-legislative veto player of the Council of the EU, change EU policy-making?
- How does the institutional choice to continue with the supranational agenda monopoly of the unreformed European Commission to draft proposals change the nature and type of EU policy-making?
- How does EU policy-making affect party competition, which polarizes between pro-integrationist ruling/mainstream and anti-integrationist challenger/periphery parties?
- How does EU policy-making impact public support of European integration at times of supranational problem-solving with mass-mobilizing EU crisis management?

According to SNP, the institutional choices have two major consequences for EU policy-making: First, veto bicameralism reduces the threat of legislative override, which promotes supranational technocracy with uncontrolled delegation of supranational experts in the first phase of deepening. Second, the failure to reform the agenda monopoly of the European Commission, which prioritizes supranational over national norms, fosters supranational camp-building between a pro-integrationist camp of ruling/mainstream and an anti-integrationist camp of challenger/periphery parties in the second phase of widening. With the Constitutional crisis in 2005, the Great Recession with the following European sovereign debt crisis between 2007 and 2010, and the Migrant crisis in 2015, the EU experiences several massmobilizing crises, which demonstrate the shortcomings of supranational problem-solving with EU crisis management in the third phase.

5.3. Veto Bicameralism and Uncontrolled Delegation

The outcomes of the institutional choices define the scale and scope of delegation to supranational experts in the EU policy-making game. In this EU policy-making game of checks-and-balances, the legislature controls the scale of delegation to the supranational executive and judiciary by the possibility of legislative override. Important for supranational governance, the subsidiarity principle defines the scope of taking supranational action in shared areas, where the EU—except in cases where it has exclusive competence—should only be active unless it is more effective than action taken at the national, regional, or local level.[1] Although supranational delegation generally aims to achieve the goal of European integration, SNP proposes that veto bicameralism reduces the control of the scope and scale of supranational delegation by reducing the threat of legislative override. A lower threat of legislative override fosters activism of supranational experts, which cannot be effectively constrained by the subsidiarity principle.

According to the proposition of SNP, the higher conflict on governance design of a deepening and widening EU, which experiences higher economic, cultural, and societal heterogeneity and intensity of interests (König and Bräuninger 2004), translates into institutional choices that establish high checks-and-balances for EU policy-making. When veto bicameralism increases checks-and-balances by adding an institutional (parliamentary) veto player, it reduces the threat of legislative override for activism of the supranational experts (Tsebelis and Garrett 2001, Carrubba et al. 2012, Junge,

---

1. Shared areas are the common market, employment and social affairs, economic, social and territorial cohesion, agriculture and fisheries, environment, consumer protection, transport, trans-European networks, energy, justice and fundamental rights, migration and home affairs, public health, research and space, development cooperation and humanitarian aid.

König, and Luig 2015). These experts are without an electoral mandate and are committed to pursuing the long-term goal of European integration. Following Caramani (2017), the delegation of authority to experts without an electoral mandate, experts who stress responsibility for long-term goals at the expense of responsiveness to the distinct public demands, is a typical characteristic of technocracy. Taken together, from the proposition that higher conflict on governance design leads to higher checks-and-balances, follows the first hypotheses on supranational technocracism:

- $H_{con}1$. With the higher conflict in EU governance design, the more technocratic will EU policy-making be.

More specifically, SNP conjectures that veto bicameralism changes the scale and scope of delegation to supranational experts in the post-Maastricht period. Compared to the unicameral consultation procedure in the pre-Maastricht period, the bicameral codecision procedure increases the discretionary power of the supranational agenda setter. To illustrate the procedural implication of veto bicameralism, one method is to compare the size of the legislative core across procedures, which defines the set of all status quo policies that cannot be changed by the legislature under the procedure (Hammond and Miller 1987). The left panel in Figure 5.1a identifies the size of the core in the unicameral consultation procedure by the intersecting median lines of seven member states (1 to 7). They pursue different positions and decide by unanimity or qualified majority (5 out of 7) in a two-dimensional policy space, which distinguishes between left versus right and a pro- versus anti-integrationist dimension.

Applying a qualified majority instead of unanimity reduces the size of the core, which makes legislative override more likely in the unicameral consultation procedure.[2] In the bicameral codecision procedure, when the adding of a parliamentary veto player expands the size of the legislative core, the threat of legislative override for the supranational agenda setter decreases. This is illustrated in the right panel of Figure 5.1b, which adds five groups of the European Parliament. They pursue similar positions to the seven member

---

2. While the size of the core under unanimity covers the area defined by the lines connecting the heptagon of the seven member states, the qualified majority core shrinks to the smaller shaded area because the positions of two of the seven member states can be excluded from changing the status quo.

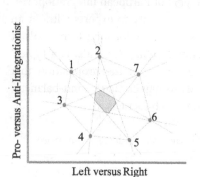
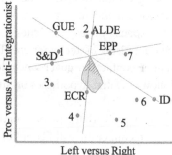

Figure 5.1. Changes of Core Size from Uni- to Bicameralism: Member States 1–7, Parliamentary Groups ALDE, ECR, EPP, GUE, ID, and S&D

states on the left versus right dimension but are slightly more integrationist on the second dimension. Because these five groups decide by a majority (3 out of 5), their core size is reduced to the median point of the intersecting lines. Although this median point is the smallest parliamentary core, the bicameral size of the legislative core almost doubles, which is illustrated by the additional striped area at the top of the shaded unicameral core.

Specifically, SNP predicts that a lower threat of legislative override for the supranational agenda setter will modify the type of EU policy-making from secondary to tertiary legislation. As illustrated in Figure 5.2, the European Commission can either propose secondary or use tertiary legislation to implement legally binding acts (Junge, König, and Luig 2015). In secondary legislation, the proposal requires approval by the legislature, which consists of the representatives of the member states in the Council and, more increasingly in the post-Maastricht period, the groups in the European Parliament. When the legislature does not approve the proposal, the status quo prevails (no act); otherwise, the member states need to comply with the secondary act, which may require further transposition into national law.[3] Unlike secondary legislation, the implementation of tertiary legislation is delegated to the European Commission, and the act enters into force when the legislature

---

3. When the member states do not comply with the act, the European Commission can start an infringement proceeding, and the European Court of Justice can sanction noncompliance. However, if the European Commission does not enforce compliance by starting an infringement proceeding or the European Court of Justice does not sanction noncompliance, the status quo prevails (no act).

Consequences of Choices

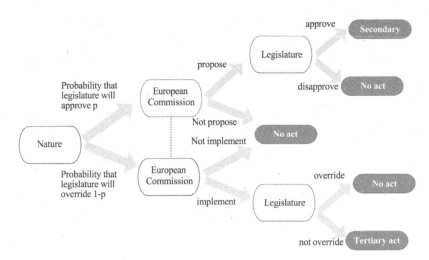

Figure 5.2. EU Policy-Making between the European Commission and the (Bicameral) Legislature

does not override it. Due to the lack of direct approval by the legislature, tertiary legislation implements nonlegislative delegated or bureaucratic acts (Junge, König, and Luig 2015).

In the lower path of Figure 5.2, the legislature needs to override the tertiary act, for example, by an action for annulment, which reestablishes the status quo (no act). When the legislature does not override the bureaucratic act, the member states need to comply with it.[4] Regarding the size of the legislative core, the European Commission will propose secondary legislation, the higher the likelihood p that the legislature will approve the act; it will implement tertiary legislation, the lower the likelihood $1-p$ of legislative override:

- $H_{con}2$. The larger the size of the legislative core, the more tertiary legislation is implemented in EU policy-making.

Following SNP, a lower threat of legislative override also offers more discretion for the choice of legislative instruments, which has implications for the amount of centralization in EU policy-making. For secondary and tertiary

---

4. In case of noncompliance, the European Commission can start an infringement proceeding and the European Court of Justice can sanction noncompliance. Again, if they do not enforce compliance or sanction noncompliance, the status quo prevails (no act).

legislation, the European Commission can propose regulations, decisions, and directives, which implement binding and enforceable acts. Unlike regulations, a decision is only binding on those to whom it is addressed. Compared to directives, which provide member states more discretion to achieve a certain result, regulations and decisions are directly and immediately applicable, which centralizes EU policy-making. Despite widening and deepening in the post-Maastricht period, which would demand more discretion to cope with higher economic, cultural, and societal heterogeneity and intensity of interests in the EU, this suggests that centralizing instruments will dominate when a larger size of the legislative core reduces the threat of legislative override:

- $H_{con}3$. The larger the size of the legislative core, the more centralizing regulations and decisions are implemented in EU policy-making.

In addition to changing the scale of supranational delegation by more bureaucratic and centralizing acts in EU policy-making, a change in the threat of legislative override may also affect the scope of supranational delegation in multilevel governance, which is defined by the subsidiarity principle. To control the scope of supranational delegation, the subsidiarity principle divides competences into the three categories of exclusive, shared, and supporting (coordinated) competences with lists of the areas covered by the three categories. In the shared areas, the EU "shall take action only if and in so far as the objectives of the proposed action cannot be sufficiently achieved by the member states."[5] However, when a larger size of the legislative core reduces the threat of legislative override, the less controlled are supranational activities in shared areas:

- $H_{con}4$. The larger the size of the legislative core, the less effective is the subsidiarity principle.

In the post-Maastricht period, the size of the legislative core raises for two reasons. First, widening and deepening increases the diversity and intensity of interests in EU policy-making. Second, the adding of a parliamentary veto

---

5. The Lisbon Treaty specifies three preconditions for supranational delegation: (a) the area concerned does not fall within the EU's exclusive competence (i.e., nonexclusive competence); (b) the objectives of the proposed action cannot be sufficiently achieved by the member states (i.e., necessity); (c) the action can therefore, by reason of its scale or effects, be implemented more successfully by the EU (i.e., added value).

player establishes an additional hurdle for legislative override. Although the political leaders introduce the subsidiarity principle to limit supranational activities in areas of shared competences, SNP predicts that the larger size of the legislative core expands the scale and scope of supranational delegation in the post-Maastricht period. In addition to uncontrolled scale and scope of supranational delegation, widening and deepening are also likely to affect compliance and the democratic deficit in the post-Maastricht period.

5.4. Compliance and Democratic Deficit

For liberal intergovernmentalism, supranational delegation assures the implementation of and compliance with acts (Moravcsik 1998: 76). In contrast to liberal intergovernmentalism (Moravcsik 2002: 607, 2008: 181) and functionalist integration by regulatory politics (Majone 1998, 2000), Follesdal and Hix (2006) outline a trend toward a democratic deficit through an increase in executive power and policy drift with overemphasis of negative integration (Scharpf 1997, 1999, Schmitter and Streeck 1991). Weiler, Haltern, and Mayer (1995) are also strongly skeptical about the weakness of the European Parliament in the interplay between the legislature on the one side and the executive and judiciary on the other side. They suggest a more democratic solution with the constitutionalization of the EU, in which supranational centralization in EU policy-making is legitimized by the procedural involvement of the European Parliament.[6]

In the post-Maastricht period, however, widening and deepening not only expand the size of the legislative core in EU policy-making but the higher diversity and intensity of interests of a larger number of member states also increases the risk of enforcement conflicts about noncompliance with legislative acts (König and Mäder 2014). According to SNP, this changes the focus of the procedural involvement of the European Parliament from democratic legitimacy of supranational centralization toward compliance in EU policy-making. Compared to centralizing regulations and decisions, the

---

6. This procedural linkage is already indicated by the Maastricht Treaty, which defines in Article 3b (2) that the Community shall take action only "if and insofar as the objectives of the proposed action cannot be sufficiently achieved by the Member States and can therefore, by reason of the scale or effect of the proposed action, be better achieved by the Community," while the preamble also states that "decisions are taken as closely as possible to the citizen."

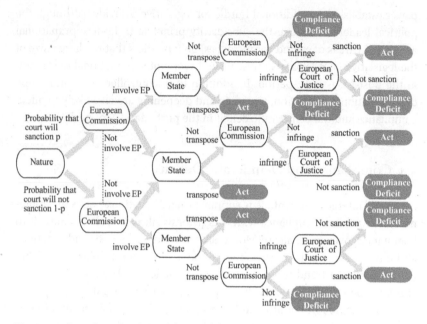

Figure 5.3. Compliance and EU Policy-Making of Directives with and without European Parliament (EP)

results to be achieved by directives need to be transposed into domestic law, which raises most enforcement conflicts about compliance (König and Luetgert 2009, Börzel 2021).[7] For SNP, the focus on compliance implies that the European Parliament is less involved in legitimizing supranational centralization through regulations and decisions than in strengthening supranational enforcement power for the implementation of directives in areas of "greater dispersion of authority" (Hooghe and Marks 2001: xii).

Regarding compliance, which is conventionally discussed between the management and enforcement schools of thought from a country-specific perspective (Chayes and Chayes 1993, Downs, Rocke, and Barsoom 1996, Tallberg 2002, Falkner, Hartlapp, and Treib 2007, Toshkov 2008, Börzel 2021), scholars have started to acknowledge the policy-specific procedural

---

7. Because correct transposition is difficult to evaluate, most research has focused on timely transposition, i.e., whether the member states notify their measures within the prescribed deadline (e.g., Mastenbroek 2003, Kaeding 2005).

Consequences of Choices 93

implications for compliance in EU policy-making (e.g., König and Mäder 2014, Fjelstul and Carrubba 2018). From a policy-seeking procedural view of sequential choices, the European Commission can involve the European Parliament to strengthen supranational enforcement power, when the European Court of Justice is more likely to sanction noncompliance with directives the European Parliament has approved.

According to Figure 5.3, the European Commission can involve the European Parliament in the making of a directive, which the member states need to transpose into domestic law. If they do not transpose the directive, the European Commission can start an infringement proceeding to enforce compliance. If the European Commission does not start an infringement or the European Court of Justice does not sanction nontransposition, a compliance deficit exists. This suggests that the risk of noncompliance is defined by the European Commission's belief p that the court will sanction nontransposition whether the European Parliament has been involved or not. Depending on the probability that the European Court of Justice will sanction nontransposition, SNP predicts that the role of the European Parliament changes when the European Commission considers the risk of noncompliance higher than the costs of supranational centralization:

- $H_{con}5$. Compared to centralizing regulations and decisions, the European Parliament is more involved in EU policy-making of directives.

The involvement of the European Parliament in EU policy-making of directives is only one procedural policy-seeking strategy to cope with a higher risk of noncompliance in the post-Maastricht period. Another procedural policy-seeking strategy is to use informal trilogue between the European Commission, the Council presidency, and a delegation of the European Parliament for early agreement during the first or second reading. An early agreement avoids the entering of a directive into the third reading of bicameral conflict resolution, which sends an observable signal of contest about a directive's result to be achieved. According to Figure 5.4, first-reading early agreements are concluded before the European Parliament approves a common position in the first reading, while second-reading early agreements are approved before the Council reaches its common position in the second reading. Because early agreements are concluded in informal trilogues, they reduce transparency and accountability in EU policy-making (Reh et al. 2011).

Compared to the Council presidency and the delegation of the European

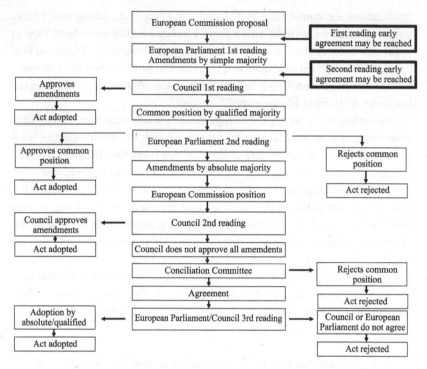

Figure 5.4. Regular EU Policy-Making and Informal Trilogues for Early Agreement

Parliament, which may benefit from informational advantages through informal trilogues, the European Commission supports an early agreement in informal trilogues for three reasons: First, the European Parliament and the Council can approve a joint text in the third reading without the consent of the European Commission; second, the European Commission can improve the proposal and has no electoral mandate, which demands more transparency and accountability in EU policy-making; third, and perhaps most importantly for an enforcement conflict about compliance, bicameral conflict resolution signals that the result to be achieved is contested.[8]

To avoid an enforcement conflict about compliance, informal trilogues allow for the improvement of a directive in consent with the European Com-

---

8. Compared to the European Commission, the decision of the Council and the European Parliament to enter into the third reading depends on the improvement of the directive in informal trilogues (Lu and König 2021).

mission and to avoid sending signals of contest on the result to be achieved at the expense of transparency and accountability. This suggests that informal trilogues will dominate EU policy-making of directives when the costs from an enforcement conflict are expected to exceed the costs from the lack of transparency and accountability:

- $H_{con}6$. Early agreements with informal trilogues reduce the risk of an enforcement conflict about compliance with directives in EU policy-making.

Both procedural strategies can solve the compliance puzzle and the parliamentarization paradox in the post-Maastricht period. Regarding compliance, it is puzzling that the rates of infringements to enforce compliance decline despite the accession of more diverse member states, while most legal acts are paradoxically approved in informal trilogues despite the European Parliament is strengthened for increasing transparency and accountability in EU policy-making. For (neo)functionalist scholars, however, the European Commission does not need to pursue such strategies, because the European Court of Justice is a promoter of European integration, which prioritizes supranational over national norms (e.g., Burley and Mattli 1993, Mattli and Slaughter 1995, Stone Sweet and Caporaso 1998, Cichowski 2004, Stone Sweet and Brunell 2012). Others find that judicial activism in favor of supranational norms is constrained by the threat of legislative override and refer to correlations between court judgments and amicus curiae briefs, which the member states send to the court (Carrubba, Gabel, and Hankla 2008, Carrubba and Gabel 2014, Larsson and Naurin 2016).

For SNP, agenda-setting of the European Commission, which can propose centralizing regulations and decisions instead of directives or conclude early agreements to avoid enforcement conflicts about compliance in EU policy-making, is also relevant to the role of the court. Furthermore, the European Commission can select to start an infringement, which it is likely to win (König and Mäder 2014). According to Figure 5.3, a compliance deficit exists when the European Commission does not start an infringement or the court does not sanction nontransposition. Before the court decides on the priority of a supranational or national norm, the European Commission and the Advocate General send opinions about a case to the court—the European Commission concerning the norm's supranational conformity, the Advocate General regarding the more general implications of the norm. In this procedure, the member states may send amicus curiae briefs about their opinions to the court, which will only control supranational activism when they send a strong signal to the court. From this proposition on the need to send a strong signal follows the seventh hypothesis on judicial activism in EU policy-making:

- $H_{con}7$. Member states can only conditionally constrain judicial activism in EU policy-making.

In addition to supranational delegation in EU policy-making, which raises concerns about compliance and the democratic foundation of supranational centralization, the political leaders also decide about the transfer of policy competences, which affects the supranational game of party competition. When supranational norms are prioritized over national norms in sensitive policy areas, this fosters supranational camp-building in EU policy-making with a pro-integrationist camp of ruling/mainstream parties and an anti-integrationist camp of challenger/periphery parties, the former supporting and the latter rejecting the priority of supranational over national norms in EU policy-making.

5.5. Agenda Monopoly and Camp-Building

For scholars of politicization, with the Maastricht Treaty the period of the permissive consensus ended (e.g., De Wilde 2011, De Wilde and Zürn 2012, Rauh 2016). Apart from referendums on the Maastricht, Nice, and Lisbon treaties, which reveal sporadically "punctuated politicization" (Grande and Kriesi 2016), Hooghe and Marks (2003, 2009) argue that transfers of policy competences for sensitive areas of asylum and migration, monetary and fiscal policies firstly politicize and mobilize national identities, which structure support of European integration. Political parties secondly respond to the voters' desires of preserving their national identities, which establishes a new transnational cleavage in party competition.[9] In particular political entrepreneurs from periphery parties are more responsive to the short-term con-

---

9. Compared to green/alternative/libertarian (or GAL), traditional/authoritarian/nationalist (or TAN) parties are pivotal in mobilization arising from the perforation of nationalism due to the transfer of policy competences for immigration, integration, and trade.

cerns of the voters and challenge mainstream parties that continue to support European integration (De Vries and Hobolt 2012, 2020).

SNP proposes to first identify the critical juncture of ideological conflict on European integration between ruling/mainstream parties and challenger/ periphery parties in the national game of party competition. Second, with the transfer of policy competences for sensitive areas, this divide is considered to consolidate through the agenda monopoly of the European Commission that fosters camp-building between a pro- and an anti-integrationist camp in EU policy-making, along which the public ideologically aligns, third, in times of supranational problem-solving with mass-mobilizing EU crisis management.

Regarding the critical juncture of ideological conflict on European integration, 20 referendums are held about accession before the prominent referendum on British membership to leave the EU in 2016, which sporadically allow challenger/periphery parties to mobilize supporters against European integration. In 1997, Denmark, Ireland, and Norway decided about their accession, United Kingdom in 1975, followed by Austria, Finland, Norway, and Sweden in 1994, Switzerland in 1997 and 2001, the Czech Republic, Estonia, Hungary, Latvia, Lithuania, Malta, Poland, Slovakia, Slovenia in 2003, and Croatia in 2012.[10] Because mainstream/ruling parties expect office- and policy-seeking benefits from European integration, they usually support accession, while challenger parties from the periphery of the party spectrum reject it (König and Luig 2017). From this proposition follows the eighth hypothesis on the critical juncture of the ideological divide between mainstream/ruling and challenger/periphery parties:

- $H_{con}8$. Accession divides mainstream/ruling and challenger/periphery parties in the national game of party competition on European integration.

SNP posits that this divide between mainstream/ruling and challenger/ periphery parties consolidates in EU policy-making by the agenda monopoly of the European Commission, which fosters camp-building in the supranational game of party competition. More specifically, SNP conjectures that veto bicameralism reduces two- or multidimensional proposals to a single pro- versus anti-integrationist conflict line. As illustrated in Figure 5.5, the two chambers form a common position within each chamber in the first and

---

10. It is noteworthy to say that mainstream/ruling parties did not support accession in Switzerland and Norway.

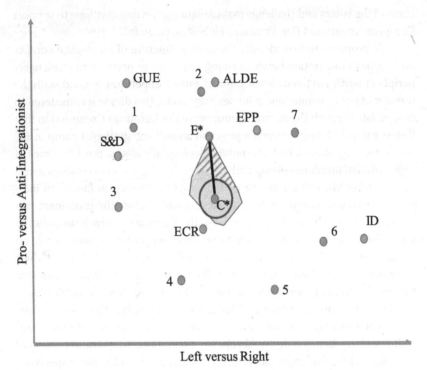

Figure 5.5. Bicameral Conflict Resolution and Polarization between Pro- and Anti-Integrationists

second reading, whereby the majority of the European Parliament pursues a more (moderate) pro-integrationist position E* than the centroid of the Council's core C*, which represents the most likely solution under qualified majority voting among the seven member states (Tsebelis 2002). Following Tsebelis and Money (1997), bicameral conflict resolution connects E* and C* on the shortest conflict line.

In veto bicameralism, the supranational experts of the European Commission prioritize supranational over national norms on the shortest conflict line, which separates a camp of pro-integrationist ruling/mainstream from anti-integrationist challenger/periphery parties in supranational party competition. In an environment of complete and perfect information, the agenda-setting European Commission can propose the most acceptable supranational norm, which the majority of the pro-integrationist camp approves in the first or second reading. In an environment of incomplete and imperfect

Consequences of Choices   99

information, the European Commission—which participates in the Council's deliberations on a common position—has an informational advantage about the pivotal position on the priority of the national norm, which excludes the strategic positioning in the third reading of bicameral conflict resolution (König et al. 2007). From this proposition on bicameral conflict resolution follows the ninth hypothesis on supranational camp-building:

- $H_{con}9$. Veto bicameralism fosters supranational camp-building of a pro- versus anti-integrationist camp in EU policy-making.

Despite deepening and widening, the institutional choices fail to reform the composition and role of the European Commission in EU policy-making. The Amsterdam Treaty postpones the reform of the European Commission's composition, the Nice Treaty only approves a review clause, while the concessions after the negative Irish referendum on the Lisbon Treaty eliminate the agreement on the reduction of the number of Commissioners. As a result, the college of Commissioners more than doubles, each holding a specific portfolio of policy competences in the post-Maastricht period. Figure 5.6 illustrates the consequences of portfolio allocation among two Commissioners with competences for two policy areas, for which a compromise X has been approved at interstate bargains.

Within each portfolio, usually connected to one or several Directorates-General (DGs), the Commissioner is responsible for drafting a proposal, which requires the approval of the Council and the European Parliament. Although X is the Pareto-efficient compromise solution between the two member states MS1 and MS2 at interstate bargains, a more pro- or anti-integrationist Commissioner Com 1 and Com 2 can autonomously draft proposals within portfolios 1 and 2 that drift from X.[11] In portfolio 2, for example, the distance between Commissioner 2 and X is larger than X', which is the shortest distance from the winset. Similarly, COM 1 can shorten the distance to the winset within portfolio 1. Such drift is likely to increase with a growing number of portfolios, which promotes polarization in EU policy-making by untying previously agreed compromise. From this proposition on portfolio

---

11. Although a Commissioner's party background matters for appointment (Wonka 2007), each Commissioner is required to recite the "solemn undertaking" to respect the treaties and the Charter of Fundamental Rights of the EU before the European Court of Justice.

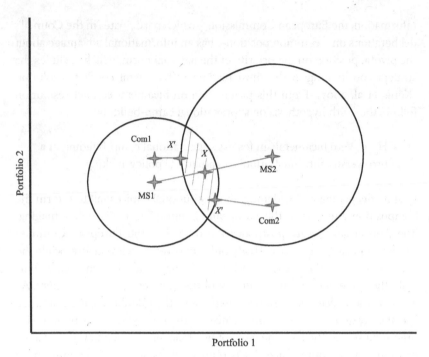

Figure 5.6. Portfolio Allocation and Agenda-Setting Power of Commissioners

allocation follows the tenth hypotheses on polarization in EU policy-making:

- $H_{con}10$. With the higher number of portfolios, the more likely is polarization in EU policy-making.

Drift from previously agreed compromise not only applies to secondary legislation, in which the Council and the European Parliament can amend the proposals of the European Commission. In tertiary legislation, which SNP predicts to dominate EU policy-making, the European Commission can autonomously implement acts when the size of the legislative core excludes legislative override. However, camp-building and polarization do not necessarily lead to noncompliance in EU policy-making. Following the propositions and hypotheses on supranational technocracism, the European Commission can avoid enforcement conflicts about compliance with directives by using regulations and decisions in secondary legislation, implementing tertiary legislation, or inviting to informal trilogue for early agreement. In this case, neither supranational technocracism in times of deepening nor supranational camp-building in times of widening mobilizes the public at the beginning of the post-Maastricht period. This changes with mass-mobilizing supranational problem-solving and EU crisis management in the third phase of the post-Maastricht period.

5.6. Affective Polarization and Ideological Alignment

For scholars of public support of European integration, whether they investigate country-specific or individual benefits from European integration (e.g., Eichenberg and Dalton 1993, Anderson and Reichert 1995, Gabel and Palmer 1995, Anderson and Kaltenthaler 1996, Gabel 1998), whether national attachment or identity is shaping support (Carey 2002, Hooghe and Marks 2005, Risse 2010), and whether the public uses heuristics regarding the performance of their national governments (e.g., Anderson 1998, Sánchez-Cuenca 2000, Kritzinger 2003, De Vries 2018) or the positions of the political parties they support (De Vries and Edwards 2009, Helbling, Hoeglinger, and Wüest 2010), benchmarking predicts an inverse relationship to public satisfaction with domestic democracy in the member states and EU governance (Sánchez-Cuenca 2000, De Vries 2018). However, benchmarking between domestic democracy in the member states and EU governance neither accounts for public (de)mobilization nor investigates the critical link between the consequences of the institutional choices for Europe and public support, which also underlies the longstanding discussion of democratic deficit and institutional reform in the EU (e.g., Weiler, Haltern, and Mayer 1995, Scharpf 1999, Moravcsik 2002, Rittberger 2003, Follesdal and Hix 2006).

According to SNP, supranational technocracism, in which experts without electoral mandate prioritize supranational over national norms, is of little responsiveness to the distinct demands of the public. When ruling/mainstream parties furthermore continue to commonly support supranational technocracism, because they have office-seeking and policy-seeking benefits from European integration, this will neither attract nor mobilize the public. Despite further transfers of policy competences, this lack of responsiveness is more likely to reduce mobilization in European and general elections and disappoint voters, especially when issues of European integration become more salient (Gabel 2000, Spoon 2012). From this proposition on the lack of responsiveness follows the eleventh hypothesis on supranational technocracism, which will decrease mobilization and public support of European integration:

- H_{con} 11. Despite transfers of policy competences for sensitive areas, supranational technocracism decreases mobilization and public support of European integration.

Part of the reason is that the ruling/mainstream parties prefer not to politicize issues that could lead to internal splits and voter defection (Aspinwall 2002, Hooghe 2003, Müller, Jenny, and Ecker 2012). When ruling/mainstream parties continue to support supranational technocracism, which overemphasizes responsibility for European integration at the expense of responsiveness to the distinct demands of the public, SNP predicts decoupling between public and partisan attitudes toward European integration. In particular, when exogenous shocks or crises demand supranational problem-solving with mass-mobilizing EU crisis management, an overemphasis of the long-term goal of European integration allows anti-integrationist challenger/periphery parties to mobilize voters with simplifying "My Population First"-slogans. From this proposition on supranational problem-solving follows the twelfth hypothesis on the rise of challenger/periphery parties of the anti-integrationist camp:

- H_{con} 12. In times of supranational problem-solving with EU crisis management, public support of anti-integrationist challenger/periphery parties increases at the expense of pro-integrationist mainstream/ruling parties.

As cleavages are rooted in durable structures of conflict, a new cleavage only arises when external shocks or crises foster the ideological alignment of the public along existing configurations in party competition. According to SNP, supranational problem-solving with mass-mobilizing EU crisis management promotes affective polarization with partisan ingroup favoritism and outgroup derogation on issues of European integration in the third phase of the post-Maastricht period. Affective polarization—most notably, the tendency for partisans to dislike and distrust those from the other group—contributes to public opinion and preference formation (Druckman et al. 2021). Due to mass-mobilization, SNP conjectures that partisan supporters ideologically align with ruling/mainstream and challenger/periphery parties along the divide between the pro- and the anti-integrationist camps. From this proposition on affective polarization follows the thirteenth hypothesis on ideological alignment along the pro- versus anti-integrationist cleavage:

- $H_{con}13$. Affective polarization promotes ideological alignment along the pro- versus anti-integrationist dimension, which establishes a new cleavage on European integration.

Emotional mobilization and ideological alignment with a new cleavage on European integration do not necessarily mean constraining dissensus that either reduces supranational problem-solving (e.g., Hooghe and Marks 2009, 2019) or demands differentiated variability in European integration (e.g., Leuffen, Rittberger, and Schimmelfennig 2012, Schmidt 2019, Schimmelfennig, Leuffen, and De Vries 2023). It only means that partisans of ruling/mainstream parties identify with the pro-integrationist camp, while partisans of challenger/periphery parties identify with the anti-integrationist camp. According to SNP, this identification can foster a superordinate supranational identity along the cleavage on European integration when the partisan identifiers overcome their national affiliation by showing solidarity and trust for outnationals.

Although there has been a growing consensus that achieving a certain sense of a supranational identity is critical for establishing a supranational democratic system with political authority over European citizens (e.g., Bruter 2005, Eriksen and Fossum 2002, Follesdal and Hix 2006, Hix 2005, 2008, Fligstein, Polyakova, and Sandholtz 2012), little attention has been paid yet to what the two components—the "self" and the "other" (Tajfel and Turner 1979)—of a supranational identity are. When partisans identify with their camp along the cleavage on European integration, they may form a supranational "self" when they show similar levels of solidarity and trust for EU outnationals, while lower levels of solidarity and trust for non-EU members may define the "other". From this proposition on the "self" and the "other" follows the fourteenth hypothesis on the formation of a supranational identity:

- $H_{con}14$. The new cleavage on European integration fosters the creation of a supranational identity with camp-specific solidarity and trust among Europeans.

Briefly summarized, SNP posits that

- veto bicameralism increases the size of the legislative core, which reduces the threat of legislative override for activism of supranational experts;
- the risk of noncompliance increases in a deepening and widening EU, which changes the role of the European Parliament and fosters informal policy-making to avoid enforcement conflicts about compliance;
- the supranational agenda monopoly prioritizes supranational over national norms, which promotes camp-building and affective polarization between a pro-integrationist camp of ruling/mainstream parties and an anti-integrationist camp of challenger/periphery parties.

The consequences of the institutional choices are predicted to establish supranational technocracism and camp-building with affective polarization as the sources of these dynamics in the post-Maastricht period, in which the EU experiences phases of approval and disapproval from political leaders, their parties, and the public. But why should one believe in the propositions and hypotheses of a new theory about the consequences of the institutional choices for Europe more than in existing insights from prominent theories such as postfunctionalism? SNP offers an examination of the explanatory power of the propositions and hypotheses, for which the next chapter presents the research design and data on legislative activities, partisan and public attitudes in the post-Maastricht period.

CHAPTER 6

Phase I: Technocracism and Compliance

6.1. Abstract

This chapter examines the propositions and hypotheses on supranational technocracism as a major consequence of the institutional choices for Europe in the post-Maastricht period. After a short introduction of the research design and the data on legislative activities, the analyses investigate EU policy-making, in which veto bicameralism reduces the threat of legislative override that expands the scale and scope of supranational delegation. In addition to uncontrolled supranational delegation, the higher risk of noncompliance fosters centralization and a lack of transparency and accountability in EU policy-making. Compared to the activism of supranational executive experts, the court is conditionally constrained through strong signals from the member states.

6.2. Legislative Activities in EU Policy-Making

For examining the consequences of veto bicameralism with regulated supranational competences for EU policy-making, a research design is warranted that allows for distinguishing between the type of act (secondary or tertiary) and the kind of instrument (regulation, decision, directive) across policy areas (exclusive, shared, coordinated) with implications for transparency (regular or informal) and compliance (with or without infringement). In the pre-Maastricht period, for example, the European Parliament has no veto right in EU policy-making, while the Maastricht Treaty introduces the bicameral codecision procedure with regulated supranational competences to increase transparency and accountability, which becomes the standard procedure with the Lisbon Treaty. The Amsterdam Treaty already introduces the possibility of approving early agreements in informal trilogue meetings between the European Commission, the Council presidency, and a delegation of the European Parliament. In the post-Maastricht period, this variation in legislative activities includes not only different procedures but also the type of act and the kind of instrument that are used in EU policy-making across policy areas and over time.

For many scholars, the introduction and expanded application of the codecision procedure reduces the democratic deficit of EU policy-making (e.g., Crombez 1996, 1997, Rittberger 2003, Hix and Follesdal 2006). The higher checks-and-balances in EU policy-making by the addition of the parliamentary veto player may also increase the discretionary power of the supranational executive and judiciary (Tsebelis and Garrett 2001). Because the supranational executive and judiciary are experts without electoral mandate and committed to pursue the goal of European integration, they prioritize supranational over national norms, which fosters supranational technocracism. In contrast to the politicization thesis, SNP contends that supranational technocracism—despite the further transfer of policy competences—demobilizes the public instead of mobilizing national identities and a desire for self-rule in a deepening EU.

For the evaluation of the propositions and hypotheses of SNP on supranational technocracism, the research design adheres to three methodological standards. To examine the proposition of SNP on uncontrolled delegation, the first standard concerns data collection of all observable legislative activities, which allows us to identify the distribution of specific acts, instruments, and procedures across policy areas and over time. Second, these data need to generate sufficient observations to evaluate the relationship between the type of act, the kind of instrument, and the level of procedural transparency and accountability for the period of study. Third, the data on legislative activities are combined with data on area-specific preferences to examine whether the threat of legislative override is responsible for uncontrolled delegation and the effectiveness of the subsidiarity principle.

For the study of the post-Maastricht period, data on more than 120,000 legislative acts are retrieved from EUR-Lex in the period from 1983 to 2015. Compared to analyses of legislative activities in secondary legislation (e.g., Schulz and König 2000, König 2007, Crombez and Hix 2015), the data also include all acts of tertiary legislation to investigate the bureaucratic trend in EU policy-making (Junge, König, and Luig 2015). To determine the level of centralization, it also lists the type of instrument (regulation, decision, directive) and specifies the procedure for each act, that is, whether the European Parliament is involved in the making of regulations and decisions or directives. The goal is to provide a comprehensive picture of all legislative activities in EU policy-making during the period of study.

This dataset on legislative acts is combined with data on informal trilogues and infringement proceedings to evaluate the implications for compliance, transparency, and accountability. Compared to existing compliance studies, which focus on country-specific characteristics (e.g., Börzel 2001, Falkner et al. 2007 Börzel and Knoll 2012, Dannwolf 2014), the analysis investigates the procedural implications by distinguishing between regular and informal EU policy-making. For the study of supranational executive and judicial activism, the legislative data are complemented with data from party manifestos to estimate the area-specific size of the legislative core, which defines the threat of legislative override across policy areas and over time (Junge, König, and Luig 2015). In addition to the analysis of supranational executive activism, which covers the time series of more than 30 years of legislative activities in secondary and tertiary legislation, the analysis of supranational judicial activism uses the data of Larsson and Naurin (2016), which cover the period from 1997 to 2008.

6.3. Uncontrolled Delegation and Threats of Legislative Override

For liberal intergovernmentalism, the institutional choices establish institutions and procedures that assure predictable, usually fair implementation and compliance (Moravcsik 1998: 69). According to Majone (1998), delegation is mainly used to implement pragmatic solutions for achieving the goal of European integration rather than defending political positions. The executive is better equipped with bureaucratic expertise, which translates into a highly technical nature of legal acts. For Majone (2004) and Moravcsik (2005: 373, 2008: 174) this regulatory nature of European integration is unproblematic and even unavoidable in the post-Maastricht period. On the contrary, Scharpf (1996, 1997, 1999) stresses the problematic aspects of the increasing imbalance between "positive" and "negative integration" by the technocratic removal of obstacles to economic competition in the common market through executive and judicial experts.

SNP predicts that with higher conflict in governance design, the more technocratic will EU policy-making be, due to a lower threat of legislative override ($H_{con}1$). A major reason for higher conflict on governance design is the widening and deepening of the EU, which increases economic, cultural, and societal heterogeneity and salience of interests among political leaders in the post-Maastricht period. This higher conflict translates into institutional choices that establish higher checks-and-balances for EU policy-making, which increase the size of the legislative core in EU policy-making. However, when a larger legislative core reduces the threat of legislative override, the executive and the judiciary become more active (Tsebelis and Garrett 2001). To measure the size of the legislative core, CMP data of national programmatic party competition are used for the area-specific estimation of the governmental positions in the Council (Budge et al. 2001) and combined with EMP data on area-specific positions of the parties in the European Parliament (Braun et al. 2007).[1] Figure 6.1 illustrates how the core size of the legislature expands in the area of competitiveness from EU15 to EU25 and from unicameral consultation to bicameral codecision in the post-Maastricht period.

The shaded areas in the upper figures, which represent the two-dimensional configuration of the 15 governmental representatives in the Council and the groups of the European Parliament in the area of competitiveness in 2004 before the enlargement of Eastern and Central European countries and the European election, show that the size of the legislative core more than doubles with the introduction of the bicameral codecision procedure. Because the Council continues to apply qualified majority voting rule among the governmental representatives, the expansion from 0.14 to 0.29 toward a more leftish pro-integrationist area results from adding the European Parliament as an institutional veto player (see for more detail, Junge, König, and Luig 2015: 781). The lower figures reveal the enlargement effect in 2005, which further increases the size of the core from 0.29 to 0.5 toward pro-integration. Compared to the left versus right dimension, the area of competitiveness particularly expands toward pro-integration with more support of the priority of supranational over national norms in the post-Maastricht period.

According to the proposition of SNP, the larger size of the legislative core reduces the threat of legislative override of supranational activism, which

---

[1]. To measure the preferences in the (bicameral) legislature, three issues with national-supranational (ns) poles and ten issues with left-right (lr) poles based on thirty-eight CMP categories and corresponding EMP categories are used. To consider the area-specific salience of each issue, the keywords of the CMP and EMP coding schemes are used to search in contents of EU legislative acts that were approved within a year (König and Luig 2012).

Phase I: Technocracism and Compliance

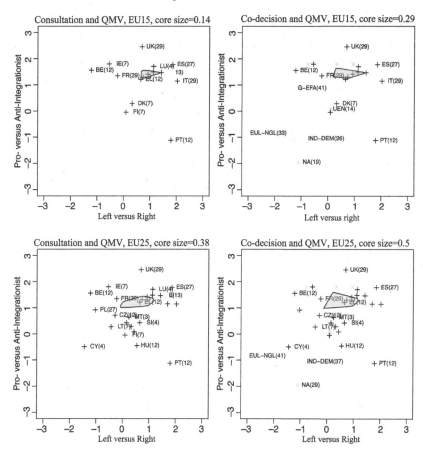

Figure 6.1. Positions of Governmental Representatives and Political Groups of the European Parliament for Competition Policy before and after 2004 European Elections

has more discretion for implementing tertiary acts ($H_{con}2$) and the choice of the instrument ($H_{con}3$), that is, more centralizing regulations and decisions instead of directives. Compared to secondary legislation, which is approved by the Council and the European Parliament in EU policy-making, tertiary legislation consists of delegated implementing acts, which the European Commission uses to supplement or amend certain elements of secondary legislation. Although the Lisbon Treaty introduces a distinction between delegated and implementing acts for tertiary legislation, they remain far from clearly defined (Bast 2016).[2] Tertiary legislation is also used where uniform conditions are needed to implement a legally binding act. Because tertiary legislation often adds more controls, adherence to rigid procedures, and attention to every detail for its own sake, Junge, König, and Luig (2015) use the amount of tertiary legislation as an indicator of the level of bureaucratization.

In secondary and tertiary legislation, the European Commission can propose three instruments for implementing legal acts and enforcing the compliance of those acts. Regulations, which are binding in their entirety and directly applicable in all member states, and decisions, which differentiate bindingness to those to whom they are addressed, centralize by fixing detailed legal supranational prescriptions. Because regulations and decisions are directly applicable, they bear a lower risk of noncompliance than directives, which require further transposition into national law. Directives set out the result that all member states must achieve but allow individual discretion for transposition regarding how and to what kind of measures are needed within a prescribed period. This means that the European Commission can propose regulations and (more differentiated) decisions instead of directives to avoid enforcement conflicts about compliance.[3] Figure 6.2 illustrates the number of regulations, decisions, and directives concerning tertiary and secondary legislation (so-called other acts excluded from the illustration). It also shows under which conditions the European Parliament is more involved.

Most of the more than 120,000 EU legal acts, which are approved as regulations, decisions, and directives between the mid-1980s and 2015, are delegated acts in tertiary legislation (about 85 percent), of which about 80 percent are regulations followed by decisions (15 percent). Directives, which provide for more discretion in a widening and deepening EU, only make up about 1.3 percent of the lower path of the tree of tertiary legislation. In addition to the very high share of regulations and decisions in tertiary legislation, these centralizing instruments also dominate secondary legislation, in which directives have a share of only about 10 percent when reviewing the upper path of the tree of secondary legislation in Figure 6.2.

---

2. Theoretically, delegated acts concern political delegation, which enters into force after a two-month period of scrutiny, in which the Council and the European Parliament may veto those acts; implementing acts refer to the technical delegation for specific cases, for which the Council and the European Parliament can demand consultation of the comitology committees.

3. Hurka and Steinebach (2020) illustrate the discretion of the European Commission by its justifications for the choice between two different, but quite similar legal acts.

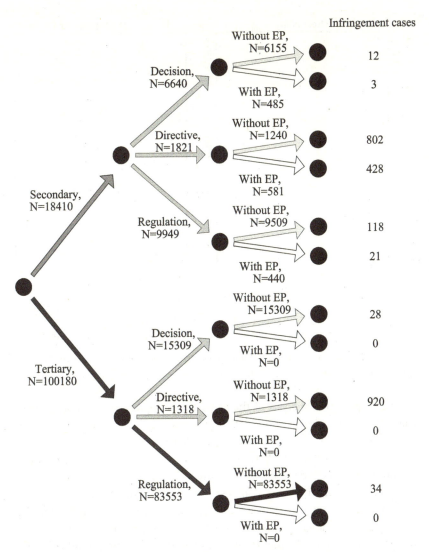

Figure 6.2. Number of Secondary and Tertiary Legislation in the Period 1983 to 2015 (by Number of Regulations, Decisions, and Directives with Parliamentary Involvement and Infringements)

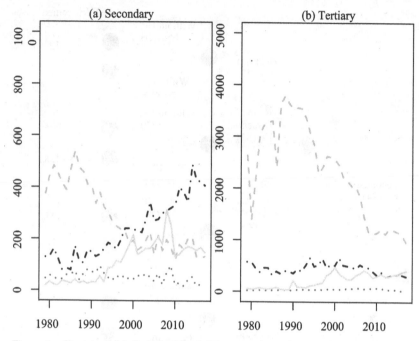

Figure 6.3. Decisions (black dashed line), Directives (gray dotted line), Regulations (gray dashed line), Other Legal Acts (gray solid line)

The explorative analysis of the more than 120,000 EU legal acts shows that EU policy-making is dominated by bureaucratic, centralizing acts. Figure 6.3 portrays the trend of secondary and tertiary legislation distinguishing by the type of instrument between the mid-1980s and 2015. Compared to the amount of secondary legislation, which does not exceed more than 600 legal acts per year, the higher share of tertiary legislation reaches a maximum of about 4,000 acts per year at the beginning of the 1990s. The following declining trend indicates that the incentive to interpret the legislative status quo is decreasing over time. However, a similar decreasing trend exists for regulations in secondary legislation, while the number of secondary decisions is increasing. Although both regulations and decisions are centralizing EU policy-making, this finding suggests differentiating between decreasing centralization through tertiary regulations with the lower incentive to interpret the status quo over time, while centralization through secondary decisions increasingly applies only to specific member states in a widening and deepening EU. This confirms the literature on differentiated integration, which

Phase I: Technocracism and Compliance

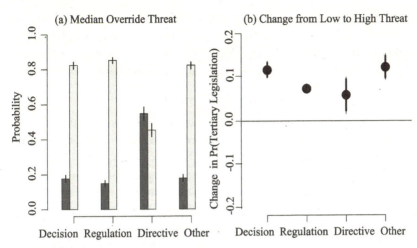

Figure 6.4. Estimation of Executive Activism in the Period 1983 to 2015. Dark Shaded = Probability for Secondary Legislation, Gray Shaded = Probability of Tertiary Legislation

finds more exemptions in the application of rules and provisions for European integration (Leuffen, Rittberger, and Schimmelfennig 2012).

SNP posits that the lower threat of legislative override reduces the control over supranational delegation, which is responsible for the trend toward bureaucratic and centralizing EU policy-making. If this mechanism is at work, more regulations and decisions are approved in tertiary legislation when the threat of legislative override declines. Because no data exist about the European Commission's own expectations of the threat of legislative override, the following analysis uses the average core size of legal acts that are approved within a policy area over the previous three years to approximate the likelihood of legislative override, which is considered to motivate supranational activism (Junge, König, and Luig 2015). The left panel in figure 6.4 shows how the median threat of legislative override affects the probability of tertiary and secondary legislation for each instrument (decision, regulation, directive, other).

Except for directives, the median override threat always increases the probability of using tertiary legislation, which confirms $H_{con}2$. Compared to directives, which provide more discretion to the member states in achieving the result, regulations, and decisions centralize EU policy-making ($H_{con}3$). These findings are also confirmed by the right panel of Figure 6.4, which illustrates the implications of a change from low to high threat of override for the probability of tertiary legislation. Overall, the likelihood of tertiary legislation significantly increases with a change in the threat of override from low to high. Like other instruments, the more differentiating instrument of a decision experiences a higher level of delegation, while directives in particular reveal more variation for this change.

Under these circumstances, SNP also predicts a change in the scope of supranational delegation with more executive activism in areas of shared competences ($H_{con}4$). This undermines the effectiveness of the subsidiarity principle, which aims at limiting taking supranational action in areas of shared competences. It rules out interventions at the EU level when a goal can be achieved at the national (or regional and local) level, while the European Commission can take supranational action when member states are unable to achieve the objectives and EU-level involvement adds valuable pressure.[4] Table 6.1 lists the share of secondary and tertiary legislation for the areas with exclusive, shared, and coordinated competences.

According to the characteristics of the more than 120,000 legal acts, which also include so-called other acts, the relationship between secondary and tertiary legislation is balanced in the (sub)areas with exclusive competences of the EU, such as in general affairs, employment and social, and agriculture and fisheries. In the exclusive (sub)areas of Ecofin and transport, secondary legislation dominates. However, the European Commission is mostly active in (sub)areas where it shares competences (about 84 percent of all acts), in particular with tertiary legislation. Secondary legislation only dominates in the shared areas of general affairs, Ecofin, justice and home affairs (JHA), employment and social, and education, while supranational executive activism is most pronounced in the shared (sub)areas of agriculture and fisheries, followed by competitiveness and environment. These findings forcefully demonstrate the explanatory power of SNP regarding the implications of the size of the legislative core for uncontrolled delegation. A larger size promotes activism of supranational executive experts without electoral mandate in EU policy-making, which the subsidiarity principle can hardly constrain.

---

4. This principle, which was formally implemented in the post-Maastricht period, delegates the subsidiarity review to the European Commission, which has agenda-setting monopoly for the type and the drafting of proposals. In particular, for delegated acts in tertiary legislation, the delegation of this review requires self-reflection, or rather self-control, of the European Commission.

Table 6.1. Secondary and tertiary legislation in areas with exclusive, shared, and coordinated competences

	Exclusive			Shared			Coordinated		
	Secondary	Tertiary	Sum	Secondary	Tertiary	Sum	Secondary	Tertiary	Sum
General affairs	4447	4477	8924	7177	1323	8500	213	275	488
	49.83%	50.17%	100.00%	84.44%	15.56%	100.00%	43.65%	56.35%	100.00%
Ecofin	1080	209	1289	481	86	567	5	22	27
	83.79%	16.21%	100.00%	84.83%	15.17%	100.00%	18.52%	81.48%	100.00%
JHA	0	0	0	788	162	950	10	13	23
	0.00%	0.00%	0.00%	82.95%	17.05%	100.00%	43.48%	56.52%	100.00%
Employment social	58	39	97	619	311	930	57	13	70
	59.79%	40.21%	100.00%	66.56%	33.44%	100.00%	81.43%	18.57%	100.00%
Competitiveness	2879	8539	11418	1066	11500	12566	428	675	1103
	25.21%	74.79%	100.00%	8.48%	91.52%	100.00%	38.80%	61.20%	100.00%
Transport	103	2	105	497	867	1364	17	17	34
	98.10%	1.90%	100.00%	36.44%	63.56%	100.00%	50.00%	50.00%	100.00%
Agriculture Fisheries	754	1377	2131	5073	84312	89385	5	22	27
	35.38%	64.62%	100.00%	5.68%	94.32%	100.00%	18.52%	81.48%	100.00%
Environment	0	0	0	419	2917	3336	104	125	229
	0.00%	0.00%	0.00%	12.56%	87.44%	100.00%	45.41%	54.59%	100.00%
Education	0	0	0	88	41	129	165	37	202
	0.00%	0.00%	0.00%	68.22%	31.78%	100.00%	81.68%	18.32%	100.00%
Sum	9321	14643	23964	16208	101519	117727	1004	1199	2203

6.4. Enforcing Compliance and Informal Policy-Making

To enforce compliance, the European Commission can start an infringement proceeding if a member state fails to fulfil EU obligations. As the last column in Figure 6.2 already shows, about 90 percent of all enforcement conflicts about compliance, for which the European Commission can start an infringement proceeding, relate to directives (920 infringements for 1,318 directives in delegated tertiary and 1,230 infringements for 1,821 directives in secondary legislation). In contrast to directives, the very high number of regulations and decisions seldom experience infringements (206 infringements for the combined 115,451 cases). To win enforcement conflicts about compliance in an infringement proceeding before the European Court of Justice, SNP contends that the European Commission more frequently involves the European Parliament in EU policy-making of directives ($H_{con}5$).

Even though the Lisbon Treaty establishes veto bicameralism as the standard procedure, the other procedures are still in use (Blom-Hansen 2019). Compared to delegated acts in tertiary legislation, the acts in secondary legislation provide a slightly higher share of directives, in which the European Parliament is more frequently involved (1,821 directives with 581 parliamentary involvements as compared to 16,589 regulations and decisions with 925 parliamentary involvements).[5] However, according to Figure 6.5, the number of infringements decreases since the end of the 1990s, even though the infringement potential, which is defined by multiplying the number of member states by the number of directives, expands through widening and deepening in the post-Maastricht period. This establishes the so-called compliance puzzle in the period of study, in which a higher number of member states with more heterogenous and salient interests enters less frequently into an enforcement conflict about compliance.

One reason for this puzzling trend is that the European Commission strategically starts infringement proceedings to enforce compliance only for those cases that it is likely to win before the European Court of Justice (König and Mäder 2014). Others refer to the conditionality of membership (Börzel and Sedelmeier 2017, Schimmelfennig and Sedelmeier 2004), that is,

---

5. Interestingly, reviewing the transposition records of the member states shows that national parliaments are more often involved in the transposition into domestic law when the European Parliament has been involved in the making of a directive (König and Luig 2014).

Phase I: Technocracism and Compliance

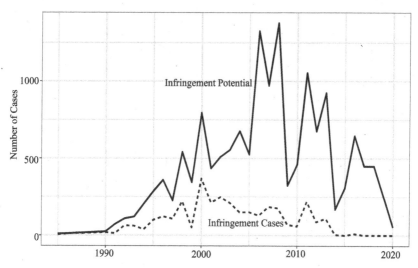

Figure 6.5. Number of Potential Infringements and Infringement Cases

that accession countries from Eastern and Central Europe had to implement acts before becoming members, socialization and "lock-in" (Checkel, 2001, Sedelmeier 2006, 2012), which assumes normative adaption of a supranational priority. Alternatively, SNP contends that the European Commission prefers informal trilogues for early agreements because they reduce the risk of an enforcement conflict about compliance with directives by reducing transparency and accountability (H_{con}6).[6] Early agreements not only make it possible to improve a proposal in collaboration with the Council presidency and a delegation of the European Parliament in informal trilogues but also avoid bicameral conflict resolution in the third reading, which signals contest about the result to be achieved. Figure 6.6 shows the share of directives that are approved in the first or second reading early agreement, and the share of third reading cases, which enter into bicameral conflict resolution of conciliation.

Since the Amsterdam Treaty offers the possibility of early agreements, the number of informal trilogues drastically increases ever since. Of the 704 directives, only about a third are approved without trilogue, mostly before

---

6. Because the European Commission has no electoral mandate, it also has no costs from the lack of transparency and accountability of informal trilogues and can avoid a third reading, in which the Council and the European Parliament can approve a joint text.

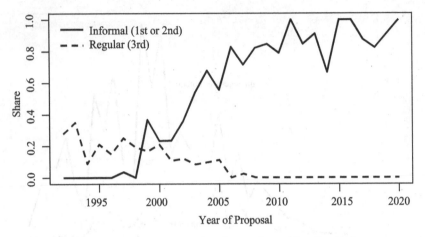

Figure 6.6. Share of Directives Approved in First or Second Reading Early Agreement or Third Reading Conciliation

1999. According to the study of König and Lu (2021), there exists a positive association between the number of prior infringement proceedings and informal trilogues, and negative associations to contested directives and infringement proceedings of directives with a high number of recitals (scope). This suggests that when the amount of enforcement conflicts about compliance increases, the likelihood of informal trilogues increases, while directives with larger scope are less likely to be infringed when they are contested. Confirming $H_{con}6$, informal trilogues reduce the likelihood of an infringement proceeding, especially under the shadow of enforcement conflicts with high numbers of previous infringement proceedings. This establishes the so-called parliamentarization paradox, according to which the European Parliament has become an institutional veto player to enhance transparency and accountability in EU policy-making, while most secondary legislation is approved by early agreements in informal trilogue.

SNP also posits that the member states can only conditionally control supranational delegation to the European Court of Justice when they send strong signals about the priority of norms. In the literature on legislative oversight of courts, scholars conventionally use amicus curiae briefs as a measure for the size of the legislative core (e.g., Carrubba, Gabel, and Hankla 2008, Carrubba and Gabel 2014, Larsson and Naurin 2016). However, amicus

Phase I: Technocracism and Compliance 119

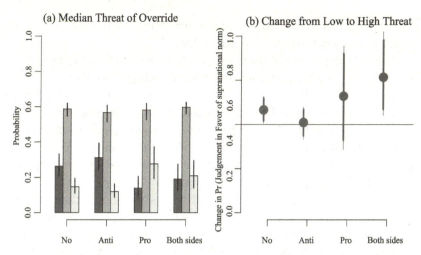

Figure 6.7. Estimation of Judicial Activism in the Period 1997 to 2008. Dark Shaded = Probability for National Norm, Gray Shaded = Probability of Neutral, White Shaded = Probability for Supranational Norm

curiae briefs can also be interpreted as signals to the court about a preference for or against the priority of supranational over national norms. This interpretation may also overcome two shortcomings of using amicus curiae briefs as a measure for the legislative core: First, in more than a third of the cases, the European Court of Justice does not receive any amicus curiae briefs (Stone Sweet and Brunell 2012). Second, the court also receives amicus curiae briefs from both sides, that is, briefs in favor and against the priority of supranational over national norms (Hilpert and König 2021).

To compare the implications of the legislative core for supranational executive with judicial activism, it is more promising to use the median threat of legislative override from the previous analysis of supranational executive activism than to use amicus curiae briefs. This measure can be combined with controls for the type of signal that the European Court of Justice receives by amicus curiae briefs: compared to cases without any amicus brief (no), one-sided briefs indicate a strong favor (pro) or against (anti) the priority of the supranational norm, while briefs from both sides indicate contest about the priority of a norm. Using data from Larsson and Naurin (2016) for the period 1997 to 2008, Figure 6.7 illustrates how the threat of legislative override affects the probability of a court decision to preserve national norms, to take a neutral decision, or to prioritize supranational norms for each type of amicus curiae brief (no, anti, pro, both sides).

Almost independent of the type of brief, the median threat of legislative override increases the probability of a neutral decision from the court. This suggests that the court responds with caution when some threat of legislative override exists. Compared to the situation of not receiving any brief (no), the receipt of one-sided briefs in favor (pro) or against (anti) the priority of a supranational norm increases the probability of the respective court decision and accordingly decreases the probability of a decision for the alternative outcome, while a brief from both sides remains in-between.

These findings suggest that the court is sensitive to both the threat of legislative override and the type of signal, which affects the court's decision about the preservation of the national norm and the primacy of the supranational norm. When the member states send strong one-sided signals, they can conditionally constrain the court in the one or other direction. Compared to supranational executive activism, the right panel indicates that supranational judicial activism provides for more variation regarding a change in the threat of legislative override from low to high. However, the member states can hardly control delegation when the court either does not receive any brief or receives briefs of a contest from both sides ($H_{con}7$).

Briefly summarized, the findings demonstrate that

- a larger size of the legislative core decreases the threat of legislative override, which fosters supranational technocracism with a dominance of bureaucratic and centralizing acts including shared areas of competences;
- a higher noncompliance risk in a widening and deepening EU either involves the European Parliament or fosters the informal approval of directives to avoid enforcement conflicts about compliance;
- compared to supranational activism of the experts of the European Commission, the European Court of Justice is conditionally constrained when the member states send a clear preference over the priority of a norm.

Confirming the hypotheses of SNP, EU policy-making becomes more bureaucratic, centralizing, and informal, especially in the beginning of the post-Maastricht period. At the same time, the European Parliament is mainly involved in the making of directives and increasingly agrees to delegate early agreements into informal trilogues, which reduces transparency and accountability. In addition to the promotion of supranational technocracism by a larger size of the legislative core, SNP predicts camp-building through the agenda monopoly of the European Commission in a widening EU, which the political leaders fail to reform in the post-Maastricht period.

CHAPTER 7

Phase II: Partisan Conflict and Supranational Camp-Building

7.1. Abstract

This chapter investigates the propositions and hypotheses on supranational camp-building in EU policy-making as another major consequence of the institutional choices for Europe, which transform the supranational game of party competition in the post-Maastricht period. After a short introduction of the research design and the data on party positions, the analysis identifies the critical juncture of the divide about European integration in the national game of party competition. This divide consolidates in EU policy-making with supranational camp-building of pro- and anti-integrationist camps with few moderates in between. The voting patterns of the European Parliament confirm this proposition and reveal cohesive support of the proposals of the European Commission by the groups of mainstream/ruling parties, which are rejected by those of challenger/periphery parties.

7.2. Party Positions on European Integration

For the study of partisan conflict and supranational camp-building in the post-Maastricht period, the research design covers time series cross-country data on parties' positions and supranational voting behavior of ruling/mainstream and challenger/periphery parties. After the signing of the Rome Treaty by the six founding members Belgium, France, Germany, Italy, Luxembourg, and the Netherlands in the 1950s, the history of European integration experiences several waves of widening, namely, the Western enlargement by Denmark, Ireland, United Kingdom in the 1970s, the Southern enlargement by Greece, Portugal, and Spain in the 1980s, the Northern enlargement by Austria, Finland, and Sweden in the 1990s, and the Eastern enlargement by Central and Eastern European countries, 10 in 2004 and two in 2007. In addition to widening, deepening by the further transfers of policy competences for sensitive areas changes the salience and importance of issues of European integration in party competition.

For many scholars, the further transfers of policy competences in the post-Maastricht period are critical and give rise to a new cleavage in European integration (e.g., Evans 1998, Kriesi 1998, Kriesi et al. 2006, 2012, Bartolini 2005, Hooghe and Marks 2009, 2018). However, the classic account of European party competition posits the salience and persistence of traditional socioeconomic cleavages, such as class, region, and religion (Lipset and Rokkan 1967, Richardson 1991, Bartolini 2005). For SNP, three preconditions have to be met for identifying a new cleavage in European integration. First, a new divide about European integration structures the national game of party competition differently from the dominant (socioeconomic) left versus right divide. Second, this new divide consolidates in EU policy-making, such as parties in the European Parliament voting in favor or against proposals of the European Commission. Third, partisan supporters are emotionally mobilized at times of EU crisis management and ideologically align along this new divide about European integration, such as their attitudes correspond to those of the stances of their party, and form a partisan identity accordingly.

Regarding the new divide about European integration, postfunctionalism argues that the conflict between ruling/mainstream and challenger/periphery parties on the further transfers of policy competences transforms the traditional left versus right conflict toward a two-dimensional U-shaped transnational configuration (Hooghe and Marks 2009, 2019). Unlike postfunctionalism, which posits

1. mass-mobilization of national identities fosters a desire for self-rule, to which
2. challenger/periphery parties are responsive, which
3. establishes a new transnational cleavage between ruling/mainstream and challenger/periphery parties,[1]

---

1. In addition to the dominant socioeconomic dimension with left and right poles, Hooghe and Marks (2003) interpret the poles of the new transnational cleavage as GAL (green/alternative/libertarian) and TAN (traditional/authoritarian/nationalist).

SNP contends that

1. a divide between ruling/mainstream and challenger/periphery parties emerges, which
2. consolidates with camp-building in EU policy-making,
3. and partisans ideologically align in times of supranational problem-solving with mass-mobilizing EU crisis management.

To identify the critical juncture of this new divide in the national game of party competition, the analysis combines the data from Chapel Hill expert surveys with data on programmatic party positions (Budge et al. 2001). It compares the likelihood that either a one-dimensional left versus right or a two-dimensional U-shaped configuration with the new divide structures national party competition in the period from 1945 to 2017.

According to the proposition of SNP, veto bicameralism and the agenda monopoly of the (unreformed) European Commission transform this divide into the building of a pro- and an anti-integrationist camp in EU policy-making. This proposition is investigated by the positional variation of political parties documented in the Chapel Hill expert survey data for the period 1999 to 2017, which also allows us to explore country-specific support of European integration by the type of parties (Polk et al. 2017). The combination of the data on legislative activities with the voting records of the European Parliament from 1979 to 2019 (EP1 to EP8) shows increasing camp-specific support of legislative proposals of the European Commission with high voting consensus, which increasingly polarizes between ruling/mainstream and challenger/periphery parties in EU policy-making (Blumenau and Lauderdale 2018).

For the evaluation of the hypotheses on supranational camp-building and polarization, the research design adheres to three methodological standards: The first is data collection of all party manifestos and expert survey data, which makes it possible to identify the critical juncture of the new divide on European integration in the game of national party competition. Second, the voting records of the European Parliament need to generate sufficient observations to evaluate the camp-specific support of legislative proposals, which also consider the portfolio-specific kind of activities of the European Commission. Third, while the temporal variation in the expert data on the partisan positions on European integration outlines a trend toward supranational camp-building between pro- and anti-integrationists with few moderates in between, the supranational voting records need to reveal the trend in support by ruling/mainstream parties and rejection by challenger/periphery parties.

7.3. The Critical Juncture of the New Divide

For liberal intergovernmentalism, important domestic societal groups do not contest European integration. These groups take the same view on transfers of national sovereignty, which political leaders execute on demand of these key domestic constituencies, while the leaders pre-commit unsupportive societal groups. This claim is disputed by Hix and Lord (1997), who find that a societal conflict "about more or less European integration derived from deep social, cultural, national and territorial traditions" is arising, which crosscuts the dominant left versus right conflict of party competition in Europe. With the further transfer of policy competences from the national to the supranational level of the EU, postfunctionalist scholars argue that domestic discourses about European integration become more politicized and mobilize national identities, which fosters the emergence of a transnational cleavage (Hooghe and Marks 2009, 2018b).

For the post-Maastricht period, the rise of anti-integrationist parties from the peripheries of the party spectrum is well documented by comparative studies (e.g., Kriesi 2007, Marks, Wilson, and Ray 2002, Szczerbiak and Taggart 2008, Taggart 1998, Topaloff 2012, Van Elsas and van der Brug 2015). Following the findings of the Chapel Hill expert surveys, an inverted U-shape—marked by periphery parties at the left and right of the party spectrum opposing European integration (Hix and Lord 1997, Marks, Wilson, and Ray 2002)—is also discernible in the game of national party competition in the newer Eastern member states, though less pronounced than in the older Western member states (Bakker et al. 2015). Figure 7.1 illustrates the configuration of left versus right and pro- versus anti-integrationist party positions of the Chapel Hill expert survey data with party families' prior density. The contours are calculated using a kernel density estimation for each party family (for more detail, see König, Marbach, and Osnabrügge 2017).

According to these expert evaluations, the relation between party families on the left versus right has an inverted U-shape. In other words, the more extreme a position concerning left or right, the more Eurosceptic is the party family.[2] The data also suggest that some Green and Conservative parties are more critical of European integration than Socialist, Liberal, and Christian Democratic parties. Using this configuration as prior information, the question between SNP and postfunctionalism is whether and when this inverted

---

2. This configuration also characterizes the current discussions about the sanctioning of the Russian aggression.

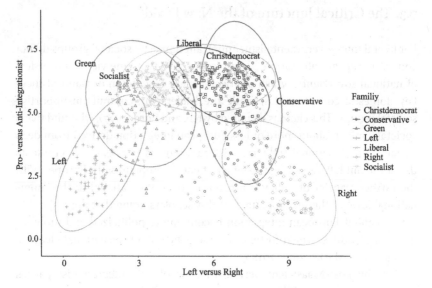

Figure 7.1. Priors for Party Families from the Chapel Hill Expert Survey and Contours from Two-Dimensional Kernel Density Estimation for Party Families

U-shaped configuration arises in the national game of party competition. Because the identification of critical junctures requires time series analysis of longer periods of study (Lipset and Rokkan 1967), data from the Comparative Manifesto Project are used as they cover the programmatic electoral declarations of all member states' parties since 1945 (Budge et al. 2001).

For the time series analysis of the configuration in national party competition, König, Marbach, and Osnabrügge (2017) introduce a Bayesian finite mixture factor model to estimate the likelihood that the configuration on the dominant left versus right dimension is replaced by another configuration, such as a two-dimensional inverted U-shaped configuration in the period from 1945 to 2012. Figure 7.2 shows for each general election (dots) until 2017 the likelihood that programmatic party competition can be represented by only a one-dimensional left versus right or a two-dimensional U-shaped configuration, in which parties with more periphery positions on the left versus right dimension are more Eurosceptic.[3]

---

3. Except for Bulgaria and Romania, which acceded in 2007, and Croatia in 2013, the analysis complements the time series until 2017 providing three sets of parameters: the

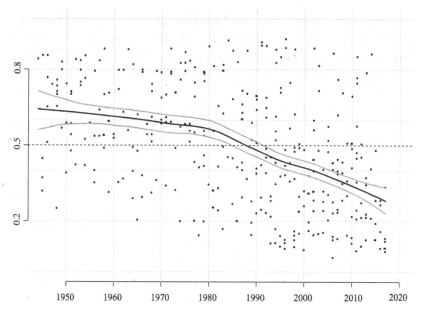

Figure 7.2. Posterior Probability for a One-Dimensional Left/Right versus a Two-Dimensional U-Shaped Policy Space with Fitted Local Polynomial Regression on Each Posterior Draw for the Period 1945 to 2017

The solid black line, which technically indicates the mean of the fitted curves from local polynomial regressions on each posterior draw, reveals a negative trend over time for the likelihood of a one-dimensional left versus right configuration from 66 percent in the 1950s to less than 30 percent in 2017. For all observations, the critical juncture is around the 1990s—the time of the Maastricht Treaty. Ever since, the likelihood of a two-dimensional inverted U-shape configuration continuously increases, which reflects the increasing importance of the pro- versus anti-integrationist dimension in party competition.

The loading pattern of the underlying factor analysis allows for a substantive interpretation of this two-dimensional representation. The pro- versus anti-integrationist dimension is mainly determined by a very large pos-

---

configuration parameters (π), factor loadings (λ), and latent positions of the parties (χ) using JAGS (Plummer 2003). Using multiple streams of pseudorandom numbers from JAGS six MCMC chains were run in parallel, from which every 10th draw of the 20,000 values were stored after the first 10,000 iterations.

itive factor loading of the EU (0.85) and internationalism (0.80). This is also associated with macroeconomics (0.50) and administration (0.40) as typical characteristics of supranational technocracism. Furthermore, the negative loading of multiculturalism (-0.42), labor, and target groups (-0.41, -0.25) indicates that this conflict goes beyond regulatory politics and also concerns the four freedoms of the common market, which is considered to reduce the welfare state (-0.33) and the quality and national way of life/immigration (-0.20, -0.14). Figure 7.3 reports the country-specific development with three types of trends:[4]

- First, the probability of a one-dimensional left versus right configuration in the national game of party competition decreases over time. Belgium, Germany, Greece, Luxembourg, and the Netherlands exhibit a strong monotone, negative trend beginning in the 1970s. Closer inspection of the founding members shows that France is more likely to have an inverted U-shaped configuration beginning in the late 1950s until the mid-1980s, and then restarts again around the early twenty-first century; in Belgium, the Netherlands, and Luxembourg, the U-shape configuration begins in the early 1980s; and Germany in the late 1990s. Austria, Sweden, and partly Finland, which acceded in 1995, show a trend toward an inverted U-shaped configuration since the beginning of the twenty-first century. Note that data for Finland are only available until 2011.
- Second, some member states have either a one- or two-dimensional configuration for almost the entire time since World War II. Denmark's electoral party competition remains a one-dimensional left versus right configuration, though data are only available until 2011. The trends of the United Kingdom, Ireland, and Spain, the two other accession countries of this period, are nonmonotonic but suggest a trend toward an inverted U-shaped configuration.
- Third, Portugal and Italy exhibit a monotone trend until the first decade of the twenty-first century and an indicative reversing trend thereafter. Note that data for Italy are only available until 2013.

Some member states from Eastern and Southern Europe with shorter time series also exhibit a negative trend toward an inverted U-shaped configura-

---

4. For some countries, such as Cyprus, Denmark, Finland, Netherlands, Poland, Slovakia, and Slovenia, the time series data are limited to 2011/2012 due to missing data.

tion in the national game of party competition, while others show a strong positive trend. The Czech Republic, Estonia, Hungary, Lithuania, Poland, Slovenia, and Slovakia are likely to have a kind of party competition that is characterized by an inverted U-shape, at least recently. Estonia and Latvia show a positive trend toward domestic discourses of programmatic party competition that is only centered on the left versus right conflict. This variation suggests that a cautious interpretation of findings is warranted, which uses regional classifications.

On closer inspection of the critical juncture in the national game of party competition, in which the probability for the one-dimensional configuration becomes smaller than the probability for the inverted U-shaped two-dimensional solution, the analysis shows—except for the six founding member states—a very high coincidence with the time of accession. Confirming SNP ($H_{con}8$), the conflict about European integration arises with the controversies between ruling/mainstream and challenger/periphery parties about accession—long before further policy competences for sensitive areas are transferred and national identities are mobilized with a desire for self-rule. For the accession of Eastern and Central European countries, which needed to implement the acquis communautaire before becoming members (Nugent 2004), the critical juncture is unsurprisingly earlier.

The analysis confirms the predictions of SNP about the critical juncture of the divide on European integration in the national game of party competition. At the time of accession, the divide translates into an inverted U-shaped configuration with anti-integrationist challenger/periphery parties on the left and right periphery of the party spectrum in many member states. This conflict addresses not only the EU and international cooperation in general, but also more specific issues of European integration such as protectionism against multiculturalism, immigration, labor and target groups, and a negative perspective on the welfare state and the national way of life/immigration. Following the procedure of De Vries and Edwards (2009), which conceives parties with at least one standard deviation below the average integrationist position as Eurosceptic, almost 300 cases of anti-integrationist parties can be identified in the post-Maastricht period, which are increasingly located in the right periphery of the party spectrum. In some countries, such as Austria, Belgium, France, the Netherlands, Slovakia, Slovenia, Spain, and Sweden, these anti-integrationist parties become a constant element in the national game of party competition.

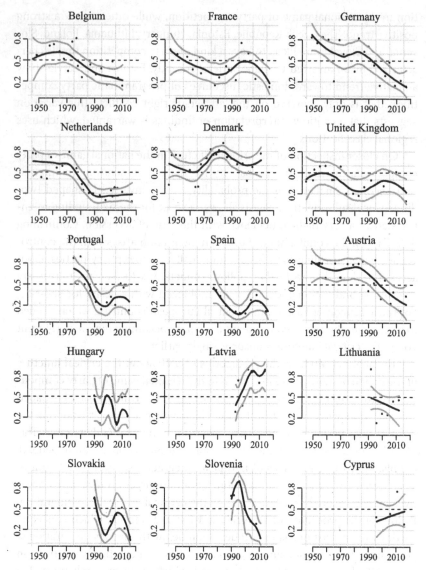

Figure 7.3. Posterior Probability for a One-Dimensional Left/Right Policy Space for Each Member State with Fitted Local Polynomial Regression on Each Posterior Draw between 1945 and 2017. Continued on second page.

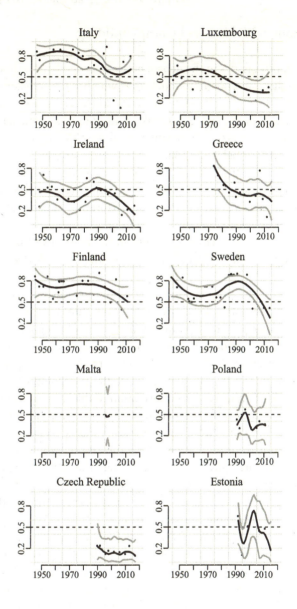

7.4. EU Policy-Making and Camp-Building

One of the central issues in the debate between proponents of liberal intergovernmentalism and postfunctionalism is whether the transfer of further policy competences from the national to the EU level has politicized European integration. Following Moravcsik (2018: 1662), the transfer of policy competences in the post-Maastricht period has few implications and is mostly symbolic. Hooghe and Marks (2018, 2019) strongly reject this consideration and argue that radical "TAN parties" (parties on the "Traditional, Authoritarian, Nationalism" end of the spectrum) are pivotal in mobilizing a transnational cleavage arising from the perforation of nationalism due to the transfer of policy competences for immigration, integration, and trade. This thesis on the politicization of European affairs suggests that EU policy-making becomes more polarized among political groups (De Wilde and Zürn 2012).

According to the proposition of SNP, ruling/mainstream parties have office-seeking and policy-seeking benefits from European integration and support it, while opposition/periphery parties hardly enjoy these benefits and reject it. Using various estimates, such as expert surveys, voter surveys, and roll call votes, Proksch and Lo (2012) already find a bipolar pattern on the European integration dimension at the beginning of the twenty-first century (for a more recent confirmation of this finding, see Blumenau and Lauderdale 2018). This bipolar pattern between a pro- and an anti-integrationist camp has two characteristics: a high correlation of all estimates that result from the extreme positions of the two camps, and only a few moderate party positions that are located in between those camps. Within the camps, the association of the parties' positions on the subranges of the data decreases over time, which means that variation of their positions only exists within but not across camps.

Using time series data from the Chapel Hill expert surveys (Polk et al. 2017), which ask country experts for the overall orientation of party leadership toward European integration between 1999 and 2017, the upper columns in Figure 7.4 show the configurations on European integration of only the same parties, while the lower columns illustrate this configuration of the time-varying set of all parties. The squares, circles, and triangles represent types of anti-integrationist, moderate, and pro-integrationist positions measured by averaging their total expert evaluations over all survey years. Values between 1 to 3 are classified as anti-integrationist positions (squares), from more than 3 to 5 as moderate positions (circles), and from more than 5 to 7 as pro-integrationist positions (triangles). Each figure compares the positions on European integration of the survey year in the diagonal with the other years of the expert data.

Despite the high number of parties, the correlations between the positions of the parties on European integration—whether in the upper right-hand figures that represent the positions of the same parties over time or in the lower left-hand figures of the set of all parties—are very strong with values between 0.85 and 0.96. In this time series, the two camps seldom overlap. On the right upper corner of each figure, the triangles of the larger pro-integrationist camp are commonly located, while the squares of the anti-integrationist parties stand in opposition in the left lower corner of each figure. All pictures indicate a bipolar pattern between the pro- and the anti-integrationist camp with only a few moderate parties (circles) in the middle. Independent from the higher number and the varying set of all parties in the lower left-hand figures, this bipolar pattern of the two camps hardly changes (correlations between 0.86 to 0.93 in the period 1999 to 2017). Most parties belong to the camp of pro-integrationist triangles, which stands in opposition to the smaller camp of anti-integrationist squares. The few circled moderate parties only barely overlap with one of the two opposed camps in the middle.

The high correlations can result from sensitivity to the extreme positional endpoints of the two camps on European integration. One way to examine this is to inspect whether a relationship appears consistently throughout narrower ranges (Proksch and Lo 2012: 324). The findings reveal a high but decreasing reliability over time for the positions in the pro-integrationist camp (from 0.85 of the same parties in 2002 to about 0.4 in 2017 for both), lower reliability for the positions in the anti-integrationist camp (from 0.81 in 2002 to .11 in 2017 for the same parties and 0.27 for all), and almost no reliability with many negative correlations among the moderates. This finding stands in contrast to results for the left versus right dimension, for which scholars report consistent relationships over time and across different measurements (e.g., Proksch and Lo 2012, König and Luig 2012). Compared to left versus right, this confirms the proposition of SNP ($H_{con}9$) on an increas-

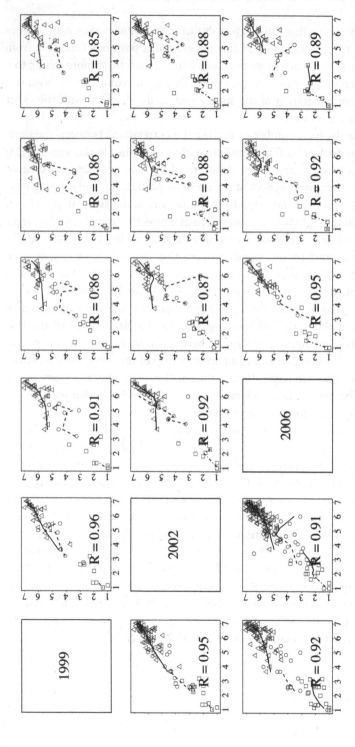

Figure 7.4. Upper Columns on the Right Side = Positional Variation of Same Parties, Lower Columns = Positional Variation of All Parties for the Period 1999 to 2017. Continued on second page.

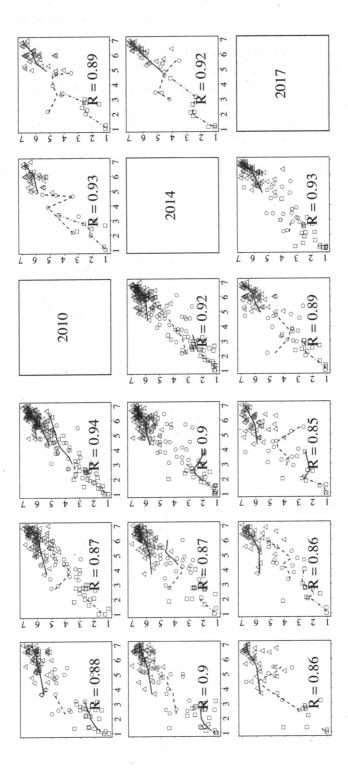

ing camp-related polarization on European integration, where party positions change within but not across camps.

According to the proposition of SNP, a major reason for this divide is that ruling/mainstream parties support European integration because they have office-seeking and policy-seeking benefits from EU policy-making. Ruling/mainstream parties not only send their governmental representatives to the Council, but they also nominate delegates for the posts in the European Commission and the European Court of Justice, while challenger/periphery parties are usually in opposition and may have only access to EU policy-making via the European Parliament. These differences in office- and policy-seeking benefits will become more pronounced between the two camps with the further transfer of policy competences in the post-Maastricht period. Using the time series data of the Chapel Hill expert surveys, Figure 7.5 shows trends in the country-specific distribution of ruling and opposition parties regarding their support of European integration.

The country-specific evaluation reveals that ruling parties highly support European integration on the horizontal axis in almost all member states, which further confirms the policy- and office-seeking proposition of SNP. They mostly peak on the right pro-integrationist side of this axis, oftentimes with a highly skewed distribution. In Belgium, Bulgaria, Czech Republic, Croatia, Denmark, Finland, France, Germany, Greece, Ireland, Italy, Netherlands, Portugal, Romania, Spain, and Sweden, ruling parties are highly concentrated on the pro-integrationist side, while the dark-shaded distribution of opposition parties indicates a more uniform attitude toward European integration. Only in Cyprus, Estonia, Latvia, Lithuania, Slovakia, and Slovenia, the support of ruling parties is similarly shared by opposition parties. However, in Austria, Hungary, Italy, Luxembourg, Poland, and the United Kingdom, the level of support of both the ruling and opposition parties is moderate and more evenly distributed.[5]

7.5. Portfolios and Polarization

Following the proposition of SNP, the failure to reform the composition and role of the European Commission has crucial implications for supranational

---

5. This pattern is reinforced when distinguishing between ruling/mainstream parties with some and opposition/periphery parties without governmental experience in the period of study.

Phase II: Partisan Conflict and Supranational Camp-Building

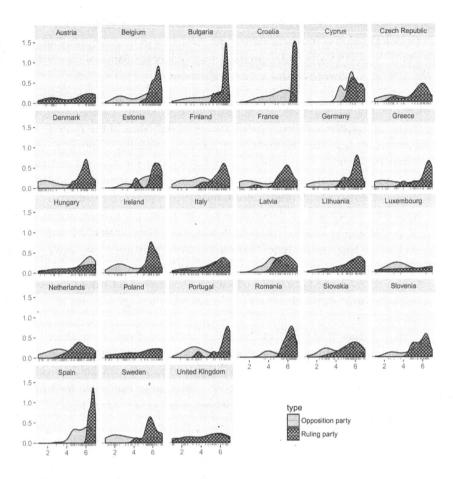

Figure 7.5. Density of European Integration Support by Ruling and Opposition Parties in the Period 1999 to 2017

camp-building and polarization in EU policy-making. As the college of Commissioners increases from 12 to 27 holding an area-specific portfolio of policy competences in the post-Maastricht period, previously agreed compromise on the transfer of policy competences for sensitive areas and the subsidiarity principle will be untied in EU policy-making. Although the European Commission can implement tertiary legislation and draft uncontested bureaucratic proposals, which are approved by early agreement in informal trilogue, SNP predicts that the prioritization of supranational over national norms will foster supranational camp-building and polarization of the two camps in secondary legislation (H_{con}10). To account for selection effects, table 7.1 lists the type of legislation across policy areas and the terms of the European Parliament (EP1 to EP8), where the number of secondary legislation results from the difference between all and tertiary legislation.

Until EP3 (1989–1994), the overall number of secondary legislation increases, but it steadily declines through the eighth term (EP8: 2014–2019) despite the further transfer of policy competences. Most of the more than 120,000 acts are tertiary legislation (83 percent), which the European Commission implements without the direct approval of the Council and the European Parliament. The vast majority of almost 110,000 tertiary acts are implemented in the areas of agriculture and fisheries (80 percent), though the overall share of tertiary legislation decreases over time due to fewer activities in this area. In the areas of competitiveness and general affairs, the activity level hardly changes over time. In the areas with fewer legislative activities, such as transport, economic and financial affairs, employment and social policy, justice and home affairs, and education, the level of activities increases albeit with lower shares of tertiary legislation, while this share is very high in environment.

These numbers suggest that the further transfers of policy competences do not necessarily foster supranational camp-building within the bicameral legislature, because tertiary legislation dominates EU policy-making in many policy areas. Furthermore, the European Commission can invite for early agreement in informal trilogue or draft proposals in secondary legislation, which the Council and the European Parliament will approve without contest (Boranbay, König, and Osnabrügge 2017). The European Parliament and the Council—in addition to the European Council—only have the right to invite the European Commission to present a proposal, essentially granting it gatekeeping power (König 2007). Although the Lisbon Treaty codifies the European Commission's obligation to provide reasons for any refusal to follow this invitation, this does not create an obligation for the European Commission to propose the legislation requested.

One way to assess this selection effect is to examine voting consensus over time.[6] Put differently, in a widening and deepening EU, the voting consensus is likely to decline if the European Commission does not preselect

---

6. Kriesi (2016) alternatively investigates vote shares of left- and right-periphery Eurosceptic parties in three regions in the 2014 European election.

Table 7.1. Legislative activities across areas and terms from 1979 to 2019

		All	1. General affairs and external relations	2. Economic and financial affairs	3. Justice and home affairs	4. Employment and social policy
EP1	Tertiary	15072 (83.1)	1240 (64.0)	33 (42.3)	0 (NaN)	30 (28.0)
	All	18118 (100)	1936 (100)	78 (100)	0 (100)	107 (100)
EP2	Tertiary	18355 (85.2)	685 (53.8)	17 (29.3)	0 (NaN)	28 (46.6)
	All	21523 (100)	1272 (100)	58 (100)	0 (100)	60 (100)
EP3	Tertiary	19785 (87.0)	593 (44.5)	11 (13.1)	0 (0)	29 (31.8)
	All	22726 (100)	1332 (100)	84 (100)	3 (100)	91 (100)
EP4	Tertiary	16105 (87.4)	497 (37.4)	17 (15.1)	0 (0)	16 (20.5)
	All	18424 (100)	1327 (100)	112 (100)	10 (100)	78 (100)
EP5	Tertiary	14817 (86.4)	508 (31.8)	40 (22.3)	10 (8.93)	35 (33.3)
	All	17141 (100)	1595 (100)	179 (100)	112 (100)	105 (100)
EP6	Tertiary	10965 (81.2)	639 (31.9)	45 (21.2)	34 (20.9)	44 (38.9)
	All	13492 (100)	2001 (100)	212 (100)	162 (100)	113 (100)
EP7	Tertiary	7723 (73.3)	540 (24.0)	41 (16.4)	50 (25.6)	62 (43.0)
	All	10529 (100)	2243 (100)	249 (100)	195 (100)	144 (100)
EP8	Tertiary	5760 (69.7)	473 (22.4)	54 (23.8)	51 (26.9)	54 (39.1)
	All	8254 (100)	2107 (100)	226 (100)	189 (100)	138 (100)
Sum	Tertiary	108582 (83.3)	5175 (37.4)	258 (21.5)	145 (21.6)	298 (35.6)
	All	130207 (100)	13813 (100)	1198 (100)	671 (100)	836 (100)

		5. Competitiveness	6. Transport	7. Agriculture/ fisheries	8. Environment	9. Education
EP1	Tertiary	1812 (68.8)	14 (24.5)	11939 (90.0)	3 (8.33)	1 (9.09)
	All	2632 (100)	57 (100)	13261 (100)	36 (100)	11 (100)
EP2	Tertiary	1389 (57.7)	32 (42.6)	16189 (92.1)	14 (21.2)	1 (6.67)
	All	2405 (100)	75 (100)	17572 (100)	66 (100)	15 (100)
EP3	Tertiary	1694 (70.2)	33 (27.0)	17346 (93.6)	76 (58.9)	3 (10.3)
	All	2412 (100)	122 (100)	18524 (100)	129 (100)	29 (100)
EP4	Tertiary	1927 (81.5)	58 (55.2)	13467 (94.5)	119 (73.0)	4 (23.5)
	All	2364 (100)	105 (100)	14248 (100)	163 (100)	17 (100)
EP5	Tertiary	1703 (83.7)	93 (57.7)	12235 (96.5)	189 (73.8)	4 (17.3)
	All	2033 (100)	161 (100)	12677 (100)	256 (100)	23 (100)
EP6	Tertiary	1401 (82.8)	123 (54.6)	8438 (96.3)	239 (81.2)	2 (6.25)
	All	1691 (100)	225 (100)	8762 (100)	294 (100)	32 (100)
EP7	Tertiary	1316 (82.8)	198 (65.7)	4805 (95.7)	679 (92.1)	32 (60.3)
	All	1589 (100)	301 (100)	5018 (100)	737 (100)	53 (100)
EP8	Tertiary	1463 (87.9)	201 (73.6)	2783 (95.4)	668 (93.6)	13 (46.4)
	All	1664 (100)	273 (100)	2916 (100)	713 (100)	28 (100)
Sum	Tertiary	12705 (75.6)	752 (57.0)	87202 (93.7)	1987 (83)	60 (28.8)
	All	16790 (100)	1319 (100)	92978 (100)	2394 (100)	208 (100)

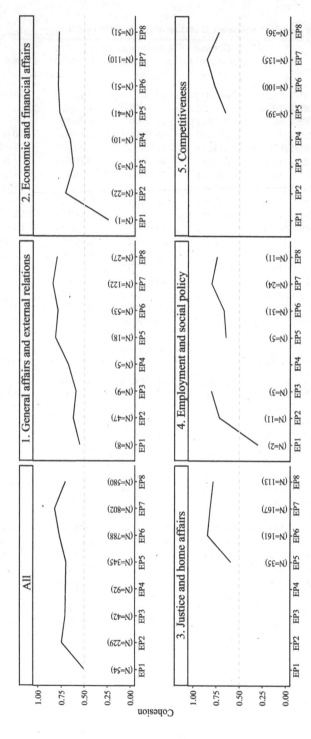

Figure 7.6. Level of Area-Specific Consensus in the Period from 1979 to 2019 Measured with Rice's "Index of Voting Likeness" ((|Yes−No|)/(Yes+No)). Continued on second page.

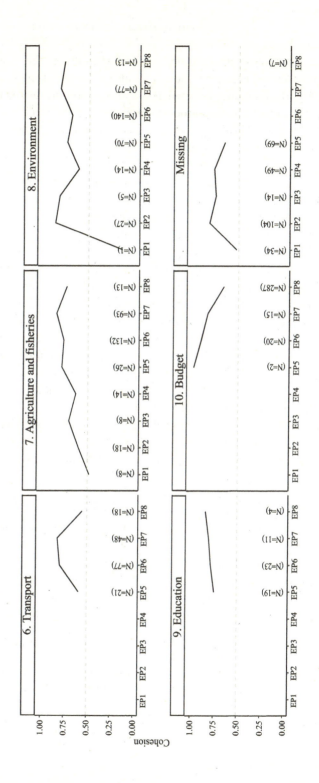

proposals, which also concern more sensitive areas due to the transfers of policy competences. Figure 7.6 shows an index of voting likeness, which is calculated by the difference between Yes- and No-votes divided by the sum of both types of votes in the European Parliament for each policy area and term.[7] A value of 1 indicates a perfect consensus in area-specific voting, while lower values suggest more contest.

Overall, there exists a very high level of consensus of about 75 percent across all areas since the second term from 1984 until 2014, though this consensus is slightly lower in both the first (1979–1984) and the eighth terms (2014–2019). On closer inspection of the eighth term, the number of votes not only decreases to 580, but 287 of those votes also concern budgetary proposals (which, across all terms, only adds to 324). In total, the highest number of votes on secondary legislation belongs to justice and home affairs (476), followed by agriculture (399) and environment (347), where tertiary legislation dominates legislative activities. However, the high level of consensus in these areas does not vanish in the more recent post-Maastricht period (only in the eighth term from 2014–2019). In competitiveness and economics, two politically more sensitive areas that follow in terms of the total number of votes (310 and 289), the level of consensus also remains high in secondary legislation. This is also true for the 289 votes in general affairs, which find increasing consensus in the period of study.

Despite widening and deepening of the EU, the voting consensus in secondary legislation never reaches a level below the 50 percent margin of parliamentary approval within a term. The European Parliament takes most votes during the sixth and seventh terms, in which the level of consensus is highest across all areas. Only in the eighth term do both the number of votes and the level of consensus slightly decrease, namely due to the very high number of budgetary proposals (about 50 percent). This high voting consensus in secondary legislation indicates a selection of uncontested proposals, which generally reduce the likelihood of building a pro- and an anti-integrationist camp in EU policy-making.

One possibility in examining camp-building is to explore the time series of voting cohesiveness across and within the political groups of the Euro-

---

7. Voting in the European Parliament is recorded in the minutes, which list all so-called roll call votes on the final passage of proposals of the European Commission; while 5 percent of votes were necessary for a roll call vote until 2009, the European Parliament takes decisions on all final passages to increase transparency (see Yordanova and Mühlböck 2015, Hug 2016).

pean Parliament, which usually votes along these lines (Hix and Noury 2009). Currently, the largest group of ruling/mainstream parties is the European People's Party (EPP) with Christian Democratic and Liberal Conservative political parties, followed by the Progressive Alliance of Socialists and Democrats (S&D) with Social Democratic parties, and the Alliance of Liberals and Democrats in Europe (ALDE), which unified with the French Movement En Marche to form Renew at the 2019 European election. Along the horizontal axis, Figure 7.7 displays the number of legislative proposals of the European Commission with a vote of the European Parliament. These numbers range from 54 votes in the first term (EP1: 1979–1984) to 580 votes in the eighth term (EP8: 2014–2019). The increasing number of votes shows the implications of expanding veto bicameralism, while the noticeably fewer number of 580 votes in the most recent eighth term indicates a drastic decline of secondary legislation from about 800 votes in the sixth and seventh terms.

According to Figure 7.7., the ruling/mainstream parties from the EPP, S&D, and ALDE share a very high support rate for legislative proposals of the European Commission, which account for about 95 percent during the latest eighth parliamentary term (EP8: 2014–2019). Since 1999 the European Green Party (EGP), the European Free Alliance (EFA), and the smaller European Pirate Party form the political group of Greens–European Free Alliance (Greens/EFA), while the European United Left/Nordic Green Left (GUE/NGL) is composed of left-wing green to far-left political parties. Both political groups follow the trend of ruling/mainstream parties from EPP, S&D, and ALDE with their increasing support of legislative proposals of the European Commission.

In contrast to this supranational pro-integrationist camp of ruling/mainstream parties, the European Conservatives and Reformists (ECR) is an anti-integrationist political group, formerly known as the Alliance of Conservatives and Reformists in Europe (2016–2019) or Alliance of European Conservatives and Reformists (2009–2016). In the eighth term, the ECR and the Europe of Freedom and Direct Democracy (EFDD), formerly the Europe of Freedom and Democracy (EFD) as a populist nationalist group mainly representing the UK Independence Party, have an almost identical support share of about 50 percent of legislative proposals of the European Commission. Nonaffiliated populist parties, the so-called Non-Inscripts (NI), such as the far-right periphery Alliance for Peace and Freedom (APF) and the Initiative of Communist and Workers' Parties, which is a far-left periphery party, also belong to this growing supranational anti-integrationist camp

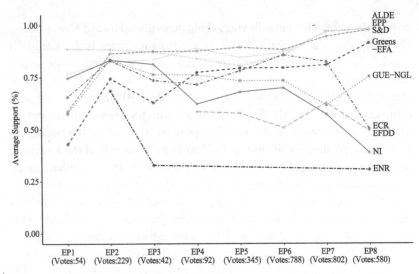

Figure 7.7. Share of Support in Final Votes of Political Groups on Legislative Proposals of the European Commission in the Period from 1979 to 2019 (EP1 to EP8)

of challenger/periphery parties. This camp is further complemented by the Europe of Nations and Freedom (ENF), which is dominated by the French Rassemblement National and the Italian Lega (in 2019 Identity and Democracy becomes the successor group to ENF).

While the existing literature on voting cohesiveness in the European Parliament devotes much attention to explaining intragroup variation in the political groups' voting behavior,[8] Figure 7.8 illustrates increasing supranational cohesiveness weighted by the size of each political group. According to their share of disapproval, the supranational groups of the ruling/mainstream parties commonly and, since the seventh term (EP7: 2009–2014), more cohesively support the legislative proposals of the European Commission, while opposition from the supranational groups of the challenger/periphery parties is becoming more visible since the eighth term (EP8: 2014–2019). This finding indicates a declining level of supranational party competition among ruling/mainstream parties, which are polarizing with challenger/periphery parties' opposition since the eighth term (EP8: 2014–2019).[9]

---

8. For example, Thiem (2006, 2009) and Finke (2015) assume that the groups use their approval for signaling purposes, while Thierse (2016) considers them as weapons of minorities having lost in the committee stage.

9. On closer inspection, the ECR has usually rejected the budgetary proposals of the European Commission in the past, while the G/EFA and the GUE/NGL supported those

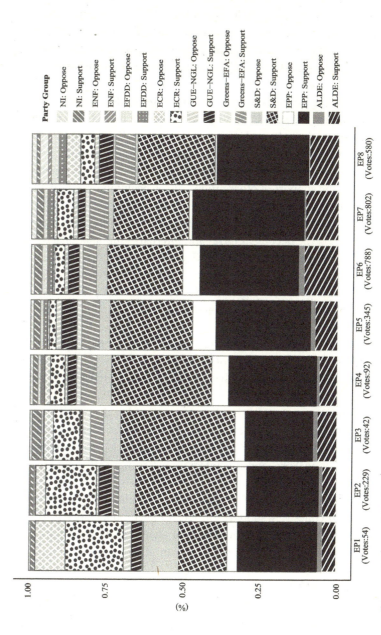

Figure 7.8. Share of (Dis)Approval in Votes on Legislative Proposals of the European Commission in the Period from 1979 to 2019 of Political Groups Weighted by Seat Share in European Parliament

Compared to the smaller pro-integrationist ALDE, the intraparty disapproval share of the EPP increases over time until the seventh term (EP7: 2009–2014), but since turns around toward almost exclusive pro-integrationist approval. The S&D—similar to GUE/NGL and Greens/EFA—is initially less supportive but becomes more pro-integrationist over time. These three political groups of ruling/mainstream parties already secure the approval of the European Commission's agenda in the post-Maastricht period. Independent from other groups, their share always exceeds the majority voting threshold of the European Parliament. In addition to increasing intraparty supranational cohesiveness of the ruling/mainstream parties, the proposals are additionally finding the support of other groups, at the beginning from the ECR, and later on from the Greens/EFA and GUE/NGL. On average, the amount of overall approval increases from 70 percent (EP1: 1979–1984) to 85 percent (EP7: 2009–2014). The decline in intra- and interparty supranational disapproval rates confirms the hypothesis of SNP on building a supranational pro-integrationist camp of ruling/mainstream parties and an anti-integrationist camp of challenger/periphery parties in the post-Maastricht period.

Briefly summarized, the findings demonstrate that

- the critical juncture of the divide on European integration in the national game of party competition is the time of accession when the likelihood of an inverted U-shaped configuration increases in many member states;
- the voting consensus in EU policy-making is high due to the rise of tertiary legislation and selection of uncontested secondary legislation, while polarization however increases in secondary legislation between the supranational pro- and anti-integrationist camps in the more recent post-Maastricht period;
- the supranational camp of pro-integrationist ruling/mainstream parties, which cohesively support European integration, stands in opposition to the anti-integrationist camp of challenger/periphery parties, which reject the proposals of the European Commission.

The analyses confirm the propositions and hypotheses of SNP on supranational camp-building between a pro-integrationist camp of ruling/mainstream parties and an anti-integrationist camp of challenger/periphery par-

---

proposals (especially those of the discharge procedure, which (dis)approves the discharge of the budget).

ties. However, these consequences do not mobilize the public in the first phases of deepening and widening in the post-Maastricht period. Neither supranational technocracism nor camp-building in EU policy-making raise the attention and interest of the public. Whether this changes in the third phase, in which the EU is confronted with supranational problem-solving and EU crisis management, will be analyzed in the next chapter.

CHAPTER 8

Phase III: Polarization and Identity-Formation

8.1. Abstract

This chapter investigates the propositions and hypotheses on public support of European integration in the post-Maastricht period. Compared to the period of permissive consensus, supranational technocracism and camp-building demobilize the public and reduce the electoral support of pro-integrationist ruling/mainstream parties, which continue to support European integration. The agenda monopoly of the supranational executive and the implementation of tertiary legislation find little public support. Furthermore, the country-specific ratings of satisfaction with domestic democracy and supranational governance design show substitution only for smaller countries. In times of supranational problem-solving with mass-mobilizing EU crisis management, the analyses show that partisan supporters ideologically align along the existing divide between the camps of pro-integrationist ruling/mainstream and anti-integrationist challenger/periphery parties.

8.2. Public and Partisan Attitudes toward European Integration

For liberal intergovernmentalism, public support varies across both countries and issues, paralleling governmental support of European integration. Regarding the variation in support, the literature on public support—which changes focus by mainly addressing the determinants of public support for European integration in the 1990s and of opposition against it in the early twenty-first century (Hobolt and De Vries 2016: 414)—conventionally asks respondents about their (perceived) countries or individual benefits from EU membership. Compared to utilitarian (e.g., Anderson and Reichert 1995, Gabel 1998) and identity (e.g., Carey 2002; Hooghe and Marks 2005, 2009)

Phase III: Polarization and Identity-Formation

determinants, cue-taking approaches acknowledge that respondents have information shortfalls about EU membership, which they can overcome by following media (e.g., De Vreese and Boomgaarden 2006) and parties (e.g., Hellström 2008). Because European affairs are too complex and remote from the daily lives of most people, the public is assumed to follow the cues of the media and parties when evaluating the benefits of EU membership (e.g., De Vries and Edwards 2009).

One of the central claims of SNP is that variation of public support exists not only across countries and issues but also within the member states between parties and voters. While deepening with the further transfer of policy competences for sensitive areas into veto bicameralism and widening without reforming the role of the European Commission change the supranational game of party competition, supranational technocracism and camp-building between pro-integrationist ruling/mainstream parties and anti-integrationist challenger/periphery parties in EU policy-making do not mobilize masses in the initial phases of the post-Maastricht period, which however changes in times of supranational problem-solving with mass-mobilizing EU crisis management. This dynamic perspective differs from linear projections on mass-mobilization and identity-formation of postfunctionalism, which argues that the transfers of policy competences for sensitive areas increasingly mobilizes national identities and explains the rise of anti-integrationist challenger/periphery parties in the post-Maastricht period.

More specifically, SNP predicts that the institutional choices for Europe in the post-Maastricht period find little public support. To identify the relative implications of governance design and transfers of policy competences for public support of European integration, a conjoint analysis uses experimental data from 13 member states (Hahm, Hilpert, and König 2019). It evaluates public preferences for proposal power, voting, and sanctioning across different policy areas. To control for substitution effects between the national and the EU level over time, Eurobarometer survey data are used to explore country-specific trends of satisfaction with domestic democracy and supranational governance. To outline demobilization and decoupling at the beginning of the post-Maastricht period, programmatic data of ruling/mainstream parties and challenger/periphery parties on the support of European integration are combined with Eurobarometer data (König and Luig 2017), which also shows country-specific trends on public and partisan support by parties with high governmental experience. Finally, affective polarization is studied by a survey in 25 member states, which combines a conjoint analysis with decision-making games that allows us to investigate ideological alignment and the formation of a supranational identity (Hahm, Hilpert, and König 2023).

The research design adheres to three methodological standards for the evaluation of the propositions and hypotheses on partisan and public support of European integration. The first is the collection of time series data for the study of trends in public support. Second, these data need to generate sufficient observations to evaluate partisan and public attitudes toward European integration, which also control for country-specific substitution effects between domestic democracy in the member states and supranational governance. Third, in addition to these explorative analyses, experimental data are used for the analysis of the relative implications of governance design and transfer of policy competences for public support of European integration and to identify the implications of affective polarization for ideological alignment and the formation of a superordinate supranational identity in the later post-Maastricht period.

8.3. Governance Design, Policy Competences, and Public Support

In the post-Maastricht period one of the central debates about European integration concern the democratic deficit and institutional reform of the EU. Proponents of liberal intergovernmentalism (Moravcsik 2002: 607, 2008: 181) and regulatory politics (Majone 1998, 2000) deny the limited effectiveness of supranational problem-solving and output legitimacy of the EU, the lack of transparency and accountability in EU policy-making. By contrast, Weiler, Haltern, and Mayer (1995) are skeptical about supranational executive dominance and the weakness of the European Parliament in EU policy-making, the interplay between the legislature on the one side, and the executive and judiciary on the other side.

Follesdal and Hix (2006) summarize the discussions about an increase in executive power and a decrease in parliamentary control (Andersen and Burns 1996, Raunio 1999), the relative weakness of the European Parliament vis-à-vis the Council (Lodge 1994), the weaknesses of a supranational party system (Schmitter 2000), the absence of issues on European integration in general and European elections (Hix 1999, Marks, Wilson, and Ray 2002, Hix and Marsh 2007), the lack of responsiveness despite the empowerment

Phase III: Polarization and Identity-Formation

of the European Parliament due to technocratic decision-making (Wallace and Smith 1995), and policy drift with overemphasis of negative integration (Scharpf 1997, 1999, Schmitter and Streeck 1991) as democratic deficit. They advocate for more supranational party competition and elections for (rational rather than affective) supranational opinion formation.

Compared to the pre-Maastricht period with permissive consensus (Lindberg and Scheingold 1970), scholars observe a trend toward "constraining dissensus" concerning the EU in the post-Maastricht period (Hooghe and Marks 2009, Hobolt and De Vries 2016, De Vries 2018). For Cramme and Hobolt (2014), this is clearly illustrated during the European debt crisis and results in a decline in trust and in an increase in support for Eurosceptic parties (Hobolt and De Vries 2015, De Vries et al. 2011, Hobolt, Spoon, and Tilley 2009, Spoon 2012). According to SNP, despite the further transfers of policy competences for sensitive areas supranational technocracism and camp-building are of little interest for the public in the initial phases of the post-Maastricht period, which changes in times of supranational problem-solving with mass-mobilizing EU crisis management. To explore the dynamics of public (de)mobilization in the period of study, Figure 8.1 illustrates the turnout trends in European and general elections, which decreases almost in parallel during both European and general elections but reverses most recently. Due to the second-order context of European elections, electoral turnout is higher in general elections because parties are more attentive to their national constituencies (Spoon and Klüver 2014) and European elections are still organized in national boundaries (König 2018).

Although the European Parliament has little procedural power and competences at the first European election in 1979, the turnout reaches almost 62 percent. During that same time, turnout in general elections is about 85 percent in the nine member states. Despite the further transfer of policy competences and the empowerment of the European Parliament, turnout in European elections continuously decreases to about 43 percent until 2009, while it drops below 70 percent in general elections in this same period in the 28 member states (note that this trend is similar for the nine member states of the end of the 1970s). Since mass-mobilizing EU management of the economic and financial crisis, the trend slightly reverses toward higher turnout in both general and European elections. This seems to confirm the dynamic perspective of SNP, which predicts that neither supranational technocracism nor camp-building in EU policy-making mobilize the masses in the begin-

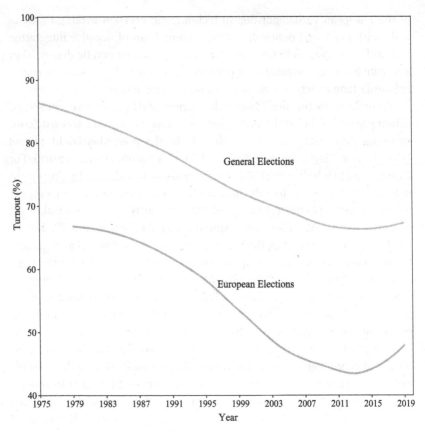

Figure 8.1. Turnout at European and General Elections in the Period from 1979 to 2019

ning of the post-Maastricht period, while supranational problem-solving with EU crisis management mobilizes masses in the latest phase.

Supranational technocracism and camp-building in EU policy-making result from the institutional choices on governance design, which establish veto bicameralism with agenda monopoly of the European Commission in the post-Maastricht period. Compared to qualified majority voting in the Council, unanimity voting not only limits the choices for Europe, but it also further reduces the threat of legislative override for supranational executive activism in EU policy-making. In addition to supranational activism of the executive experts, the European Court of Justice has sanctioning power and supremacy to decide about the priority of supranational over national norms. In the post-Maastricht period, the institutional choices not only change governance design, but also transfer further policy competences for sensitive policy areas. To identify the implications of the institutional choices for public support, Figure 8.2 combines the findings of a large-scale survey experiment on public support of governance design characteristics (Hahm, Hilpert, and König 2019) with data on the evaluation of transfers of area-specific policy competences conducted in 13 member states from December 2017 to March 2018.[1]

For the identification of the public's evaluation of the institutional choices on governance design characteristics, the analysis first distinguishes between proposal power, procedural approval, voting rule, and sanctioning in EU policy-making. The experiment shows respondents a screen with characteristics of two alternative governance designs, and they are asked about their preference for one of the two (Hainmueller, Hopkins, and Yamamoto 2014). The results express the average effects, where the average is computed based on all the other characteristics (AMCE). They indicate how much respondents support a specific governance design different from the status quo arrangement ($sq = 0$). Second, all respondents are asked whether they prefer policy competences for nine policy areas to be located at the domestic or EU level (agriculture, employment, environment and energy, health and social security, industry, market regulation and competition, security and defense, trade, and migration). As a control, the left panel lists those respondents who prefer that the EU should do less, and the right panel do more activities than the governments of the member states.

The first three items on governance design characteristics concern proposal power, for which the European Commission has a monopoly (sq). Accordingly, independent from their preference for more or less EU activities,

---

1. The sample largely represents different characteristics of the current 28 member states using Survey Sampling International (SSI). Overall, 13,000 respondents (about 1,000 respondents per country) were recruited from Austria, the Czech Republic, Denmark, France, Germany, Greece, Hungary, Ireland, Italy, the Netherlands, Poland, Spain, and Sweden. SSI recruits panel members through various opt-in methods (including website banners, television advertisements, e-mails, apps, social media, and websites) and employs a probability-weighted random process to select panel members. In this study, quotas were established based on respondent age and gender to ensure that the sample was representative of each country. The sampling algorithm continued to recruit SSI participants until all quotas were reached.

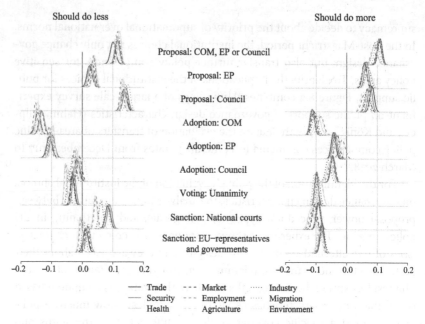

Figure 8.2. Public Support for Governance Design and Transfer of Policy Competences

and independent from the level-specific competences for a policy area, the public prefers to replace the supranational executive monopoly with a more competitive agenda setting that would provide the Council or the European Parliament with the right to submit proposals. Compared to shared proposal power by the Council and the European Parliament, the European Parliament alone finds lower public support as an additional agenda setter from those who want the EU to do less. Unsurprisingly, these respondents also prefer the Council alone as an agenda setter.

The next three items refer to whether the bicameral approval of proposals (*sq*) by the Council and the European Parliament should be replaced by approval of only the European Commission, the European Parliament, or the Council. Compared to bicameral approval of secondary legislation, approval of proposals only by the European Commission—as for tertiary legislation—is the least preferred alternative. Again, those who want the EU to do less unsurprisingly prefer the Council against the European Parliament, while bicameral approval remains the most preferred solution. Similar to proposal power, these findings are robust for all policy areas. This is also simi-

Phase III: Polarization and Identity-Formation

lar to majority voting which is publicly preferred over unanimity, in particular among those who prefer more EU activities.

The only fundamental variation on governance design characteristics among respondents exists for the supremacy of the European Court of Justice (*sq*), which is supported by those who prefer more EU activities, while those who prefer fewer EU activities favor the supremacy of national courts, in particular for the areas of trade, market regulation and competitiveness, migration, health and social security, environment and energy. Note that the experimental design allows controlling for further subgroups, such as the level of the respondents' information, their perception of benefits, and member states. Except for the variation of the court's supremacy, these subgroups hardly matter.

The disapproval of the agenda monopoly of the European Commission and the executive's adoption of tertiary legislation confirms the negative implications of supranational technocracism for public support ($H_{con}11$). Accordingly, the public prefers more competitive agenda setting, which can signal pluralist competition on the priority of supranational over national norms. Interestingly, neither those who prefer more or less EU activities, are in favor of the unanimity rule, which would foster supranational technocracism by decreasing the threat of legislative override. Finally, those who are concerned about more EU activities, do not support the supremacy of the European Court of Justice vis-à-vis national courts.

To control for country-specific variation over time, the evaluation of democracy at the domestic level may provide a contrasting lens producing an inverse relationship to satisfaction with the EU level. When the public is dissatisfied with domestic democracy, it is more likely to be satisfied with supranational governance and to support European integration (Sánchez-Cuenca 2000). Vice versa, when the public considers domestic democratic institutions to be working well, it displays much lower levels of satisfaction with supranational governance regardless of respective performance evaluations of EU policy-making (Anderson 1998, Kritzinger 2003). The simple reason is that the public perceives EU policy-making to be democratically deficient (Rohrschneider 2000). Figures 8.3, 8.4, and 8.5 illustrate how satisfied the public is with supranational governance as compared to satisfaction with domestic democracy using Eurobarometer data from 1999 to 2017. They also illustrate how this corresponds with trust in the European Commission (EC) and the European Parliament (EP):

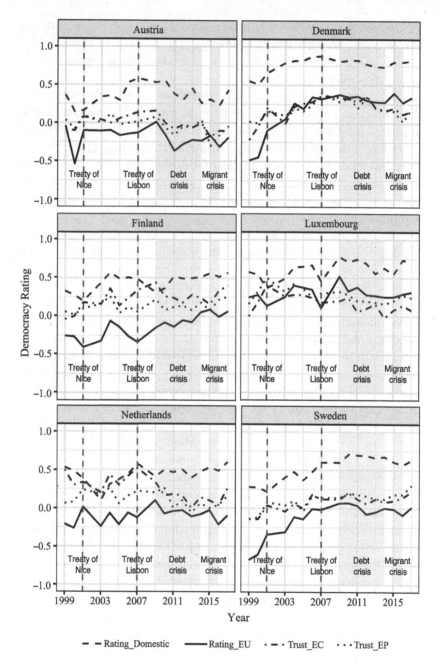

Figure 8.3. Group 1: More Satisfaction with Domestic Democracy Than with EU Governance in the Period 1999 to 2017

Phase III: Polarization and Identity-Formation

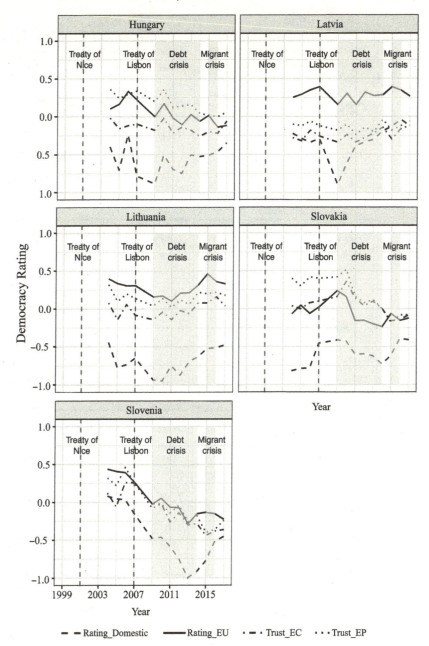

Figure 8.4. Group 2: More Satisfaction with EU Governance than with Domestic Democracy in the Period 1999 to 2017

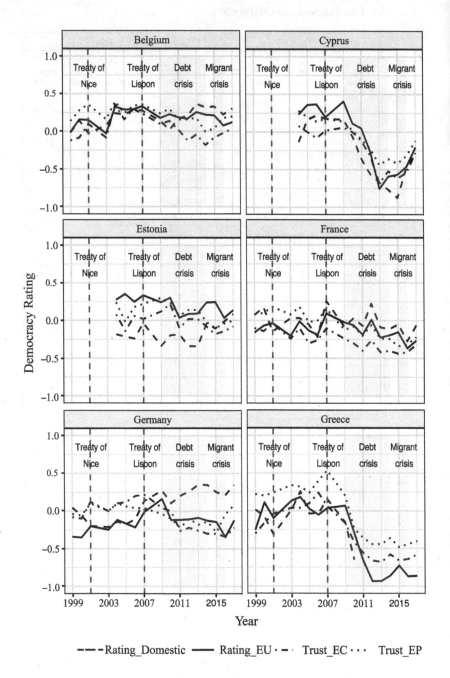

Figure 8.5. Group 3: Similar Satisfaction with EU Governance and Domestic Democracy in the Period 1999 to 2017

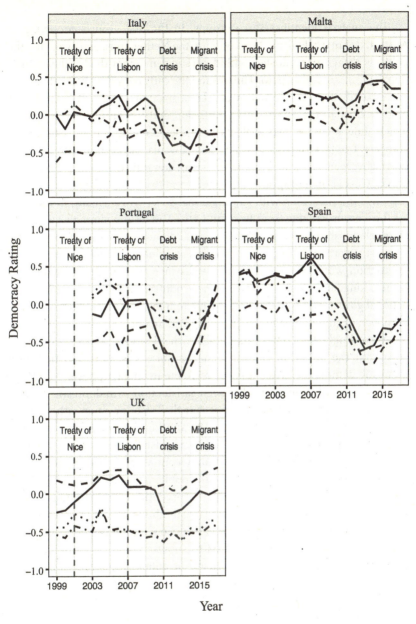

The analysis identifies three groups. In the first group—consisting of Austria, Denmark, Finland, Luxembourg, the Netherlands, and Sweden—the public is always more satisfied with domestic democracy than with supranational governance. Except for Finland and the early period in the Netherlands and Luxembourg, the level of (lower) EU satisfaction is highly associated with modest trust in the European Commission and the European Parliament, which show a very similar evaluation. In the second group, represented by Hungary, Latvia, Lithuania, Slovakia, and Slovenia, satisfaction with supranational governance is always higher than with domestic democracy. Except for Latvia, trust in the European Commission and the European Parliament corresponds to satisfaction with supranational governance. Finally, in the largest third group ranging from Belgium to the United Kingdom, there exists a close relationship between satisfaction with domestic democracy and supranational governance. Since the economic and financial crisis in 2007/2008, satisfaction with domestic democracy has increased in Germany and the United Kingdom. Compared to all other countries, satisfaction with supranational governance is in the United Kingdom much higher than trust in the European Commission and the European Parliament.

Accordingly, benchmarking between the domestic and EU level suggests that the public in smaller richer countries is more satisfied with domestic democracy, while it is the opposite in smaller poorer countries. However, substitution effects between satisfaction with domestic democracy and supranational governance hardly exist for most other larger countries. According to De Vries (2018), another differential concerns the regime and policies, which requires distinguishing between governance design and the further transfer of policy competences. Compared to the period of permissive consensus, where public support existed for policy competences and governance design, Euroscepticism might differ regarding these two dimensions.[2] Euroscepticism about governance design, as the British example for trust in the European Commission and the European Parliament indicates, is related to supranational institutions, while policy skepticism relates to the transfer of policy competences from the domestic to the EU level.

---

2. De Vries (2018) also advocates benchmarking between the domestic and the EU level, which—as the previous analysis showed—only distinguishes between small rich and poor countries.

8.4. Partisan and Public Support of European Integration

For liberal intergovernmentalism, public support of European integration varies across countries and issues. In addition to the variation of public support of European integration across countries and issues, SNP predicts variation across parties and the public over time (König 2018). According to Ezrow et al. (2011), ruling/mainstream parties are particularly sensitive to preference shifts of the (mean) voter. Regarding European integration, this is confirmed by Franklin and Wlezien (1997) for the pre-Maastricht period, in which public support of European integration reacts "with precision and almost instantaneously" to the output of EU policy-making.[3] However, in a more recent analysis, Toshkov (2011) shows that the number of directives in secondary legislation follows the level of public support in the period 1973–1995, while it disappears afterward.[4]

In contrast to Wratil (2019), Williams and Bevan (2019) reveal that EU legislative activities continue to increase despite public opposition. This is in line with the previous chapters, which show that tertiary legislation dominates EU policy-making and a divide between pro-integrationist ruling/mainstream parties and anti-integrationist challenger/periphery parties characterizes secondary legislation. Using Eurobarometer and manifesto data, Figure 8.6 illustrates the trend for public support, which is retrieved from Eurobarometer by using the difference in respondents' appreciation of their country's membership as a "good thing" from those seeing it as a "bad thing," and partisan support of European integration measured from the programmatic declarations by parties with high and low governmental experiences between 1980 and 2015 (König and Luig 2017).

Although the level of support for European integration from the Eurobarometer and programmatic manifesto scales cannot be compared directly, their individual trends indicate important differences. Until the time around the Maastricht Treaty, public and partisan support of parties with high gov-

---

[3] This is in line with studies that report that governments adjust their position on the scope of integration to closer align to the partisan composition of national parliaments as well as to public opinion on European integration (e.g., Aspinwall 2002, 2007; Finke 2010b; Koenig-Archibugi 2004).

[4] Bølstadt (2015) confirms this finding with a public impulse by founding member states, while public support in countries of 1970s Western enlargement began declining in the mid-1980s before starting a rapid climb that once again slowed down somewhat after the Maastricht Treaty.

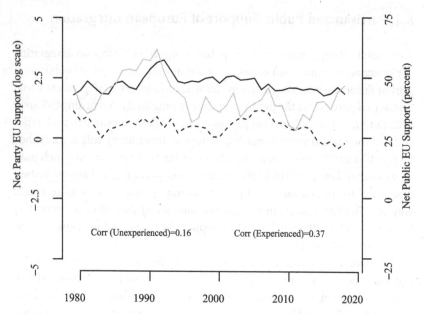

Figure 8.6. Attitudes toward European Integration: Parties with High Governmental Experience (Top 25%-black solid line), Low Governmental Experience (Bottom 25%-black dotted line) between 1979 and 2019, Public Opinion (gray solid line)

ernmental experience develop almost in parallel, confirming the findings of Toshkov (2011). Compared to the support of parties with high governmental experience, which slightly declines afterward, public support is more volatile: it drastically declines around the beginning of the 1990s in the supranational technocracism phase of deepening and remains at this level in the camp-building phase of widening (see also Hoboldt and De Vries 2016). The correlation between public and partisan support is relatively low with 0.16 for parties with low and 0.37 for those with high governmental experience.

Compared to a more parallel trend of public and partisan support by parties with high governmental experience in the period until the mid-1990s, these parties continue to support European integration almost independently of the sharp decline of public support at the beginning of the post-Maastricht period. While public support again declines with the Great Recession, support of parties with high governmental experience does not change. Furthermore, public support increases after 2011/2012 independently from the trends of support of parties with low and high governmental experience. In

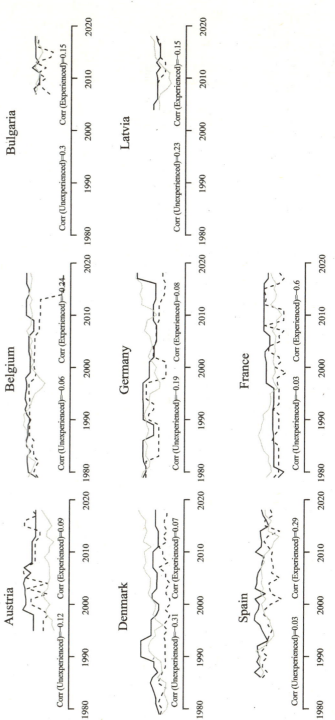

Figure 8.7. Country-Specific Attitudes toward European Integration: Parties with High Governmental Experience (black solid line), Low Governmental Experience (black dotted line), Public Opinion (gray solid line) between 1979 and 2019

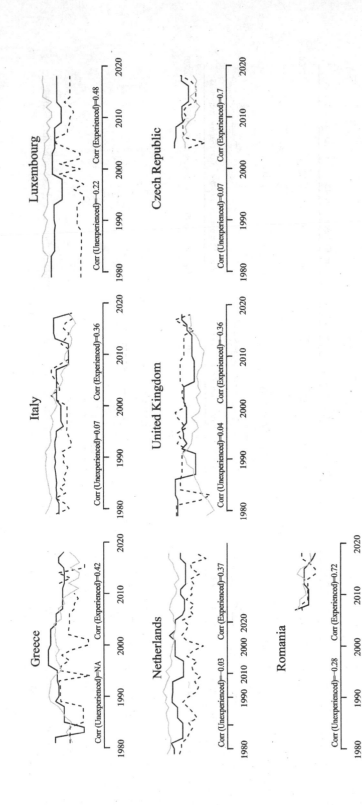

Figure 8.7—Continued

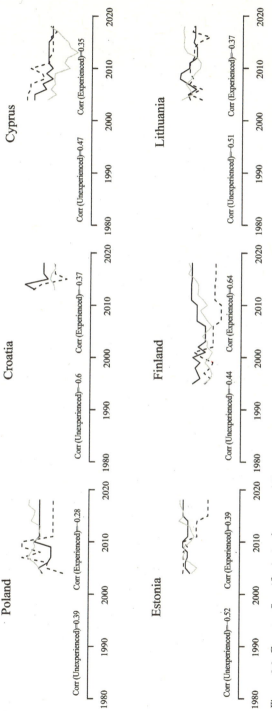

Figure 8.8. Country-Specific Attitudes toward European Integration: Parties with High Governmental Experience (black solid line), Low Governmental Experience (black dotted line), Public Opinion (gray solid line) between 1979 and 2019

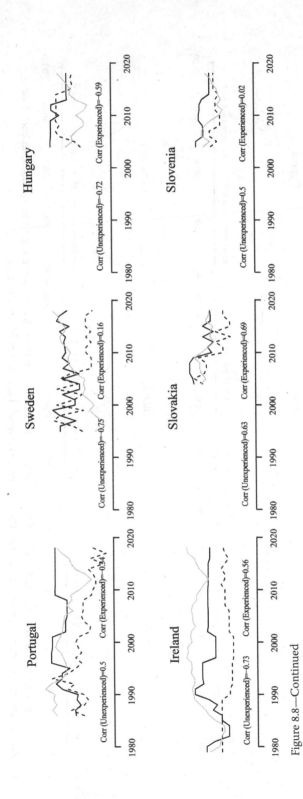

Figure 8.8—Continued

addition to cross-issue and cross-country support, the continuous support of parties with high governmental experience suggests a decoupling of partisan and public support for ruling/mainstream parties. Figures 8.7 and 8.8 control for country-specific trends of public and partisan support with low and high governmental experience.

According to Figure 8.7, the support of European integration of neither the parties with high nor those with low governmental experience is associated with public support of European integration. This is the case for those ruling/mainstream parties in Austria, Belgium, Bulgaria, Denmark, Germany, Latvia, and Spain. In France, Greece, Italy, Luxembourg, the Netherlands, the United Kingdom, the Czech Republic, and Romania, a higher association (between 0.36 and 0.6) exists between public and partisan support of European integration by parties with high governmental experience, though it is negatively correlated in France and the United Kingdom.

Figure 8.8 reveals that the association between public and partisan support is particularly high for parties with low governmental experience in Poland, negatively in Croatia, Cyprus, Estonia, Finland, Lithuania, Portugal, Sweden, Hungary, Ireland, Slovakia, and Slovenia, which is sometimes accompanied by high correlations of parties with high governmental experience. In Croatia, Estonia, Finland, Lithuania, Sweden, Hungary, and Ireland, these associations between public and partisan support of parties with low governmental experience are however negative.

In almost all member states, the support of European integration by parties with high governmental experience (top 25 percent) is almost always higher than that by parties with low governmental experience (bottom 25 percent). In some member states, such as Italy, Cyprus, Hungary, Latvia, Lithuania, Romania, and the United Kingdom, these differences disappear over time, while they are increasingly visible in Belgium, Germany, Finland, Portugal, and Sweden. Accordingly, the findings on partisan and public support indicate an increasing disconnect between the support of European integration by the public and the parties with high governmental experience.

While this decoupling between partisan and public support is of little relevance in the initial phases of the post-Maastricht period, SNP predicts that ruling/mainstream parties are particularly sanctioned for their continuous support of European integration at times of supranational problem-solving with mass-mobilizing EU crisis management, from which anti-integrationist challenger/periphery parties profit. Figure 8.9 shows how the relative vote share of ruling/mainstream parties—defined by their governmental partic-

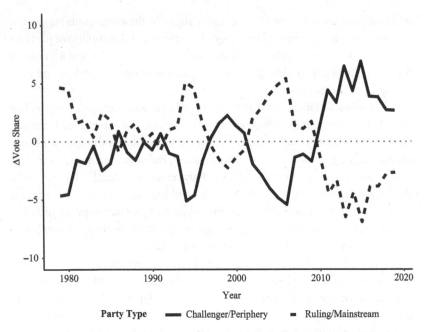

Figure 8.9. Relative Votes of Ruling/Mainstream and Challenger/Periphery Parties without Governmental Experience over Past Six Elections in the Period 1979 to 2019

ipation in the last six terms during the period of study—and other parties from the member states change over time.

Until the Great Recession the gains and losses of the ruling/mainstream are mirrored by the losses and gains of challenger/periphery parties. This changes in the latest phase of the post-Maastricht period, in which challenger/periphery parties continuously win in elections at the expense of ruling/mainstream parties. In fact, this suggests that public demobilization with decreasing turnout hardly changes the relative distribution of votes (and seats) of ruling/mainstream parties in the initial phases of the post-Maastricht period. Confirming $H_{con}12$, the findings show that challenger/periphery parties profit from the continuous support of ruling/mainstream parties of European integration in times of supranational problem-solving with mass-mobilizing EU crisis management in the latest phase of the post-Maastricht period.

This does not mean that challenger/periphery parties always win until ruling/mainstream parties are in the minority. The 2019 European election experiences the highest turnout of 50.66 in this century, in which challenger/periphery parties surprisingly fail to achieve the expected electoral breakthrough. Although migration becomes the most prominent issue in autumn 2018 and the migrant crisis mobilizes masses, the question is whether affective polarization on issues of European integration fosters identification and ideological alignment of partisans of pro-integrationist ruling/mainstream and those of anti-integrationist challenger/periphery parties, the former winning in the 2019 European election most of the seats.

8.5. Solidarity and Trust for Co- and Outnationals

Following the literature on affective polarization in the United States (e.g., Iyengar and Westwood 2015, Iyengar et al. 2019), a growing number of studies investigates the transformation of the national game of party competition in Europe toward affective polarization with ingroup favoritism and outgroup derogation from an identity-based perspective (e.g., Gidron, Adams, and Horne 2020, Bassan-Nygate and Weiss 2022, Boxell, Gentzkow, and Shapiro 2020, Harteveld 2021, Helbling and Jungkunz 2020, Hernandez, Anduiza, and Rico 2021, Hobolt, Tilley, and Leeper 2022, Lauka, McCoy, and Firat 2018, Reiljan 2020, Wagner 2021, Westwood et al. 2018). In the literature on European integration, this has stimulated a vivid debate about the role of ruling/mainstream and challenger/periphery parties and their partisan supporters (e.g., Hobolt and Tilley 2016, De Vries and Hobolt 2020), in which postfunctionalism posits that the activation of national identities "disrupts the established party systems ... and constrains supranational problem-solving" (Hooghe and Marks 2019: 1117).

Following postfunctionalism, the mobilization of national identities increases polarization with the rise of Eurosceptic left- and right-wing challenger parties (Hooghe and Marks 2009, 2019). When issues such as "immigration, exacerbated cultural and economic insecurity" impose a cultural threat to national identities (Hooghe and Marks 2018b: 110), public support for European integration declines (Carey 2002, De Vries, Hakhverdian, and Lancee 2013, Norris and Inglehart 2019). According to postfunctionalism, this allows radical left- and right-wing periphery parties to establish constraining dissensus, which will undermine solidarity and trust—two important components of a supranational identity (Scharpf 1999, Zürn 2000). Although Hooghe and Marks (2009: 17) admit that "we do not measure directly: national identity," their identity-based proposition on the mobilization of national identities suggests that conationals will receive more solidarity and trust than outnationals, in particular by supporters of challenger/periphery parties.

For SNP, ideological alignment of partisan supporters of ruling/mainstream and challenger/periphery parties on the pro- versus anti-integrationist divide is a necessary condition for a new cleavage on issues of European integration and the formation of a supranational identity with solidarity and trust for outnationals. SNP contends that affective polarization—the tendency of partisan ingroup favoritism and outgroup derogation—emotionally mobilizes partisan supporters of ruling/mainstream and challenger/periphery parties, who become aware of their pro- and anti-integrationist stances in times of supranational problem-solving with EU crisis management. To examine affective polarization between partisan in- and outgroups, Hahm, Hilpert, and König (2023) fielded a survey in 25 European democracies in 2019, which combines a conjoint analysis with two prominent games, the dictator and the trust game to measure solidarity and trust among partisan in- and outgroups.[5] The experimental data are collected in a survey fielded in 25 European democracies at the beginning of 2019 before the European election.[6]

The following analysis combines the experimental data with respondents' ideological positions to examine whether ideological alignment on the left versus right has similar moderating effects for solidarity and trust to ideological alignment on the pro- versus anti-integrationist dimension.[7] Only

---

5. The dictator game presents a simple one-shot setup where respondents (considered as Player 1) receive a certain number of tokens and are asked how much they would like to donate to another person (introduced as Player 2), described by a short profile. The trust game extends this basic setup, adding a stage where respondents are told that the researchers will triple the number of tokens allocated to Player 2 and that Player 2 will have a chance to transfer some, none, or all of these tokens back to the respondent, Player 1.

6. Combining the threat of cultural diversity with the anti-establishment rhetoric of challenger/periphery parties, the migration crisis—which mainly concerns immigration of outnationals from non-EU members in the period of study—can be conceived as an exogenous shock that constitutes a critical juncture for ideological alignment along the pro-integrationist camp of ruling/mainstream and the anti-integrationist camp of challenger/periphery parties.

7. It calculates an ideological alignment score with a range from -10 to +10 by subtracting the ideological distance to the in-party (ranging from 0 to 10) from the respondent's average ideological distance to outparties (ranging from 0 to 10). -10 indicates that distance to one's own party is much larger than the average distance to the other parties, which represents poor alignment or sorting. +10 indicates that the average distance to the other parties is much larger than the distance to one's own party, which reflects good alignment. Intermediate levels of alignment are in between.

Phase III: Polarization and Identity-Formation 171

when these effects are similar, the new cleavage on European integration has a similar importance for solidarity and trust than ideological alignment on the dominant socioeconomic left- versus right-dimension. To compare the moderating effect of ideological alignment for solidarity and trust on both dimensions, Figure 8.10 displays the interaction with the treatment indicator of Player 2's affiliation to either a ruling/mainstream or a challenger/periphery party in both games.

According to Figure 8.10, ideologically aligned partisans of ruling/mainstream and challenger/periphery parties show considerably less solidarity to the partisan outgroup than to copartisans in the dictator game, while unaligned individuals do not distinguish as much between co- and outpartisans on both dimensions.[8] While the confidence intervals for those of ruling/mainstream and challenger/periphery parties overlap strongly on the left versus right dimension, showing no statistically significant differences for solidarity, notably, ideological alignment matters more for partisans of ruling/mainstream parties (straight line) than those of challenger/periphery parties (dotted line) on the pro- versus anti-integration dimension.

The findings do not change substantially for the trust game. Trust for copartisans increases for aligned partisans along the left versus right and the pro- versus anti-integrationist dimension. For partisans of ruling/mainstream and challenger/periphery parties, ideological alignment increases differences between in- and outgroups on both dimensions in a similar manner. Confirming $H_{con}13$, ideological alignment on the pro- versus anti-integrationist dimension has very similar implications for solidarity and trust than alignment on the left versus right dimension for partisans of ruling/mainstream and challenger/periphery parties.

Ideological alignment is a necessary condition for a new cleavage in European integration, which does not necessarily mean constraining dissensus that either reduces supranational problem-solving (e.g., Hooghe and Marks 2009, 2019) or demands differentiated variability in European integration (e.g., Leuffen, Rittberger, and Schimmelfennig 2012, Schmidt 2019). According to SNP, ideological alignment on the new cleavage on European integration only means that aligned partisans of ruling/mainstream and challenger/periphery parties show more solidarity and trust for co- than outpartisans. Regarding European integration, the more interesting question is whether

---

8. The histograms depict the distribution of observations in the sample on ideological alignment displayed on the horizontal axis.

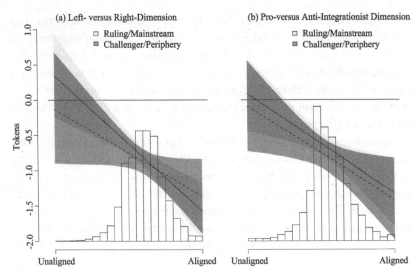

Figure 8.10. Dictator Game: Solidarity and Ideological Alignment on the Left versus Right and the Pro- versus Anti-Integrationist Dimension

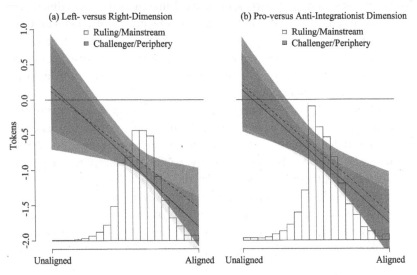

Figure 8.11. Trust Game: Trust and Ideological Alignment on the Left versus Right and the Pro- versus Anti-Integrationist Dimension

Phase III: Polarization and Identity-Formation

this alignment also fosters the formation of a superordinate supranational identity with solidarity and trust for outnationals.

Figure 8.12, which also considers the self-placement of respondents (left, center, right) on the left versus right dimension, approximates solidarity for partisans of ruling/mainstream and those of challenger/periphery parties by the dictator and trust game. To identify a superordinate supranational identity with a "self" and an "other," the figure also distinguishes between solidarity and trust for conationals and EU outnationals as well as non-EU outnationals. Positive values indicate higher solidarity or trust than for conationals, and negative values lower solidarity or trust than for conationals of each type of outnational.

On closer inspection of each type of outnational, only right-leaning supporters of ruling/mainstream and challenger/periphery parties show less solidarity for EU outnationals on the left versus right-dimension. This is different for non-EU outnationals, who are discriminated from center- and right-leaning supporters of ruling/mainstream and challenger/periphery parties. Only left-leaning supporters do not discriminate non-EU outnationals. These results only slightly change for outnational trust. Figure 8.13 shows the findings for solidarity and trust with the self-placement (pro, moderate, anti) on the pro- versus anti-integrationist dimension of respondents for each type of outnational. Independent from the camp, respondents with an anti-integrationist attitude always discriminate outnationals from EU and non-EU members. This suggests that respondents do not completely behave according to the stances of their parties on European integration. Compared to EU outnationals, those with moderate or pro-integrationist attitudes in particular of ruling/mainstream parties also discriminate non-EU outnationals. Compared to left-leaners on the left versus right-dimension, pro-integrationist respondents of ruling/mainstream parties show lower solidarity and trust for non-EU outnationals. In sum, the findings reveal that:

- Differences between solidarity and trust are of minor relevance. Except for a few cases, the results show similar patterns of discrimination.
- Discrimination is more pronounced on the pro- versus anti-integrationist than on the left versus right dimension. In particular, anti-integrationists discriminate outnationals from both EU and non-EU members.
- Compared to EU outnationals, who are discriminated from anti-integrationists and right-leaning partisans, non-EU outnationals expe-

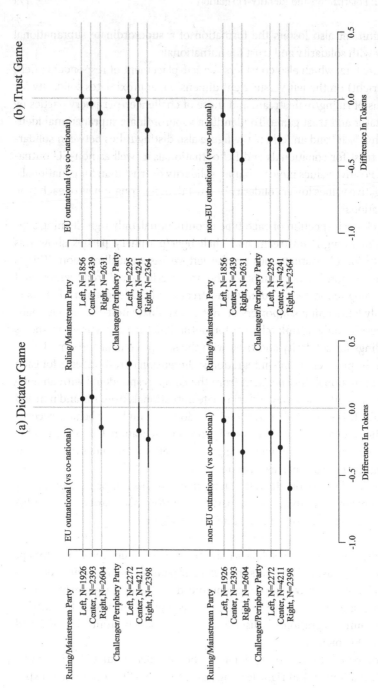

Figure 8.12. Left versus Right Solidarity and Trust for Co- and Outnationals from EU and Non-EU Members of Ruling/Mainstream and Challenger/Periphery Parties

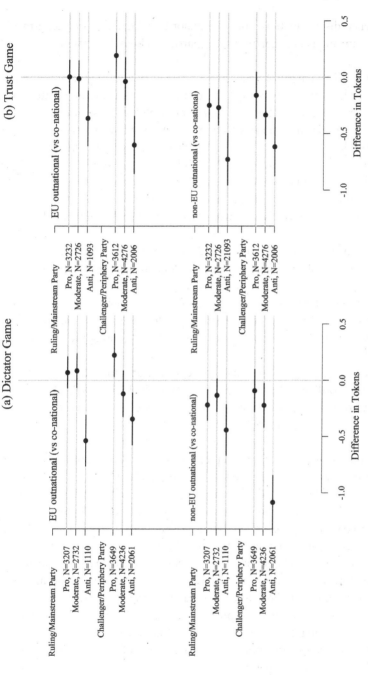

Figure 8.13. Pro- versus Anti-Integrationist Solidarity and Trust for Co- and Outnationals from EU and Non-EU Members of Ruling/Mainstream and Challenger/Periphery Parties

rience discrimination from the majority of partisans of ruling/mainstream and challenger/periphery parties on both dimensions.

Confirming $H_{con}14$, partisan identification and ideological alignment promote affective polarization between the two camps, which have similar patterns on the left versus right and the pro- versus anti-integrationist dimension. The new cleavage on European integration changes not only party competition between ruling/mainstream and challenger/periphery parties but also intensifies discrimination of outnationals. While the majority of partisans show similar levels of solidarity and trust for EU outnationals on both dimensions, non-EU outnationals experience more discrimination from the majority of partisan supporters. Briefly summarized, the findings demonstrate that

- supranational technocracism and camp-building in EU policy-making do not mobilize the masses despite deepening and widening in the initial phases of the post-Maastricht period;
- in times of mass-mobilizing supranational problem-solving and EU crisis management, the partisan supporters of ruling/mainstream and challenger/periphery parties ideologically align along the existing two camps;
- the new cleavage on European integration promotes the formation of a superordinate supranational identity with similar levels of solidarity and trust for EU outnationals as for conationals, while non-EU outnationals are discriminated.

The findings confirm the three-step proposition of SNP, according to which the critical juncture for the divide between ruling/mainstream and challenger/periphery parties, which consolidates in EU policy-making, is around the time of accession. Supranational technocracism and camp-building in EU policy-making do not mobilize masses despite deepening and widening in these initial phases of the post-Maastricht period. Instead of the mobilization of national identities with a desire for self-rule, supranational problem-solving with mass-mobilizing EU crisis management promote the ideological alignment of partisans along the existing divide between pro- and anti-integrationists in the latest phase pf the post-Maastricht period. Finally, unlike constraining dissensus, the findings suggest the formation of a superordinate supranational identity with similar levels of solidarity and trust for EU outnationals as for conationals among the majority of partisans in Europe.

These findings draw a dynamic picture on the causes and consequences of the institutional choices in the post-Maastricht period. Although political leaders are unable to effectively reform the institutional model of the EU, the consequences of their institutional choices for Europe change the patterns of partisan and public support in the one or other direction over time, which can finally promote supranational consensus rather than constraining dissensus. In particular, supranational problem-solving with mass-mobilizing EU crisis management accomplishes what many scholars missed in times of permissive consensus: the public is mobilized and aligns along the new cleavage, in which the vast partisan and public majority is in favor of European integration, while a minority attracts the most attention for their anti-integrationist, oftentimes Eurosceptic stances.

CHAPTER 9

Conclusion and Outlook

Before continuing to the conclusion and the outlook, it should be noted that a major goal of this book is to fascinate a new generation of scholars who are interested in falsifiable predictions, and to frame important research agendas by outlining empirical puzzles of the institutional choices for Europe. From a dynamic perspective, SNP can provide an answer for most paradoxes of the post-Maastricht period, such as the integration paradox of new intergovernmentalism regarding the further transfers of functions without reforming the EU (Bickerton, Hodson, and Puetter 2015), the democratic deficit paradox of announcing more referendums in order to enhance democracy though they were ultimately ignored when political leaders agreed to continue with European integration (Finke et al. 2012), the parliamentarization paradox of strengthening the role of the European Parliament though legislative proposals are negotiated in informal trilogues (Lu and König 2021), and the challenger paradox of ruling/mainstream parties, which support establishment of veto bicameralism with regulated supranational competences that promotes the rise of anti-integrationist challenger/periphery parties (Schneider 2018, De Vries and Hobolt 2020).

Concerning the classical debates about European integration (e.g., Haas 1958, Hoffmann 1966, Lindberg and Scheingold 1970, Moravcsik 1998, 2018, Sandholtz and Stone Sweet 1998, Bickerton, Hodson, and Puetter 2015, Hooghe and Marks 2009, 2019), this book introduces SNP as a broader theory about the causes *and* consequences of the institutional choices for Europe and empirically investigates the explanatory power of the propositions and hypotheses of SNP on European integration in the post-Maastricht period. In part 1 of this book on the causes, the findings confirm that political leaders perform a double role in the interstate summit game: they pursue country-specific interests in governance design ($H_{cau}1$) and party-specific interests in the transfer of policy competences ($H_{cau}2$), which are more likely to shift when the government changes ($H_{cau}3$). For example, political leaders from smaller

Conclusion and Outlook

countries prefer a "one state one vote" allocation rule for power and offices on governance design, while political leaders of ruling/mainstream parties with higher governmental experience support the transfer of policy competences.

In interstate bargains, power and capabilities are mainly derived from two components, the distance to the status quo and the environment in which political leaders of noncooperative member states pursue vote-seeking strategies to receive one-sided concessions. Political leaders of member states are more likely to approve a treaty with a larger distance to the status quo ($H_{cau}4$). This also implies that a political leader of a noncooperative member state, which is more likely to prefer failure over treaty approval by announcing a referendum with a credible veto threat, is more powerful in interstate bargains ($H_{cau}5$). In contrast to conventional wisdom, political leaders from smaller member states, which economically profit from European integration, are able to reduce a reform of the institutional model of the EU to the lowest common denominator despite approaching enlargement ($H_{cau}6$).

With widening toward more diverse interests among a larger number of member states and deepening toward more salient interests in sensitive policy areas, uncertainty about the environment increases at interstate bargains, which raises the risk of failure and inefficiency of institutional choices for Europe ($H_{cau}7$). For the Council presidency, it becomes more difficult, if not impossible, to infer the (non)cooperative type of 25 and more member states. At Lisbon, the survival of ratification consequently dominates in a way that fosters inefficiency and incomplete contracting among the member states. Such incompleteness explains unintended negative and positive consequences of institutional choices for Europe, such as uncontrolled delegation and the rise of Euroscepticism but also the formation of a superordinate supranational identity.

For the consequences of the institutional choices for Europe, SNP articulates propositions and hypotheses on the implications of veto bicameralism with regulated supranational competences for supranational technocracism and building of a pro- and an anti-integrationist camp in EU policy-making, along which the public ideologically aligns in times of supranational problem-solving with mass-mobilizing EU crisis management. In part 2 of this book on the consequences, the empirical analyses confirm the relationship between higher conflict in governance design and supranational technocracism ($H_{con}1$), which produces more bureaucratic tertiary legislation ($H_{con}2$) with centralizing regulations and decisions ($H_{con}3$) when a larger size of the legislative core decreases the threat of legislative override. This also applies to areas of shared competences, which the subsidiarity principle unsuccessfully aims to protect against supranational activism ($H_{con}4$).

The higher heterogeneity and salience of interests also raise the risk of noncompliance in a deepening and widening EU, in which the European Commission involves the European Parliament in the making of directives ($H_{con}5$) and approves early agreements in informal trilogues ($H_{con}6$) to avoid enforcement conflicts on compliance. Confirming SNP, the analyses show that the activism of supranational executive and judicial experts is associated with the size of the legislative core, which reduces the threat of legislative override. Compared supranational executive activism of the European Commission, the European Court of Justice more cautiously responds to the threat of legislative override and conditionally interprets the priority of norms in the one or other direction ($H_{con}7$).

In addition to supranational technocracism, the results reveal the building of a pro- and an anti-integrationist camp in the supranational game of party competition as another consequence of the institutional choices for Europe in the post-Maastricht period, which fail to reform the role and composition of the European Commission in a widening EU. The analyses show that the critical juncture for the divide between pro-integrationist ruling/mainstream and anti-integrationist challenger/periphery parties in the national game of party competition is the time of accession in most member states ($H_{con}8$). This conflict consolidates in the supranational game of party competition through veto bicameralism, in which the European Commission's agenda monopoly promotes the building of a pro- and an anti-integrationist camp in EU policy-making ($H_{con}9$). Due to the higher number of portfolios from 12 to 27 in the post-Maastricht period, this monopoly also increases polarization between the camps of pro-integrationist and anti-integrationist parties over time ($H_{con}10$).

For the public, the divide between the pro-integrationist camp of ruling/mainstream and the anti-integrationist camp of challenger/periphery parties is of little relevance in the initial phases of the post-Maastricht period, because supranational technocracism and camp-building do not mobilize masses ($H_{con}11$). Furthermore, the camp of pro-integrationist ruling/mainstream parties continues to support European integration despite decreasing support of a demobilized public, from which challenger/periphery parties sporadically profit when a referendum is required for treaty ratification ($H_{con}12$). In times of supranational problem-solving with mass-mobilizing EU crisis management, affective polarization promotes ideological alignment

Conclusion and Outlook 181

along the pro- versus anti-integrationist divide, which establishes a new cleavage on European integration ($H_{con}13$). In contrast to constraining dissensus, the new cleavage on European integration fosters the formation of a superordinate supranational identity with solidarity and trust among co- and EU outnationals ($H_{con}14$).

These findings on the causes *and* consequences of the institutional choices for Europe break with the conventional wisdom of liberal intergovernmentalism and postfunctionalism by rejecting the idea that European integration is only driven by economic problem-solving in times of globalization. They reveal the importance of partyism at the national and supranational level, and how phases of approval and disapproval of European integration by political leaders, parties, and the public dynamically change over the period of study. From a game-theoretical perspective, SNP distinguishes between the interstate summit game and the national game of party competition to understand the causes of these dynamics, and between the game of EU policy-making and supranational party competition to understand their consequences. Because the conditions of the data generation change in the period of study, a design is warranted that allows us to draw inferences and conclusions from multiple datasets on the past and future of European integration.

Instead of only presenting one dataset to draw inferences and conclusions on the past and future of European integration, this book engages in the evaluation of the post-Maastricht period with multiple datasets, which cover the causes by data on the major turning points in the post-Maastricht history and their consequences by data on EU policy-making, party competition, and public support. Although a growing number of empirical studies on European integration infer associations among variables of one dataset, this is only possible when the conditions of the data generation process remain the same. To outline associations among variables under changing conditions in the post-Maastricht period, the analyses of this book examine different datasets by using measurement and graphical models, counterfactual analysis, and experimental designs.

Admittedly, some associational analyses only explore trends in European integration or use data that only allow showing trends of some variables of interest, which however aim to set an empirical standard of careful observation, and skepticism about what is significantly observed, given that personal views and omitted variables can distort the interpretation of observation. Because many questions that motivate research on European integration are not associational but causal in nature, more knowledge of the data-generating process, measurement models and new designs with experimental data are required to draw inferences and conclusions about the past and future of European integration.

This conclusion distinguishes two perspectives on the future of European integration. If one considers that the institutional model of the EU is in disequilibrium, one "differentiating" possibility would be to renationalize policy competences for sensitive areas. It is noteworthy to distinguish between EU migration and immigration, which postfunctionalism posits to mobilize national identities and the desire for self-rule. If this desire evolves against non-EU outnationals from immigration, the recommendation would be to secure external borders, while a desire for self-rule against EU outnationals from EU migration would need to constrain free movement within the common market.

Compared to differentiated integration, a further widening by the six Balkan countries and Ukraine, and a deepening to cope with climate change, aging European societies, migration, and the Russian aggression demand to address the four fundamental questions on institutional reform—the preparation for widening, the provision of efficiency, the balance between supranational and national norms, as well as between responsibility and responsiveness. The findings of this book suggest that a major precondition for institutional reform—a superordinate supranational identity—already exists among co- and EU outnationals. However, because the attempts to reform the institutional model of the EU bear a high risk of failure and inefficiency, as the events around the Constitutional Treaty show, the outlook discusses two scenarios, a regular and a crisis scenario.

For both scenarios, the outlook presents alternatives for institutional reform of the EU that are likely to find public support and approval by political leaders. The simple reason for this condition is that the lesson of the post-Maastricht period is that political leaders will pursue vote-seeking strategies that mobilize the public against any change of the status quo. Following the findings on public support, the reform of the European Commission's agenda monopoly is on top. Public support will increase through a more competitive agenda-setting right that provides the European Parliament or the Council with the right to submit proposals that will also overcome the bipolar voting pattern on the priority of supranational over national norms in EU policymaking (Hahm, Hilpert, and König 2019).

Although Majone (2002) criticizes that EU policy-making is already politicized by the empowerment of the European Parliament, a more import-

Conclusion and Outlook

ant implication of competitive agenda-setting is that it can transform the two camps into a more pluralist configuration with moderates in between. Competitive agenda-setting encourages, if not demands, to submit own proposals about the relationship between responsibility for European integration and responsiveness to the distinct demands of the public. Depending on the effectiveness of the supranational party system—competitive agenda-setting can be established with or without a threshold in secondary legislation, which requires finding compromise for building coalitions.

Another institutional shortcoming is uncontrolled supranational delegation through the overuse of tertiary legislation, which results from a larger size of the legislative core. Of course, the simplest solution for decreasing the size of the legislative core would be to apply majority voting in a unicameral procedure. However, the findings of this book show that the public prefers the bicameral procedure against any unicameral procedure, in which the Council, the European Parliament, or the European Commission legislates alone. Instead of distinguishing between delegated and implementing acts which are—as the ineffectiveness of the subsidiarity principle shows—difficult to implement when the size of the legislative core increases, a more promising solution for the control of supranational delegation is to introduce sunshine clauses, as they define an expiry day for each tertiary act and cease the provisions of the act unless further legislative action is taken to extend it.

Finally, to prepare for widening, a priority of directives over centralizing regulations and decisions is warranted for areas in which the costs exceed the benefits from supranational centralization. Compared to listing areas with priority of national or supranational norms, this reform applies to the type of instrument. The supranational discretion of the usage of instruments can be supervised more effectively by establishing the office of an independent prosecutor that will enhance the credibility of commitments for European integration. This prosecutor can also prepare cases independent of the European Commission to the European Court of Justice, the European Court of Auditors, and eventually the European Court of Human Rights.

In addition to these specific reform alternatives which answer three of the four fundamental questions on the consequences of the institutional choices for EU policy-making, a reform of the supranational electoral system is necessary when supranational problem-solving with mass-mobilizing EU crisis management becomes the rule rather than the exception. In this crisis scenario, which answers the fourth fundamental question on the impact of EU policy-making for public support, it is necessary to strengthen supranational party competition for improving the quality of candidates and agenda setting to internalize the country-specific costs of European integration, which foster nativist "My Population First"-slogans. One option is a more active supranational representation principle that, for example, first allocates seats according to the vote share of supranational party groups, which are then, secondly, distributed according to population size of their members. Once this active supranational representation principle is established, one further option is to move toward responsible supranational party government by appointing European Commissioners and the President of the European Commission through the ruling parties, which can subsequently be held accountable by the voters in European elections.

Another option is a change of the ballot structure within the national boundaries of the current electoral system. Instead of using a close ballot structure with the descriptive representation principle where voters can only choose between parties within relatively large districts, the alternative solution will set up electoral districts of small sizes with open ballot structure, which allows voters to choose candidates, eventually by single transferable votes to strengthen the relationship between individual representatives and district voters. As Hix and Hagemann (2009) show, the responsiveness of representatives is determined by smaller district size and the openness of the ballot structure.

Whether the political leaders will take action to reform the EU's institutional model is difficult to predict. However, when the reform clearly signals to improve responsiveness to the distinct demands of the public by competitive agenda-setting, sunshine clauses for tertiary legislation, the office of an independent prosecutor, and a reform of the supranational electoral system, political leaders of anti-integrationist parties will have a hard time mobilizing the public against its own interests. This book ends with the optimistic view derived from evidence-based insights into the causes *and* consequences of the institutional choices for Europe. The findings on a superordinate supranational identity suggest that solidarity and trust already exist among a majority of co- and EU outnationals. How large this majority is, which provides an empirical foundation for public support of European integration, will also depend on the implementation of the outlined reform options.

REFERENCES

Achen, Christopher. 2006. "Evaluating Political Decision-Making Models." In *European Union Decides*, edited by Robert Thomson, Frans Stokman, Christopher Achen, and Thomas König, 264–98. Cambridge: Cambridge University Press.

Andersen, Svein, and Tom R. Burns. 1996. "The European Union and the Erosion of Parliamentary Democracy: A Study of Post-Parliamentary Governance." In *European Union—How Democratic Is It?*, edited by Svein S. Andersen and Kjell A. Eliassen, 227–52. London: Sage Publications.

Anderson, Christopher. 1998. "Parties, Party Systems, and Satisfaction with Democratic Performance in the New Europe." *Political Studies* 46: 572–88.

Anderson, Christopher, and Karl Kaltenthaler. 1996. "The Dynamics of Public Opinion toward European Integration, 1973–93." *European Journal of International Relations* 2(2): 175–99.

Anderson, Christopher, and Shawn Reichert. 1995. "Economic Benefits and Support for Membership in the EU: A Cross-National Analysis." *Journal of Public Policy* 15: 231–49.

Aspinwall, Mark. 2002. "Preferring Europe: Ideology and National Preferences on European Integration." *European Union Politics* 3: 81–111.

Aspinwall, Mark. 2007. "Government Preferences on European Integration: An Empirical Test of Five Theories." *British Journal of Political Science* 37(1): 89–114.

Bakker, Ryan, Catherine De Vries, Erica Edwards, Liesbet Hooghe, Seth Jolly, Gary Marks, Jonathan Polk, Jan Rovny, Marco Steenbergen, and Milada Anna Vachudova. 2015. "Measuring Party Positions in Europe: The Chapel Hill Expert Survey Trend File, 1999–2010." *Party Politics* 21(1): 143–52.

Bardi, Luciano, Stefano Bartolini, and Alexander Trechsel. 2014. "Responsive and Responsible? The Role of Parties in Twenty-First Century Politics." *West European Politics* 37(2): 235–52.

Bartolini, Stefano. 2005. *Restructuring Europe: Centre Formation, System Building, and Political Structuring between the Nation State and the European Union*. Oxford: Oxford University Press.

Bassan-Nygate, Lotem, and Chagai Weiss. 2022. "Party Competition and Cooperation Shape Affective Polarization: Evidence from Natural and Survey Experiments in Israel." *Comparative Political Studies* 55(2): 287–318.

Bast, Jürgen. 2016. "Is There a Hierarchy of Legislative, Delegated and Implementing Acts?" In *Rulemaking by the European Commission: The New System for Delegation of Pow-*

ers, edited by Carl Fredrik Bergström and Dominique Ritleng, 55–86. Oxford: Oxford University Press.

Benoit, Kenneth, and Michael Laver. 2012. "The Dimensionality of Political Space: Epistemological and Methodological Considerations." *European Union Politics* 13(2): 194–218.

Bickerton, Christopher, Dermot Hodson, and Uwe Puetter. 2015. "The New Intergovernmentalism: European Integration in the Post-Maastricht Era." *Journal of Common Market Studies* 53: 703–22.

Blom-Hansen, Jens. 2019. "Studying Power and Influence in the European Union: Exploiting the Complexity of Post-Lisbon Legislation with EUR-Lex." *European Union Politics* 30(4): 692–706.

Blumenau, Jack, and Benjamin Lauderdale. 2018. "Never Let a Good Crisis Go to Waste: Agenda Setting and Legislative Voting in Response to the EU Crisis." *Journal of Politics* 80(2): 462–78.

Bølstad, Jørgen. 2015. "Dynamics of European Integration: Public Opinion in the Core and Periphery." *European Union Politics* 16(1): 23–44.

Boranbay-Akan, Serra, Thomas König, and Moritz Osnabrügge. 2017. "The Imperfect Agenda-Setter: Why Do Legislative Proposals Fail in the EU Decision-Making Process?" *European Union Politics* 18(2): 168–87.

Börzel, Tanja. 2001. "Non-Compliance in the European Union: Pathology or Statistical Artefact?" *Journal of European Public Policy* 8: 803–24.

Börzel, Tanja. 2021. *Why Noncompliance. The Politics of Law in the European Union*. Ithaca, NY: Cornell University Press.

Börzel, Tanja, and Moritz Knoll. 2012. "Quantifying Non-compliance in the EU. A Database on EU Infringement Proceedings." *Berlin Working Paper on European Integration* 15.

Börzel, Tanja, and Diana Panke. 2013. "Europeanization." In *European Union Politics*, edited by Michele Cini and Nieves Pères-Solòrzano Borragàn, 110–21. Oxford: Oxford University Press.

Börzel, Tanja, and Ulrich Sedelmeier. 2017. "Larger and More Law Abiding? The Impact of Enlargement on Compliance in the European Union." *Journal of European Public Policy* 24(2): 197–215.

Boxell, Levi, Matthew Gentzkow, and Jesse Shapiro. 2020. *Cross-Country Trends in Affective Polarization*. Technical Report no. 26669. Cambridge, MA: National Bureau of Economic Research.

Braun Daniela, Maike Salzwedel, Christian Stumpf, and Andreas Wüst. 2007. *Euromanifesto Documentation*. Mannheim: Mannheimer Zentrum für Europäische Sozialforschung.

Bruter, Michael. 2005. *Citizens of Europe? The Emergence of a Mass European Identity*. Heidelberg: Springer.

Budge, Ian, Hans-Dieter Klingemann, Andrea Volkens, Judith Bara, and Eric Tanenbaum. 2001. *Mapping Policy Preferences: Estimates for Parties, Electors, and Governments, 1945–1998*. Oxford: Oxford University Press.

References

Burley, Anne-Marie, and Walter Mattli. 1993. "Europe before the Court." *International Organization* 47(1): 41–76.

Caramani, Daniele. 2017. "Will vs. Reason: The Populist and Technocratic Forms of Political Representation and Their Critique to Party Government." *American Political Science Review* 111: 54–67.

Carey, Sean. 2002. "Undivided Loyalties: Is National Identity an Obstacle to European Integration?" *European Union Politics* 3: 387–413.

Carrubba, Clifford, Barry Friedman, Andrew Martin, and Georg Vanberg. 2012. "Who Controls the Content of Supreme Court Opinions?" *American Journal of Political Science* 56(2): 400–412.

Carrubba, Clifford, and Matthew Gabel. 2014. *International Courts and the Performance of International Agreements: A General Theory with Evidence from the European Union*. Cambridge: Cambridge University Press.

Carrubba, Clifford, Matthew Gabel, and Charles Hankla. 2008. "Judicial Behavior under Political Constraints: Evidence from the European Court of Justice." *American Political Science Review* 102: 435–52.

Chayes, Abram, and Antonia Handler Chayes. 1993. "On Compliance." *International Organization* 47(2): 175–205.

Checkel, Jeffrey. 2001. "Why Comply? Social Learning and European Identity Change." *International Organization* 55(3): 553–88.

Cichowski, Rachel. 2004. "Women's Rights, the European Court, and Supranational Constitutionalism." *Law and Society Review* 38(3): 489–512.

Cramme, Olaf, and Sara Hobolt, eds. 2014. *Democratic Politics in a European Union under Stress*. Oxford: Oxford University Press.

Crombez, Christophe. 1996. "Legislative Procedures in the European Community." *British Journal of Political Science* 26(2): 199–228.

Crombez, Christophe. 1997. "The Co-Decision Procedure in the European Union." *Legislative Studies Quarterly* 22(1): 97–119.

Crombez, Christophe. 2000. "Institutional Reform and Co-decision in the European Union." *Constitutional Political Economy* 11: 41–57.

Crombez, Christophe, and Simon Hix. 2015. "Legislative Activity and Gridlock in the European Union." *British Journal of Political Science* 45(3): 477–99.

Dannwolf, Tanja. 2014. *Achieving Compliance with the Help of the Public? A Quantitative Study of the European Commission's Decision to Enforce the Implementation of EC Directives*. Dissertation at the University of Mannheim.

De Swaan, Abram. 1973. *Coalition Theories and Cabinet Formations*. Amsterdam: Elsevier Scientific.

De Vreese, Claes, and Hajo Boomgaarden. 2006. "News, Political Knowledge and Participation: The Differential Effects of News Media Exposure on Political Knowledge and Participation." *Acta Politica* 41(4): 317–41.

De Vries, Catherine. 2018. *Euroscepticism and the Future of European Integration*. Oxford: Oxford University Press.

De Vries, Catherine, and Erica Edwards. 2009. "Taking Europe to Its Extremes: Extremist Parties and Public Euroscepticism." *Party Politics* 15: 5–28.

De Vries, Catherine, Armen Hakhverdian, and Bram Lancee. 2013. "The Dynamics of Voters' Left/Right Identification: The Role of Economic and Cultural Attitudes." *Political Science Research and Methods* 1(2): 223–38.

De Vries, Catherine, and Sara Hobolt. 2012. "When Dimensions Collide: The Electoral Success of Issue Entrepreneurs." *European Union Politics* 13: 246–68.

De Vries, Catherine, and Sara Hobolt. 2020. *Political Entrepreneurs: The Rise of Challenger Parties in Europe*. Princeton: Princeton University Press.

De Vries, Catherine, Wouter van der Brug, Marcel van Egmond, and Cees van der Eijk. 2011. "Individual and Contextual Variation in EU Issue Voting: The Role of Political Information." *Electoral Studies* 30: 16–28.

De Wilde, Pieter. 2011. "No Polity for Old Politics? A Framework for Analyzing the Politicization of European Integration." *Journal of European Integration* 33(5): 559–75.

De Wilde, Pieter, and Michael Zürn. 2012. "Can the Politicization of European Integration Be Reversed?" *Journal of Common Market Studies* 50: 137–53.

Downs, George, David Rocke, and Peter Barsoom. 1996. "Is the Good News about Compliance Good News about Cooperation?" *International Organization* 50(3): 379–406.

Druckman, James, Samara Klar, Yanna Krupnikov, Matthew Levendusky, and John Barry Ryan. 2021. "Affective Polarization, Local Contexts and Public Opinion in America." *Nature Human Behaviour* 5(1): 28–38.

Eichenberg, Richard, and Russell Dalton. 1993. "Europeans and the European Community: The Dynamics of Public Support for European Integration." *International Organization* 47(4): 507–34.

Eriksen, Erik Oddvar, and John Erik Fossum. 2002. "Indigenous Rights and the Limitations of the Nation State." In *Democracy in the European Union*, edited by Erik Oddvar Eriksen and John Erik Fossum, 244–69. London: Routledge.

Evans, Geoffrey. 1998. "Euroscepticism and Conservative Electoral Support: How an Asset Became a Liability." *British Journal of Political Science* 28(4): 573–90.

Ezrow, Lawrence, Catherine De Vries, Marco Steenbergen, and Erica Edwards. 2011. "Mean Voter Representation and Partisan Constituency Representation: Do Parties Respond to the Mean Voter Position or to Their Supporters?" *Party Politics* 17(3): 275–301.

Falkner, Gerda, Miriam Hartlapp, and Oliver Treib. 2007. "Worlds of Compliance: Why Leading Approaches to the Implementation of EU Legislation Are Only 'Sometimes-True Theories.'" *European Journal of Political Research* 64: 395–416.

Finke, Daniel. 2009. "Domestic Politics and European Treaty Reform: Understanding the Dynamics of Governmental Position-Taking." *European Union Politics* 10: 482–506.

Finke, Daniel. 2010a. "Estimating the Effect of Non-Separable Preferences in EU Treaty Negotiations." *Journal of Theoretical Politics* 21: 543–69.

Finke, Daniel. 2010b. *European Integration and Its Limits: Intergovernmental Conflicts and Their Domestic Origins*. Colchester: ECPR Press.

Finke, Daniel. 2015. "The burden of authorship: how agenda-setting and electoral rules shape legislative behaviour." *Journal of European Public Policy* 23: 604-623.

Finke, Daniel, and Thomas König. 2009. "Why Risk Popular Ratification Failure? A Comparative Analysis of the Choice of the Ratification Instrument in the 25 Member States of the EU." *Constitutional Political Economy* 20: 341–65.

References

Finke, Daniel, Thomas König, Sven-Oliver Proksch, and George Tsebelis. 2012. *Reforming the European Union: Realizing the Impossible*. Princeton: Princeton University Press.

Fjelstul, Joshua C., and Clifford J. Carrubba. 2018. "The Politics of International Oversight: Strategic Monitoring and Legal Compliance in the European Union." *American Political Science Review* 112(3): 429–45.

Fligstein, Neil, Alina Polyakova, and Wayne Sandholtz. 2012. "European Integration, Nationalism and European Identity." *Journal of Common Market Studies* 50: 106–22.

Follesdal, Andreas, and Simon Hix. 2006. "Why There Is a Democratic Deficit in the EU: A Response to Majone and Moravcsik." *Journal of Common Market Studies* 44: 533–62.

Franklin, Mark N., and Christopher Wlezien. 1997. "The Responsive Public: Issue Salience, Policy Change, and Preferences for European Unification." *Journal of Theoretical Politics* 9: 347–63.

Gabel, Matthew. 1998. "Public Support for European Integration: An Empirical Test of Five Theories." *Journal of Politics* 60: 333–54.

Gabel, Matthew. 2000. "Review of Political Theory and the European Union: Legitimacy, Constitutional Choice and Citizenship." *Journal of Politics* 62(4): 1256–58.

Gabel, Matthew, and Harvey Palmer. 1995. "Understanding Variation in Public Support for European Integration." *European Journal of Political Research* 27(1): 3–19.

Garrett, Geoffrey, and George Tsebelis. 1996. "An Institutional Critique of Intergovernmentalism." *International Organization* 50: 269–99.

Gidron, Noam, James Adams, and Will Horne. 2020. *American Affective Polarization in Comparative Perspective*. Cambridge: Cambridge University Press.

Gilligan, Thomas, and Keith Krehbiel. 1987. "Collective Decisionmaking and Standing Committees: An Informational Rationale for Restrictive Amendment Procedures." *Journal of Law, Economics, and Organization* 3(2): 287–335.

Grande, Edgar, and Hanspeter Kriesi. 2016. "The Euro Crisis: A Boost to the Politicisation of European Integration?" In *Politicising Europe*, edited by Swen Hutter, Edgar Grande, and Hanspeter Kriesi, 240–76. Cambridge: Cambridge University Press.

Haas, Ernst. 1958. *The Uniting of Europe: Political, Social, and Economical Forces 1950–1957*. London: Stevens.

Hahm, Hyeonho, David Hilpert, and Thomas König. 2019. "Institutional Reform and Public Attitudes toward EU Decision Making." *European Journal of Political Research* 59(3): 599–623.

Hahm, Hyeonho, David Hilpert, and Thomas König. 2023. "Divided We Unite: The Nature of Partyism and the Role of Coalition Partnership in Europe." *American Political Science Review* (forthcoming).

Hainmueller, Jens, Daniel Hopkins, and Teppei Yamamoto. 2014. "Causal Inference in Conjoint Analysis: Understanding Multidimensional Choices via Stated Preference Experiments." *Political Analysis* 22(1): 1–30.

Hammond, Thomas, and Gary Miller. 1987. "The Core of the Constitution." *American Political Science Review* 81(4): 1155–74.

Harteveld, Eelco. 2021. "Ticking All the Boxes? A Comparative Study of Social Sorting and Affective Polarization." *Electoral Studies* 72: 102–337.

Helbling, Marc, Dominic Hoeglinger, and Bruno Wüest. 2010. "How Political Parties Frame European Integration." *European Journal of Political Research* 49(4): 495–521.

Helbling, Marc, and Sebastian Jungkunz. 2020. "Social Divides in the Age of Globalization." *West European Politics* 43(6): 1187–1210.

Hellström, Johan. 2008. "Who Leads, Who Follows? Re-Examining the Party–Electorate Linkages on European Integration." *Journal of European Public Policy* 15(8): 1127–44.

Hernandez, Enrique, Eva Anduiza, and Guillem Rico. 2021. "Affective Polarization and the Salience of Elections." *Electoral Studies* 69: 102–23.

Hilpert, David, and Thomas König. 2021. "International Courts, Judicial Activism, and Types of Signals under Uncertainty." Unpublished Manuscript. Mimeo.

Hix, Simon. 1999. "Dimensions and Alignments in European Union Politics: Cognitive Constraints and Partisan Responses." *European Journal of Political Research* 35(1): 69–106.

Hix, Simon. 2005. "Neither a Preference-Outlier nor a Unitary Actor: Institutional Reform Preferences of the European Parliament." *Comparative European Politics* 3(2): 131–54.

Hix, Simon. 2008. "Towards a Partisan Theory of EU Politics." *Journal of European Public Policy* 15: 1254–65.

Hix Simon, and Andreas Follesdal. 2006. "Why There Is a Democratic Deficit in the EU: A Response to Majone and Moravcsik." *Journal of Common Market Studies* 44: 533–62.

Hix Simon, and Sara Hagemann. 2009. "Could Changing the Electoral Rules Fix European Parliament Elections?" *Politique Européenne* 2: 37–52.

Hix, Simon, and Christopher Lord. 1997. *Political Parties in the European Union*. New York: St. Martin's Press.

Hix, Simon, and Michael Marsh. 2007. "Punishment or Protest? Understanding European Parliament Elections." *Journal of Politics* 69(2): 495–510.

Hix, Simon, and Abdul Noury. 2009. "After Enlargement: Voting Patterns in the Sixth European Parliament." *Legislative Studies Quarterly* 34(2): 159–74.

Hobolt, Sara, and Catherine De Vries. 2015. "Issue Entrepreneurship and Multiparty Competition." *Comparative Political Studies* 48: 1159–85.

Hobolt, Sara, and Catherine De Vries. 2016. "Public Support for European Integration." *Annual Review of Political Science* 19: 413–32.

Hobolt, Sara, Jae-Jae Spoon, and James Tilley. 2009. "A Vote against Europe? Explaining Defection at the 1999 and 2004 European Parliament Elections." *British Journal of Political Science* 39: 93–115.

Hobolt, Sara, and James Tilley. 2016. "The Polls—Trends: British Public Opinion towards EU Membership." *Public Opinion Quarterly* 85(4): 1126–50.

Hobolt, Sara, James Tilley, and Thomas Leeper. 2022. "Policy Preferences and Policy Legitimacy after Referendums: Evidence from the Brexit Negotiations." *Political Behavior* 44: 839–58.

Hoffmann, Stanley. 1966. "Obstinate or Obsolete? The Fate of the Nation-State and the Case of Western Europe." *Daedalus* 95(3): 862–915.

Holzinger, Katharina, and Frank Schimmelfennig. 2012. "Differentiated Integration in the European Union: Many Concepts, Sparse Theory, Few Data." *Journal of European Public Policy* 19(2): 292–305.

Hooghe, Liesbet. 2003. "Europe Divided? Elites vs. Public Opinion on European Integration." *European Union Politics* 4(3): 281–304.

References

Hooghe, Liesbet, and Gary Marks. 2001. *Multi-Level Governance and European Integration.* Oxford: Rowman and Littlefield.
Hooghe, Liesbet, and Gary Marks. 2003. "Unraveling the Central State, but How? Types of Multi-Level Governance." *American Political Science Review* 97(2): 233–43.
Hooghe, Liesbet, and Gary Marks. 2005. "Calculation, Community and Cues: Public Opinion on European Integration." *European Union Politics* 6: 419–43.
Hooghe, Liesbet, and Gary Marks. 2009. "A Postfunctionalist Theory of European Integration: From Permissive Consensus to Constraining Dissensus." *British Journal of Political Science* 39: 1–23.
Hooghe, Liesbet, and Gary Marks. 2018a. "Is Liberal Intergovernmentalism Regressive? A Comment on Moravcsik." *Journal of European Public Policy* 27(4): 501–8.
Hooghe, Liesbet, and Gary Marks. 2018b. "Cleavage Theory Meets Europe's Crises: Lipset, Rokkan, and the Transnational Cleavage." *Journal of European Public Policy* 25: 109–35.
Hooghe, Liesbet, and Gary Marks. 2019. "Grand Theories of European Integration in the 21st Century." *Journal of European Public Policy* 26(8): 1113–33.
Hooghe, Liesbet, and Gary Marks. 2020. "A Postfunctionalist Theory of Multilevel Governance." *British Journal of Politics and International Relations* 22(4): 820–26.
Hug, Simon. 2016. "Party Pressure in the European Parliament." *European Union Politics* 17(2): 201–18.
Hug, Simon, and Thomas König. 2002. "In View of Ratification: Governmental Preferences and Domestic Constraints at the Amsterdam Intergovernmental Conference." *International Organization* 56: 447–76.
Hug, Simon, and Tobias Schulz. 2005. "Federalism in the European Union: The View from Below (If There Is Such a Thing)." *Journal of European Public Policy* 12: 488–508.
Hug, Simon, and George Tsebelis. 2002. "Veto Players and Referendums around the World." *Journal of Theoretical Politics* 14: 465–515.
Hurka, Steffen, and Yves Steinebach. 2020. "Legal Instrument Choice in the European Union." *Journal of Common Market Studies* 59(2): 278–96.
Hutter, Swen, Edgar Grande, and Hanspeter Kriesi, eds. 2016. *Politicising Europe.* Cambridge: Cambridge University Press.
Iida, Keisuke. 1993. "When and How Do Domestic Constraints Matter? Two-Level Games with Uncertainty." *Journal of Conflict Resolution* 37(3): 403–26.
Iyengar, Shanto, Yphtach Lelkes, Matthew Levendusky, Neil Malhotra, and Sean Westwood. 2019. "The Origins and Consequences of Affective Polarization in the United States." *Annual Review of Political Science* 22: 129–46.
Iyengar, Shanto, Guarav Sood, and Yphtach Lelkes. 2012. "Affect, Not Ideology: A Social Identity Perspective on Polarization." *Public Opinion Quarterly* 76: 405–31.
Iyengar, Shanto, and Sean J. Westwood. 2015. "Fear and Loathing across Lines: New Evidence on Group Polarization." *American Journal of Political Science* 59(3): 690–707.
Jackman, Simon. 2008. *Pscl: Classes and Methods for R Developed in the Political Science Computational Laboratory.* United States Studies Centre, University of Sydney. https://github.com/atahk/pscl/.
Jones, Erik, Daniel Kelemen, and Sophie Meunier. 2021. "Failing Forward? Crises and Patterns of European Integration." *Journal of European Public Policy* 28(10): 1519–36.

Junge, Dirk, Thomas König, and Bernd Luig. 2015. "Legislative Gridlock and Bureaucratic Politics in the European Union." *British Journal of Political Science* 45: 777–97.

Kaeding, Michael. 2005. "The World of Committee Reports: Rapporteurship Assignment in the European Parliament." *Journal of Legislative Studies* 11: 82–104.

Katzenstein, Peter. 1997. *Tamed Power: Germany in Europe*. Ithaca: Cornell University Press.

Koenig-Archibugi, Mathias. 2004. "International Governance as New Raison d'État? The Case of the EU Common Foreign and Security Policy." *European Journal of International Relations* 10: 147–88.

Kölliker, Alkuin. 2001. "Bringing Together or Driving Apart the Union? Towards a Theory of Differentiated Integration." *West European Politics* 24: 125–51.

Kölliker, Alkuin. 2006. *Flexibility and European Unification: The Logic of Differentiated Integration*. Boulder: Rowman and Littlefield.

König, Thomas. 2005. "Methods and Measuring Positions on European Constitution Building." *European Union Politics* 6: 259–67.

König, Thomas. 2007. "Discontinuity: Another Source of the EU's Democratic Deficit?" *European Union Politics* 8(3): 411–32.

König, Thomas. 2018. "Still the Century of Intergovernmentalism? Partisan Ideology, Two-Level Bargains and Technocratic Governance in the Post-Maastricht Era." *Journal of Common Market Studies* 56(6): 1240–62.

König, Thomas, and Thomas Bräuninger. 2004. "Accession and Reform of the European Union. A Game Theoretical Analysis of Eastern Enlargement and the Constitutional Reform." *European Union Politics* 5: 419–40.

König, Thomas, Stephanie Daimer, and Daniel Finke. 2008. "The Treaty Reform of the EU: Constitutional Agenda-Setting, Intergovernmental Bargains and the Presidency's Crisis Management of Ratification Failure." *Journal of Common Market Studies* 46(2): 337–63.

König, Thomas, and Daniel Finke. 2009. "Why Risk Popular Ratification Failure? A Comparative Analysis of the Choice of the Ratification Instrument in the 25 Member States of the EU." *Constitutional Political Economy* 20: 341–65.

König, Thomas, Daniel Finke, and Stephanie Daimer. 2005. "Ignoring the Non-Ignorables? Missingness and Missing Positions." *European Union Politics* 6(3): 269–90.

König, Thomas, and Simon Hug. 2000. "Ratifying Maastricht: Parliamentary Votes on International Treaties and Theoretical Solution Concepts." *European Union Politics* 1: 89–122.

König, Thomas, Björn Lindberg, Sandra Lechner, and Winfried Pohlmeier. 2007. "Bicameral Conflict Resolution in the European Union: An Empirical Analysis of Conciliation Committee Bargains." *British Journal of Political Science* 37: 281–312.

König, Thomas, and Xiao Lu. 2020. "Should I Stay or Should I Go? British Voter You Got to Let Me Know! Prime Ministers, Intra-Party Conflict, and Membership Referendums in the British Westminster Model." *Journal of Theoretical Politics* 32(4): 557–81.

König, Thomas, and Xiao Lu. 2021. "Helping or Sanctioning? Heterogeneous Effects in the Strategic Analysis of International Compliance." Paper presented at the 11th Annual Conference of the European Political Science Association.

References

König, Thomas, and Brooke Luetgert. 2003. *The Treaty of Nice: Intergovernmental Conferences, Domestic Constraints and the Reform of European Institutions.* First ECPR General Conference. Marburg.

König, Thomas, and Brooke Luetgert. 2009. "Troubles with Transposition? Explaining Trends in Member-State Notification and the Delayed Transposition of EU Directives." *British Journal of Political Science* 39(1): 163–94.

König, Thomas, Brooke Luetgert, and Tanja Dannwolf. 2006. "Quantifying European Legislative Research: Using CELEX and PreLex." *European Union Politics* 7(4): 553–74.

König, Thomas, and Bernd Luig. 2012. "Party Ideology and Legislative Agendas: Estimating Contextual Policy Positions for the Study of EU Decision-Making." *European Union Politics* 13(4): 604–25.

König, Thomas, and Bernd Luig. 2014. "Ministerial Gatekeeping and Parliamentary Involvement in the Implementation Process of EU Directives." *Public Choice* 160 (3–4): 501–19.

König, Thomas, and Bernd Luig. 2017. "The Impact of EU Decision-Making on National Parties' Attitudes towards European Integration." *European Union Politics* 18(3): 362–81.

König, Thomas, and Lars Mäder. 2014. "The Strategic Nature of Compliance: An Empirical Evaluation of Law Implementation in the Central Monitoring System of the European Union." *American Journal of Political Science* 58(1): 246–63.

König, Thomas, Moritz Marbach, and Moritz Osnabrügge, 2017. "Left/Right or U? Estimating the Dimensionality of National Party Competition in Europe." *Journal of Politics* 79(3): 1101–5.

König, Thomas, and Jonathan Slapin. 2006. "From Unanimity to Consensus: An Analysis of the Negotiations at the EU's Constitutional Convention." *World Politics* 58: 413–45.

Kriesi, Hanspeter. 1998. "Restructuration of Partisan Politics and the Emergence of a New Cleavage Based on Values." *West European Politics* 33(3): 673–85.

Kriesi, Hanspeter. 2007. "The Role of European Integration in National Election Campaigns." *European Union Politics* 8: 83–108.

Kriesi, Hanspeter. 2016. "The Politicization of European Integration." *Journal of Common Market Studies* 54: 32–47.

Kriesi, Hanspeter, Edgar Grande, Martin Dolezal, Marc Helbling, Dominic Höglinger, Swen Hutter, and Bruno Wüest. 2012. *Political Conflict in Western Europe.* Cambridge: Cambridge University Press.

Kriesi, Hanspeter, Edgar Grande, Romain Lachat, Martin Dolezal, Simon Bornschier, and Timotheus Frey. 2006. "Globalization and the Transformation of the National Political Space: Six European Countries Compared." *European Journal of Political Research* 45(6): 921–56.

Kritzinger, Sylvia. 2003. "The Influence of the Nation-State on the Individual Support for the European Union." *European Union Politics* 4: 219–41.

Kuhn, Thomas S. 1970. *The Structure of Scientific Revolutions.* Chicago: University of Chicago Press.

Larsson, Olof, and Daniel Naurin. 2016. "Judicial Independence and Political Uncertainty: How the Risk of Override Affects the Court of Justice of the EU." *International Organization* 70(2): 377–408.

Lauka, Alban, Jennifer McCoy, and Rengin Firat. 2018. "Mass Partisan Polarization: Measuring a Relational Concept." *American Behavioral Scientist* 62(1): 107–26.

Laursen, Finn. 2002. *The Amsterdam Treaty: National Preference Formation, Interstate Bargaining and Outcome*. Portland, OR: Odense University Press.

Laursen, Finn, ed. 2006. *The Treaty of Nice: Actor Preferences, Bargaining and Institutional Choice*. Leiden: Brill.

Laursen, Finn, ed. 2008. *The Rise and Fall of the EU's Constitutional Treaty*. Leiden: Martinus Nijhoff.

Leuffen, Dirk, Berthold Rittberger, and Frank Schimmelfennig. 2012. *Differentiated Integration: Explaining Variation in the European Union*. Basingstoke: Palgrave Macmillan.

Lindberg, Leon, and Stuart Scheingold. 1970. *Regional Integration: Theory and Research*. Cambridge: Cambridge University Press.

Lipset, Seymour, and Stein Rokkan. 1967. *Party Systems and Voter Alignments*. New York: Free Press.

Lodge, Juliet.1994. "Transparency and Democratic Legitimacy." *Journal of Common Market Studies* 32(3): 343–68.

Lu, Xiao, and Thomas König. 2021. "Legislative Decision Making and Law Compliance in the EU." Paper presented at the 79th MPSA Conference, Chicago.

Mair, Peter. 2000. "The Limited Impact of Europe on National Party Systems." *West European Politics* 23(4): 27–51.

Majone, Giandomenico. 1996. *Regulating Europe*. London: Routledge.

Majone, Giandomenico. 1998. "Europe's 'Democratic Deficit': The Question of Standards." *European Law Journal* 4: 5–28.

Majone, Giandomenico. 2000. "The Credibility Crisis of Community Regulation." *Journal of Common Market Studies* 38(2): 273–302.

Majone, Giandomenico. 2002. "The European Commission: The Limits of Centralization and the Perils of Parliamentarization." *Governance* 15: 375–92.

Majone, Giandomenico. 2004. "Information, Commitment, and the Transformation of European Governance." In *The State of Europe: Transformations of Statehood from a European Perspective*, edited by Sonja Puntscher Riekmann, Monika Mokre, and Michael Latzer, 289–305. Frankfurt: Campus Verlag.

Majone, Giandomenico. 2006. "The Common Sense of European Integration." *Journal of European Public Policy* 13: 607–26.

Marks, Gary, David Attewell, Jan Rovny, and Liesbet Hooghe. 2017. "Dealignment Meets Cleavage Theory." Paper presented at the APSA Meeting, San Francisco.

Marks, Gary, Carole Wilson, and Leonard Ray. 2002. "National Political Parties and European Integration." *American Journal of Political Science* 46(3): 585–94.

Mastenbroek, Ellen. 2003. "Surviving the Deadline: The Transposition of EU Directives in the Netherlands." *European Union Politics* 4: 371–95.

Mattli, Walter, and Anne-Marie Slaughter. 1995. "Law and Politics in the European Union: A Reply to Garrett." *International Organization* 49(1): 183–90.

Maurer, Andreas. 2005. "Negotiating the Nice Treaty: a joint but failed search for efficiency

References

building." In *The European Union in the Wake of Enlargement*, edited by Amy Verdun, and Osvaldo Croci, 174-199. Manchester: Manchester University Press.

Meret, Susi. 2010. *The Danish People's Party, the Italian Northern League and the Austrian Freedom Party in a Comparative Perspective: Party Ideology and Electoral Support*. Institut for Historie, Internationale Studier og Samfundsforhold, Aalborg Universitet. Spirit PhD Series No. 25.

Moravcsik, Andrew. 1991. "Negotiating the Single European Act: National Interests and Conventional Statecraft in the European Community." *International Organization* 45: 19–56.

Moravcsik, Andrew. 1992. "Liberalism and International Relations Theory." Harvard University and University of Chicago. Working Paper 92–6.

Moravcsik, Andrew. 1993. "Preferences and Power in the European Community: A Liberal Intergovernmentalist Approach." *Journal of Common Market Studies* 31: 473–524.

Moravcsik, Andrew. 1998. *The Choice for Europe: Social Purpose and State Power from Messina to Maastricht*. Ithaca: Cornell University Press.

Moravcsik, Andrew. 2002. "In Defense of the 'Democratic Deficit': Reassessing Legitimacy of the European Union." *Journal of Common Market Studies* 40: 603–24.

Moravcsik, Andrew. 2005. "The European Constitutional Compromise and the Neofunctionalist Legacy." *Journal of European Public Policy* 12: 349–86.

Moravcsik, Andrew. 2008. "The European Constitutional Settlement." *World Economy* 31: 158–83.

Moravcsik, Andrew. 2018. "Preferences, Power and Institutions in 21st-Century Europe." *Journal of Common Market Studies* 56: 1648–74.

Moravcsik, Andrew, and Kalypso Nicolaidis. 1999. "Explaining the Treaty of Amsterdam: Interests, Influence, Institutions." *Journal of Common Market Studies* 37: 59–85.

Moravcsik, Andrew, and Frank Schimmelfennig. 2019. "Liberal Intergovernmentalism." In *European Integration Theory*, edited by Antje Wiener, Tanja Börzel, and Thomas Risse, chapter 4. Oxford: Oxford University Press.

Müller, Wolfgang, Marcelo Jenny, and Alejandro Ecker. 2012. "The Elites–Masses Gap in European Integration." In *The Europe of Elites: A Study into the Europeanness of Europe's Political and Economic Elites*, edited by Heinrich Best, György Lengyel, and Luca Verzichell, 167–91. Oxford: Oxford University Press.

Norris, Pippa, and Ronald Inglehart. 2019. *Cultural Backlash: Trump, Brexit, and Authoritarian Populism*. Cambridge: Cambridge University Press.

Nugent, Neill, ed. 2004. *European Union Enlargement*. Basingstoke: Palgrave Macmillan.

Pahre, Robert. 1997. "Endogenous Domestic Institutions in Two-Level Games and Parliamentary Oversight of the European Union." *Journal of Conflict Resolution* 41(1): 147–74.

Plummer, Martyn. 2003. "JAGS: A Program for Analysis of Bayesian Graphical Models Using Gibbs Sampling." DSC 2003 Working Papers.

Polk, Jonathan, Jan Rovny, Ryan Bakker, Erica Edwards, Liesbet Hooghe, Seth Jolly, Jelle Koedam, Filip Kostelka, Gary Marks, Gijs Schumacher, Marco Steenbergen, Milada Vachudova, Marko Zilovic. 2017. "Explaining the Salience of Anti-Elitism and Reducing Political Corruption for Political Parties in Europe with the 2014 Chapel Hill Expert Survey Data." *Research and Politics* 4(1): 1–9.

Proksch, Sven-Oliver. 2007. "Ideology and the Politics of Constitution Making: The Institutional Organization of the European Convention." Paper presented at 10th Biennial Conference of the European Union Studies Association, Montreal.

Proksch, Sven-Oliver, and James Lo. 2012. "Reflections on the European Integration Dimension." *European Union Politics* 13(2): 317–33.

Putnam, Robert. 1988. "Diplomacy and Domestic Politics: The Logic of Two-Level Games." *International Organization* 42: 427–60.

Rauh, Christian. 2016. *A Responsive Technocracy? EU Politicization and the Consumer Policies of the European Commission.* Colchester: ECPR Press.

Rauh, Christian, Bart Joachim Bes, and Martijn Schoonvelde. 2020. "Undermining, Defusing or Defending European Integration? Assessing Public Communication of European Executives in Times of EU Politicisation." *European Journal of Political Research* 59(2): 397–423.

Raunio, Tapio. 1999. "Always One Step Behind? National Legislatures and the European Union." *Government and Opposition* 34(2): 180–202.

Reh, Christine, Adrienne Héritier, Edorado Bressanelli, and Christel Koop. 2011. "The Informal Politics of Legislation: Explaining Secluded Decision Making in the European Union." *Comparative Political Studies* 46(9): 1112–42.

Reif, Karlheinz, and Hermann Schmitt. 1980. "Nine Second-Order National Elections: A Conceptual Framework for the Analysis of European Election Results." *European Journal of Political Research* 8(1): 3–44.

Reiljan, Andres. 2020. "'Fear and Loathing across Party Lines' (Also) in Europe: Affective Polarisation in European Party Systems." *European Journal of Political Research* 59(2): 376–96.

Richardson, Bradley. 1991. "European Party Loyalties Revisited." *American Political Science Review* 85(3): 751–75.

Riker, William. 1962. *The Theory of Political Coalitions*. New Haven: Yale University Press.

Risse, Thomas. 2010. "No Demos? Identities and Public Spheres in the Euro Crisis." *Journal of Common Market Studies* 52(6): 1207–15.

Rittberger, Berthold. 2003. "Creation and Empowerment of the European Parliament." *Journal of Common Market Studies* 41(2): 203–25.

Rohrschneider, Robert. 2000. "The New Politics of the Right: Hans-Georg Betz and Stefan Immerfall." *Journal of Politics* 62(2): 619–20.

Rosamond, Ben. 2000. *Theories of European Integration*. Basingstoke: Palgrave.

Sánchez-Cuenca, Ignacio. 2000. "The Political Basis of Support for European Integration." *European Union Politics* 1: 147–71.

Sandholtz, Wayne, and Alec Stone Sweet, eds. 1998. *European Integration and Supranational Governance*. Oxford: Oxford University Press.

Sandholtz, Wayne, and Alec Stone Sweet. 2012. *Neo-Functionalism and Supranational Governance*. Oxford: Oxford Handbook of the European Union.

Scharpf, Fritz. 1996. "Democratic Policy in Europe." *European Law Journal* 2(2): 136–55.

References

Scharpf, Fritz. 1997. *Games Real Actors Play: Actor-Centered Institutionalism in Policy Research*. Boulder: Westview Press.

Scharpf, Fritz. 1999. *Governing in Europe: Effective and Democratic*. Oxford: Oxford University Press.

Schimmelfennig, Frank. 2019. "The Choice for Differentiated Europe: An Intergovernmentalist Theoretical Framework." *Comparative European Politics* 17: 176–91.

Schimmelfennig, Frank, Dirk Leuffen, and Catherine De Vries. 2023. "Differentiated Integration in the European Union: Institutional Effects, Public Opinion, and Alternative Flexibility Arrangements." *European Union Politics* 24: 3–20.

Schimmelfennig, Frank, and Ulrich Sedelmeier. 2004. "Governance by Conditionality: EU Rule Transfer to the Candidate Countries of Central and Eastern Europe." *Journal of European Public Policy* 11(4): 661–79.

Schimmelfennig, Frank, and Thomas Winzen. 2020. *Ever Looser Union? Differentiated European Integration*. Oxford: Oxford University Press.

Schmidt, Vivien A. 2019. "The Future of Differentiated Integration: A 'Soft-Core,' Multi-Clustered Europe of Overlapping Policy Communities." *Comparative European Politics* 17(2): 294–315.

Schmitter, Philippe. 2000. *How to Democratize the European Union—and Why Bother?* Boulder: Rowman and Littlefield.

Schmitter, Philippe, and Wolfgang Streeck. 1991. "From National Corporatism to Transnational Pluralism: Organized Interests in the Single European Market." *Politics and Society* 19(2): 133–64.

Schneider, Christina. 2018. *The Responsive Union: National Elections and European Governance*. Cambridge: Cambridge University Press.

Schulz, Heiner, and Thomas König. 2000. "Institutional Reform and Decision-Making Efficiency in the European Union." *American Journal of Political Science* 44(4): 653–66.

Sedelmeier, Ulrich. 2006. "The EU's Role as a Promoter of Human Rights and Democracy: Enlargement Policy Practice and Role Formation." In *The European Union's Roles in International Politics*, edited by Ole Elgström and Michael Smith, 138–55. London: Routledge.

Sedelmeier, Ulrich. 2012. "Is Europeanisation through Conditionality Sustainable? Lock-In of Institutional Change after EU Accession." *West European Politics* 35(1): 20–38.

Slapin, Jonathan. 2008. "Bargaining Power at Europe's Intergovernmental Conferences: Testing Institutional and Intergovernmental Theories." *International Organization* 62: 131–62.

Slapin, Jonathan. 2011. *Veto Power: Institutional Design in the European Union*. Ann Arbor: University of Michigan Press.

Spoon, Jae-Jae. 2012. "How Salient Is Europe? An Analysis of European Election Manifestos, 1979–2004." *European Union Politics* 13(4): 558–79.

Spoon, Jae-Jae, and Heike Klüver. 2014. "Do Parties Respond? How Electoral Context Influences Party Responsiveness." *Electoral Studies* 35: 48–60.

Stegmueller, Daniel. 2013. "How Many Countries for Multilevel Modeling? A Comparison of Frequentist and Bayesian Approaches." *American Journal of Political Science* 57(3): 748–61.

Steunenberg, Bernhard. 1994. "Decisionmaking under Different Institutional Arrangements: Legislation by the European Community." *Journal of Theoretical and Institutional Economics* 150: 642–69.

Stimson, James, Michael Mackuen, and Robert Erikson. 1995. "Dynamic Representation." *American Political Science Review* 89(3): 543–65.

Stone Sweet, Alec, and Thomas Brunell. 2012. "The European Court of Justice, State Non-Compliance, and the Politics of Override." *American Political Science Review* 106(1): 204–13.

Stone Sweet, Alec, and James Caporaso. 1998. *From Free Trade to Supranational Polity: The European Court and Integration.* Berkeley: University of California.

Stone Sweet, Alec, and Wayne Sandholtz. 1997. "European integration and supranational governance." *Journal of European Public Policy* 4: 297-317.

Sunstein, Cass. 2015. *Partyism.* University of Chicago Legal Forum.

Szczerbiak, Aleks, and Paul Taggart. 2008. *Opposing Europe? The Comparative Party Politics of Euroscepticism.* Vol. 1, *Case Studies and Country Surveys.* Oxford: Oxford University Press.

Taggart, Paul. 1998. "A Touchstone of Dissent: Euroscepticism in Contemporary Western European Party Systems." *European Journal of Political Research* 33: 363–88.

Tajfel, Henri, and John Turner. 1979. "An Integrative Theory of Intergroup Conflict." In *The Social Psychology of Intergroup Relations*, edited by Walter Austin and Stephen Worchel, 33–47. Monterey: Brooks/Cole.

Tallberg, Jonas. 2002. "Paths to Compliance: Enforcement, Management, and the European Union." *International Organization* 56: 609–43.

Tallberg, Jonas. 2004. "The agenda-shaping powers of the Council Presidency." *Journal of European Public Policy* 10(1): 1-19.

Tallberg, Jonas. 2006. *Leadership and Negotiation in the European Union.* Cambridge: Cambridge University Press.

Thiem, Janina. 2006. "Explaining Roll Call Vote Request in the European Parliament." MZES Working Paper 21.

Thiem, Janina. 2009. *Nationale Parteien im Europäischen Parlament: Delegation, Kontrolle und politischer Einfluss.* Wiesbaden: VS Verlag für Sozialwissenschaften.

Thierse, Stefan. 2016. "Going on Record: Revisiting the Logic of Roll-Call Vote Requests in the European Parliament." *European Union Politics* 17(2): 219–41.

Thomson, Robert. 2008. "The Council Presidency in the European Union: Responsibility with Power." *Journal of Common Market Studies* 46(3): 593–617.

Thurner, Paul, and Franz Urban Pappi. 2009. *European Union Intergovernmental Conferences: Domestic Preference Formation, Transgovernmental Networks and the Dynamics of Compromise.* London: Routledge.

Thurner, Paul, Franz Urban Pappi, and Michael Stoiber. 2002. "EU Intergovernmental Conferences: A Quantitative Analytical Reconstruction and Data-Handbook of Domestic Preference Formation, Transnational Networks, and Dynamics of Compromise during the Amsterdam Treaty Negotiations." MZES Working Paper 60.

References

Topaloff, Liubomir. 2012. *Political Parties and Euroscepticism*. New York: Palgrave Macmillan.

Toshkov, Dimiter. 2008. "Embracing European Law: Compliance with EU Directives in Central and Eastern Europe." *European Union Politics* 9(3): 379–402.

Toshkov, Dimiter. 2011. "Public Opinion and Policy Output in the European Union: A Lost Relationship." *European Union Politics* 12: 169–91.

Tsebelis, George. 2002. *Veto Players: How Political Institutions Work*. Princeton: Princeton University Press.

Tsebelis, George. 2006. "The European Convention and the Rome and Brussels IGCs: A Veto Players Analysis." In *Policy-Making Processes and the European Constitution: A Comparative Study in Member States and Accession Countries*, edited by Thomas König and Simon Hug, 9–22. ECPR Studies in European Political Science. London: Routledge.

Tsebelis, George, and Geoffrey Garrett. 2001. "The Institutional Foundations of Intergovernmentalism and Supranationalism in the European Union." *International Organization* 55: 357–90.

Tsebelis, George, and Jeannette Money. 1997. *Bicameralism*. Cambridge: Cambridge University Press.

Van Elsas, Erika, and Wouter van der Brug. 2015. "The Changing Relationship between Left–Right Ideology and Euroscepticism, 1973–2010." *European Union Politics* 16(2): 194–215.

Wagner, Markus. 2021. "Affective Polarization in Multiparty Systems." *Electoral Studies* 69: 102–22.

Wallace, William, and Julie Smith. 1995. "Democracy or Technocracy? European Integration and the Problem of Popular Consent." *West European Politics* 18(3): 137–57.

Weiler, Joseph, Ulrich Haltern, and Franz Mayer. 1995. "European Democracy and Its Critique." *West European Politics* 18: 4–39.

Weingast, Barry, and William Marshall. 1988. "The Industrial Organization of Congress; or, Why Legislatures, Like Firms, Are Not Organized as Markets." *Journal of Political Economy* 96: 132–68.

Westwood, Sean, Shanto Iyengar, Stefaan Walgrave, Rafael Leonisio, Luis Miller, and Oliver Strijbis. 2018. "The Tie That Divides: Cross-National Evidence of the Primacy of Partyism." *European Journal of Political Research* 57(2): 333–54.

Williams, Christopher, and Shaun Bevan. 2019. "The Effect of Public Attitudes on European Commission Policy Activity." *European Union Politics* 30(4): 608–28.

Wonka, Arndt. 2007. "Technocratic and Independent? The Appointment of European Commissioners and Its Policy Implications." *Journal of European Public Policy* 14(2): 169–89.

Wratil, Christophe. 2019. "Territorial Representation and the Opinion–Policy Linkage: Evidence from the European Union." *American Journal of Political Science* 63(1): 197–211.

Yataganas, Xenophon. 2001. "The Treaty of Nice: The Sharing of Power and the Institutional Balance in the European Union—A Continental Perspective." *European Law Journal* 7: 242–91.

Yordanova, Nikoleta, and Monika Mühlböck. 2015. "Tracing the Selection Bias in Roll Call Votes: Party Group Cohesion in the European Parliament." *European Political Science Review* 7(3): 373–99.

Zürn, Michael. 2000. "Democratic Governance beyond the Nation-State: The EU and Other International Institutions." *European Journal of International Relations* 6(2): 183–221.

INDEX

accession, 7, 14, 16, 37, 47, 48, 60, 66, 73, 95, 97, 117, 128, 129, 145, 176, 180, 192, 197, 199
accountability, 15, 42, 44, 55, 93, 94, 95, 105, 106, 107, 117, 118, 121, 150
affective polarization, 3, 7, 9, 10, 11, 13, 15, 83, 101, 102, 103, 104, 149, 150, 169, 170, 176, 180, 185, 188, 189, 190, 191, 199
agenda-setting monopoly, 21, 85, 114
Amsterdam Treaty, 5, 6, 8, 21, 30, 34, 35, 37, 38, 41, 42, 47, 57, 58, 67, 68, 70, 74, 76, 99, 105, 117, 194, 198
anti-integrationist, 3, 7, 11, 12, 15, 16, 20, 36, 48, 85, 87, 97, 98, 102, 103, 104, 122, 124, 125, 127, 129, 132, 133, 141, 144, 145, 147, 148, 149, 157, 163, 169, 170, 171, 172, 173, 175, 176, 177, 178, 179, 180, 181, 184

bargaining, 11, 12, 13, 22, 25, 26, 28, 30, 36, 55, 65, 72, 73, 77, 194, 197
Bayesian, 41, 61, 126, 195, 198
benchmarking, 101, 156
bicameral conflict resolution, 93, 94, 98, 99, 117
blocking minorities, 43

camp-building, 7, 9, 11, 14, 15, 83, 86, 96, 97, 99, 100, 104, 121, 122, 123, 124, 125, 127, 129, 132, 133, 136, 138, 141, 145, 147, 148, 149, 151, 153, 176, 180
camps, 9, 10, 11, 16, 52, 102, 122, 132, 133, 136, 138, 145, 148, 176, 180, 183
capabilities, 25, 179
Central and Eastern Europe, 7, 14, 21, 37, 47, 58, 60, 61, 66, 67, 71, 108, 117, 123, 129, 197, 199
centralizing regulations, 90, 91, 93, 95, 109, 179, 183
challenger paradox, 12
challenger/periphery parties, 3, 7, 9, 11, 12, 16, 25, 85, 96, 97, 98, 102, 103, 104, 122, 123, 124, 129, 136, 144, 145, 147, 148, 149, 157, 163, 168, 169, 170, 171, 172, 173, 174, 175, 176, 178, 180
checks-and-balances, 86, 87, 106, 108
cleavage, 2, 7, 10, 12, 66, 84, 85, 96, 102, 103, 123, 125, 132, 170, 171, 172, 176, 177, 181, 191, 193, 194
codecision procedure, 6, 38, 43, 48, 58, 59, 65, 70, 71, 72, 87, 105, 106
Common Foreign and Security Policies, 38
compliance, 15, 88, 89, 91, 92, 93, 94, 95, 96, 100, 104, 105, 107, 109, 110, 116, 117, 118, 120, 180, 186, 187, 188, 189, 193, 194, 198, 199
conationals, 170, 173, 176, 177
constitutional, 30, 40, 48, 51, 54, 68, 73, 74, 77, 86, 189, 192, 193, 195
Constitutional Treaty, 14, 35, 51, 67, 68, 73, 74, 77, 78, 182, 194
constraining dissensus, 5, 6, 103, 172, 177, 191
consultation procedure, 87
Council presidency, 15, 25, 26, 27, 28, 29, 30, 55, 67, 69, 72, 73, 93, 106, 117, 179, 198
country-specific interests, 12, 19, 23, 24, 35, 53, 66, 77
Covid-19, 6, 25

crisis management, 3, 8, 9, 11, 12, 15, 16, 20, 85, 86, 97, 101, 102, 123, 123, 147, 148, 151, 152, 163, 168, 170, 176, 177, 179, 180, 183, 192
critical juncture, 3, 11, 16, 97, 122, 123, 124, 126, 127, 129, 145, 170, 176, 180

data generation, 1, 7, 8, 13, 181
decisions, 15, 21, 37, 48, 77, 83, 89, 90, 91, 92, 93, 95, 100, 106, 109, 110, *111*, *112*, 113, 116, 140, 179, 183
deepening, 3, 5, 7, 9, 11, 14, 16, 19, 20, 21, 31, 72, 78, 83, 85, 86, 90, 91, 99, 100, 104, 106, 108, 110, 116, 120, 123, 140, 147, 149, 162, 176, 179, 180, 182
delegation, 9, 12, 15, 16, 21, 42, 85, 86, 87, 90, 91, 93, 96, 105, 106, 107, 110, 113, 114, 117, 118, 120, 183, 185, 198
democratic deficit paradox, 12, 178
descriptive representation, 16, 184
dimensions, 11, 26, 33, 34, 36, 38, 40, 41, 43, 48, 52, 55, 56, 58, 59, 65, 157, 171, 172, 173, 176, 188, 190
directive, 15, 89, 90, 91, 92, 93, 94, 95, 100, 105, 109, 110, *111*, *112*, 113, 114, 116, 117, 118, 120, 121, 157, 180, 183, 193, 194, 199
distributive theory, 12, 23
dual role, 14, 23, 74
dynamic, 1, 2, 8, 9, 10, 11, 13, 24, 73, 104, 149, 151, 177, 178, 181, 185, 186, 188, 198

early agreement, 15, 42, 93, *94*, 95, 100, 105, 117, *118*, 121, 138, 180
efficiency, 8, 20, 21, 28, 42, 43, 51, 67, 68, 72, 74, 79, 182, 195
electoral breakthrough, 6
empirical implications, 2, 8, 13
enforcement conflicts, 15, 91, 95, 100, 104, 110, 116, 118, 120, 180
EU policy-making game, 9, 11, 86
European debt crisis, 6, 86, 151
Europeans, 2, 3, 10, 13, 103, 188
Eurosceptic parties, 6, 21, 151, 169

Euroscepticism, 6, 7, 67, 72, 84, 85, 156, 179, 187, 188, 198, 199
executive activism, 107, *113*, 114, 120, 152, 180
experts, 1, 2, 9, 15, 83, 85, 86, 87, 98, 101, 103, 105, 106, 107, 114, 120, 132, 152, 180

failure, 9, 11, 13, 15, 27, 28, 29, 30, 31, 35, 47, 53, 54, 68, 69, 71, 72, 73, 77, 78, 85, 136, 179, 182, 188, 192

globalization, 24, 84, 181, 190, 193
governance design, 3, 5, 6, 8, 11, 14, 22, 23, 26, 33, 35, 38, 41, 42, 43, 44, 46, 48, 55, 56, 58, 59, 61, 64, 65, 66, 67, 70, 71, 74, 76, 77, 78, 86, 87, 107, 148, 149, 150, 152, 153, 155, 156, 159, 178, 179
governmental experience, 8, 60, 61, 66, 136, 149, 162, 163, 168, 179
Great Recession, 6, 86, 162, 168

heads of state and government, 2, 5, 8, 22

identity, 2, 10, 11, 12, 13, 37, 101, 103, 123, 144, 146, 150, 169, 170, 173, 176, 177, 179, 181, 182, 186, 187, 189, 191
ideological alignment, 9, 10, 12, 102, 103, 150, 169, 170, 171, 172, 176, 180
imperfect, 13, 14, 21, 27, 54, 78, 79, 98, 186
incomplete, 8, 13, 14, 21, 27, 54, 78, 79, 98, 179
individual summits, 34, 55
informal trilogues, 12, 15, 93, 94, 95, 107, 117, 118, 121, 178, 180
infringement, 88, 89, 93, 95, 105, 107, 111, 116, *117*, 118, 186
institutional choices, 1, 2, 3, 5, 6, 8, 9, 10, 11, 12, 13, 14, 19, 20, 21, 25, 26, 29, 30, 31, 32, 34, 35, 52, 53, 55, 66, 72, 77, 78, 83, 85, 86, 99, 101, 104, 105, 107, 108, 122, 149, 152, 153, 177, 178, 179, 180, 181, 184
institutional mismatch, 3, 13, 72, 84
integration paradox, 12, 77, 178
intergovernmentalism, 6, 12, 13, 19, 22, 25,

28, 61, 73, 77, 91, 107, 125, 148, 150, 157, 191, 192, 195
interstate bargains, 3, 6, 8, 11, 13, 14, 19, 25, 26, 27, 28, 29, 30, 31, 32, 33, 34, 35, 47, 52, 53, 54, 55, 66, 67, 78, 69, 72, 73, 77, 78, 99, 179
interstate summit game, 8, 22, 29, 30, 76, 78
issue-specific positions, 34, 35

Judicial Activism, 43, 95, 96, 107, *119*, 120, 190
Justice and Home Affairs, 20, 37, 38, 46, 114, 138, 140

latent, 14, 22, 33, 34, 36, 37, 52, 55, 56, 57, 59, 65, 127
left versus right, 16, 87, 108, 123, 124, 125, 126, 127, 128, 129, 133, 170, 171, 172, 173, *174*, 176
leftovers, 21, 38, 40, 42, 46, 67, 74
legislative core, 15, 51, 87, 88, 89, 90, 91, 100, 103, 107, 108, 114, 118, 119, 120, 121, 179, 180, 183
legislative override, 9, 15, 86, 87, 88, 89, 90, 95, 100, 103, 105, 106, 107, 108, 113, 119, 120, 152, 155, 179, 180
legitimacy, 42, 43, 46, 47, 91, 150, 189, 194, 195
Lisbon Treaty, 8, 21, 27, 33, 34, 35, 47, 50, 56, 58, 68, 70, 71, 72, 73, 74, 74, 76, 78, 90, 96, 99, 105, 109, 116, 138
long-term, 20, 86, 102
lowest common denominator, 8, 19, 29, 30, 31, 35, 53, 68, 73, 77, 179

Maastricht Treaty, 1, 2, 5, 6, 19, 20, 37, 46, 66, 67, 70, 73, 91, 96, 105, 127, 157, 192, 195
macroeconomic interests, 66
mass-mobilization, 102, 123
measurement model, 13, 14, 34, 36, 182
migrant crisis, 6, 86, 168
multi-dimensional bargaining spaces, 13, 25
multi-level governance, 90, 191

national game of party competition, 8, 16, 23, 29, 30, 31, 65, 66, 72, 73, 77, 79, 97, 122, 123, 124, 125, 126, 128, 129, 145, 169, 180, 181
national identities, 5, 16, 84, 85, 96, 106, 123, 125, 129, 149, 169, 170, 176, 182
national norms, 9, 20, 21, 52, 79, 85, 95, 96, 98, 101, 106, 108, 119, 138, 153, 182, 183
neo-functionalism, 197
Next Generation Fund, 6, 25
noncompliance, 8, 88, 89, 91, 93, 100, 104, 105, 110, 120, 180, 186

office-seeking, 8, 12, 19, 22, 23, 24, 35, 53, 64, 65, 66, 77, 101, 132, 133, 136
outgroup derogation, 102, 169, 170
outnationals, 12, 16, 103, 169, 170, 173, *174*, *175*, 176, 177, 181, 182
overemphasis, 12, 91, 102, 151

paradigmatic, 1, 2, 6, 10
parliamentarization paradox, 12, 118, 178
partisan composition, 24, 157
partisan ingroup favoritism, 102, 170
party competition, 7, 8, 9, 10, 11, 12, 13, 16, 20, 23, 29, 30, 31, 58, 65, 66, 72, 73, 77, 79, 83, 84, 85, 96, 97, 102, 108, 122, 123, 124, 125, 126, 127, 128, 129, 145, 149, 151, 169, 176, 180, 181, 183, 185, 193
party system, 10, 150, 169, 183, 185, 194, 196, 198, 199
party-specific interests, 8, 19, 23, 24, 35, 53, 65, 178
Permissive Consensus, 5, 7, 20, 66, 84, 85, 96, 148, 151, 156, 191
polarization, 3, 7, 8, 9, 10, 11, 13, 15, 16, 83, 85, 98, 99, 100, 102, 103, 104, 124, 133, 136, 145, 149, 150, 169, 170, 176, 180, 185, 186, 188, 189, 190, 191, 194, 199
policy-seeking, 11, 12, 15, 22, 23, 31, 35, 53, 64, 65, 66, 73, 77, 78, 92, 93, 97, 101, 132, 133, 136

political leaders, 2, 5, 6, 8, 11, 12, 13, 14, 19, 21, 22, 23, 24, 25, 29, 30, 31, 32, 33, 34, 35, 36, 37, 38, 40, 41, 42, 43, 44, 46, 47, 48, 51, 53, 54, 55, 56, 58, 59, 60, 61, 65, 66, 68, 71, 73, 74, 76, 77, 78, 90, 96, 104, 108, 121, 125, 177, 178, 179, 181, 182, 184
politicization, 7, 12, 65, 85, 96, 106, 132, 188, 193, 196
populism, 72, 195
populist movements, 21, 73
portfolio allocation, 99, *100*
portfolios, 99, 100, 180
positions, 14, 22, 33, 34, 35, 36, 52, 56, 59, 85, 87, 101, 107, 108, *109*, 122, 124, 125, 126, 127, 132, 133, 170, 185, 192, 193
postfunctionalism, 3, 6, 11, 16, 72, 84, 85, 104, 125, 132, 149, 169, 181, 182
power, 12, 13, 19, 21, 22, 24, 25, 27, 29, 31, 32, 35, 38, 41, 44, 46, 48, 54, 55, 56, 57, 58, 61, 64, 65, 66, 68, 70, 71, 72, 77, 78, 87, 91, 92, 93, 100, 104, 106, 114, 138, 149, 150, 151, 152, 153, 154, 178, 179, 186, 192, 195, 196, 197, 198, 199
preference fundamentals, 3, 11, 14, 19, 22, 23, 34, 35, 52, 53, 55, 59, 60, 64, 65
pro-integrationist, 9, 85, 96, 97, 98, 102, 103, 104, 108, 132, 133, 136, 141, 145, 147, 148, 149, 157, 169, 170, 173, 180
public demobilization, 168
public demands, 20, 79, 84, 87, 101, 102, 183, 184
public support, 6, 16, 83, 101, 102, 148, 149, 150, 153, 154, 155, 156, 157, 159, 162, 163, 169, 177, 181, 182, 188, 189, 190
punctuated politicization, 7, 96

qualified majority voting, 38, 42, 43, 45, 46, 72, 98, 108, 152

referendum, 7, 9, 11, 12, 13, 15, 16, 20, 27, 28, 30, 31, 37, 40, 41, 45, 46, 48, 51, 53, 54, 67, 68, 70, 71, 72, 73, 74, 76, 77, 78, 84, 96, 97, 99, 178, 179, 180, 190, 191, 192

regulations, 15, 89, 90, 91, 92, 93, 95, 100, 106, 109, 110, *111*, 112, 113, 116, 179, 183
responsibility, 20, 21, 54, 79, 83, 102, 182, 183, 198
responsiveness, 7, 20, 21, 79, 84, 87, 101, 102, 150, 183, 184, 197
risk of failure and inefficiency, 11, 30, 31, 35, 53, 54, 68, 69, 72, 77, 78, 179, 182
ruling/mainstream parties, 3, 8, 9, 11, 12, 15, 16, 21, 66, 85, 96, 97, 98, 102, 104, 122, 123, 124, 129, 132, 133, 136, 144, 145, 148, 149, 157, 163, 168, 169, 170, 171, 172, 173, 174, *175*, 176, 178, 179, 180

sensitive areas, 6, 14, 16, 20, 45, 46, 55, 65, 71, 72, 84, 96, 97, 102, 123, 129, 136, 140, 149, 151, 153, 179, 182
sequential choices, 14, 22, 25, 26, 27, 29, 30, 54, 59, 63
shared areas, 15, 20, 86, 90, 91, 114, 120, 180
shocks, 1, 2, 8, 9, 13, 102
short-term, 20, 96
Single European Act, 20, 195
size of the core, 15, 51, 87, 88, 89, 90, 91, 100, 103, 107, 108, 113, 114, 118, 120, 121, 179, 180, 183
solidarity, 2, 3, 10, 12, 13, 16, 103, 169, 170, 171, 172, 173, *174*, *175*, 176, 177, 181, 189
static, 7
status quo, 7, 26, 27, 28, 29, 31, 35, 36, 44, 46, 58, 68, 69, 70, 71, 72, 74, 76, 77, 78, 79, 87, 88, 89, 112, 153, 179, 182
subsidiarity principle, 15, 20, 21, 86, 90, 106, 114, 180, 183
Summit Game, 8, *28*, 29, 30, 76, 77, 178, 181
supranational activism, 15, 86, 95, 103, 105, 107, 108, 114, 120, 152, 180
supranational consensus, 6, 177
supranational delegation, 15, 21, 85, 86, 90, 91, 96, 105, 113, 114, 118, 183
supranational game of party competition, 9, 10, 11, 16, 20, 96, 145, 149, 180, 181
supranational governance, 5, 7, 8, 9, 10, 11, 23, 86, 48, 155, 156, 198

Index

supranational identity, 2, 12, 13, 103, 150, 169, 170, 173, 176, 177, 179, 181, 182
supranational norm, 9, 20, 21, 52, 79, 85, 95, 96, 98, 101, 104, 106, 108, *119*, 120, 138, 153, 182, 183
supranational problem-solving, 3, 6, 7, 9, 11, 12, 15, 16, 20, 85, 86, 97, 101, 102, 103, 147, 148, 149, 150, 151 152, 163, 168, 169, 170, 172, 176, 177, 180, 183

technocracism, 7, 9, 11, 14, 15, 83, 85, 87, 100, 101, 102, 104, 105, 106, 120, 121, 128, 147, 148, 149, 151, 152, 155, 162, 176, 179, 180
technocratic, 83, 84, 87, 107, 151, 187, 192, 199
tertiary acts, 196, 109, 110, 112, 116, 138
tertiary legislation, 88, 89, 100, 106, 107, 109, 110, 111, 112, 113, 114, 116, 138, 145, 148, 155, 157, 179, 183, 184
transfer of policy competences, 3, 5, 7, 8, 11, 14, 22, 23, 24, 25, 26, 33, 35, 38, 40, 41, 43, 45, 46, 48, 50, 55, 56, 58, 59, 61, 64, 65, 66, 71, 72, 76, 77, 84, 96, 97, 101, 102, 106, 123, 125, 132, 136, 138, 140, 149, 150, 151, 153, 156, *159*, 178, 179
transparency, 15, 42, 68, 93, 94, 95, 105, 106, 107, 117, 118, 121, 140, 150, 194

transposition, 88, 92, 93, 110, 116, 193, 194
trust, 2, 3, 10, 12, 13, 16, 103, 151, 155, 156, 169, 170, 171, 172, 173, *174*, *175*, 176, 177, 181
trustee model, 83, 84
Two-level Games, 30, 191, 195, 196
two-stage sequential choices, 25, 30, 54, 72

unanimity, 72, 87, 152, 155, 193
uncertainty, 3, 13, 14, 22, 30, 31, 53, 54, 56, 72, 73, 76, 77, 78, 179, 190, 191, 194
uncontrolled delegation, 9, 15, 16, 91, 105, 106, 114, 183

veto bicameralism, 7, 8, 11, 14, 15, 20, 21, 45, 46, 48, 56, 65, 72, 85, 86, 87, 97, 98, 99, 103, 105, 116, 124, 141, 149, 152, 178, 179, 180
Veto Players, 8, 85, 191, 199
veto threats, 13, 14, 78
vote-seeking, 11, 13, 14, 19, 53, 66, 68, 73, 77, 78, 179, 182

widening, 5, 7, 9, 11, 14, 16, 19, 20, 27, 30, 31, 78, 83, 86, 90, 91, 99, 100, 104, 108, 110, 112, 116, 120, 121, 122, 140, 147, 149, 162, 176, 179, 180, 182, 183
winset, 26, 27, 29, 99